Praise for *Don't Tell Me What To Do, Just Send Money*

"This concrete, easy-to-use guide is designed to help anxious parents support and understand their newly fledged children. Johnson and Schelhas-Miller possess decades of professional experience as college counselors and their easy expertise is obvious. Situations are discussed in level, clear language designed to help parents allow their children to cope. Both a useful guide and a literary security blanket . . . good, solid, clear, consistent, and grounded advice."   —*Kirkus Reviews*

"In addition to humerous dialogues and Doonesbury cartoons that introduce each chapter, this book is chock-full of sound, practical tips for reshaping relationships between parents and their emerging adult offspring and for coping with the challenges families face during this crucial time."   —Jennifer Wolcott,
The Christian Science Monitor

"This indispensable book provides practical advice to parents navigating the rough water of letting go of their children. The authors honest dialogues and meaty analysis also guide parents who are sending their children to boarding school or summer camp."   —Thomas Hassan, Dean of Admissions and
former Director of College Counseling, Phillips Exeter Academy

"College may look like a great investment, but don't let your children hit the quad without first making purchase of this wise, advice-filled book. From helping your child prepare the dorm room through your child's postgraduate years and first job, this comprehensive book will provide the reason and reassurance you're looking for."   —Verna Noel Jones,
Denver Rocky Mountain News

"Helen Johnson and Christine Schelhas-Miller have done us all a great service. This book is well grounded in the psychological and practical challenges of college life—for parents and students. As a college professor and the father of college students, I welcome this book with open arms. I wish it had been available to my parents!"
—James Garbarino, Ph.D., author of *Lost Boys*, and
Elizabeth Lee Vincent, Professor of Human Development, Cornell University

"*Don't Tell Me What To Do, Just Send Money* is down-to-earth, sensible, and wise. The book offers firm direction, yet it is also full of warmth, humor, and hope. It is brilliantly organized, useful, and fun."   —Russ Muirhead,
Assistant Professor of Government, Harvard University

"This book is a perfect balance of theoretical foundation with anecdotes and arrestingly useful insights. Working with parents on a daily basis, I know this is an important guide for any parent navigating the transition to college."

—Randy S. Stevens,
Dean of Student Life, Northfield Mount Hermon School

"Based on sound theory and research, *Don't Tell Me What To Do, Just Send Money* is a substantial new contribution to our profession. It is an excellent reference for university administrators as we respond to a new generation of parents and their needs and expectations for involvement." —Susan T. Kitchen,
Vice Chancellor for Student Affairs, University of North Carolina at Chapel Hill

"*Don't Tell Me What To Do, Just Send Money* is one of the most practical guides I've read for parents who are sending their student off to college. An honest look at college life that offers straightforward advice on issues your student may face. You'll find yourself referring back to this book time and time again."

—Susan Brown, National Chair,
APPI (Administrators Promoting Parent Involvement),
Director, Parents and Family Programs, Northeastern University

"This wonderful guide leads nervous parents through one of the most difficult transitions of their lives. I wish a copy of this book could be sent to every parent who's sending a child to college." —Susan Murphy, Vice President for
Student and Academic Affairs, Cornell University

"Subtitled, *The Essential Parenting Guide to the College Years*, this book, by two experts in the field of college counseling, does in fact cover the waterfront, effectively and with good examples, and charming writing to boot."

—David Brudnoy, *Brudnoy's Bookshelf*, WBZ (Boston)

"This tremendous guide provides anxious parents with great insight into how they can advise their child in making good career decisions."

—Tom Devlin, Director, Career Center,
University of California Berkeley

"This book hits the target! It is the best guidebook for parents with college students that I have seen. I work with parents of college students on a regular basis and know for certain that this book will be invaluable to them, whether they are first-time parents or veterans who have sent several sons or daughters to college."

—Thomas E. Miller, Vice President for Student Affairs, Eckerd College

"Don't Tell Me What to Do, Just Send Money"

The Essential Parenting Guide to the College Years

Helen E. Johnson
Christine Schelhas-Miller

 St. Martin's Griffin   New York

·

www.stmartins.com

Library of Congress Cataloging-in-Publication Data

Johnson, Helen E.
     Don't tell me what to do, just send money : the essential parenting guide to the college years / Helen E. Johnson and Christine Schelhas-Miller.—1st ed.
          p.   cm.
     ISBN 0-312-26374-0 (pbk.)
     1. College students—United States—Psychology.   2. Parenting—United States.   I. Schelhas-Miller, Christine.   II. Title.

LA229 .J55 2000
378.1'98—dc21
                                                                                        00-026428

10   9   8   7   6   5   4

Contents

3. Roommates, Fraternity Parties, All-nighters, Changing Majors, and Hanging Out   51
Adjustment During the First Year

Acknowledgments

We are deeply grateful to those who have contributed so much to the development of this book. As our ideas began to take form, we had the benefit of generous support and encouragement from Tom Devlin, Joan Jacobs Brumberg, Marnie Cochran, Toby VanderVorm, Cindy Klein Roche, JoAnn Miller, and Bob Frank. When we began to write, many people provided information that has made this a better book. They include (in alphabetical order): Toby Cookingham, Nina Cummings, Lisa Diamond, Sharon Dittman, Bob Everett, Mary Agnes and Steve Hamilton, Marcia Harris, Laura Horn, Peter Hurst, Roz Kenworthy, Phil Meilman, Patti Papapietro, Sharon Policello, Laurimar Reveron-Medina, Rebecca Sparrow, Jan Talbot, Sharon Thrasher, as well as students in Human Development 216 at Cornell University who let us read their adolescent autobiographies.

As we moved forward with the writing process, the following people read our drafts and provided invaluable feedback: Meghan Brown, Nancy Busch, Mon Cochran, Susie Criswell, Janet and Carl Eskridge, Nancy Fuchs, Rhoda Linton, Mary Lou Meier, Jane Miller, Margaret Miller, Virginia Nelson, Eileen Rock, John Schelhas, Sandy Stein, and Peggy Ulrich-Nims. We extend special thanks to our agent, Jill Kneerim, of the Palmer & Dodge Agency and to Cassie Jones, our initial editor.

This book could not have been produced without the extraordinary efforts of Lara Asher, our editor at St. Martin's Press. Her intelligence, skill, and willingness to put in long hours at crucial moments have literally made this book possible. Moreover, her unfailing enthusiasm, good humor, and warmth made working with her a pleasure.

I (Helen) would like to thank several special people: My late husband, Tom, whose love, irreverent sense of humor, insight, and encouragement still grace my life; my sons, Travis and Jay, whose college experiences provided inspiration for this book and whose continuing love and support is a daily blessing; my new daughter-in-law, Jennifer Cook Johnson, whose spirit and loving presence enriches our family. I also want to thank other friends and family members who have provided support and inspiration: Mon and Eva Cochran; Joan and David Brumberg; Christiann Dean, Carol Groneman, Steve Curry, Jeff Collins, Jane Sims,

Emily Votruba, Rhoda Linton, Anne Brodie, Jeri Vargo, Page Madison, Pat Donelan, and Norma Prendergast.

Many close friends have listened to and encouraged me (Chrissie) during the writing of this book. Peggy Ulrich-Nims, Bonnie Buettner, and Marjory Rinaldo-Lee proved, yet again, that they are the kind of friends who are always there for me. In addition, my brother John Schelhas and my sister-in-law Susie Criswell provided both advice and emotional support. I am indebted and grateful to the following people, who cheerfully entertained and chauffeured my children while I was writing: Silvia Arrillaga, Rhonda Lathwell, Lisa Stankus, and Bev Chin.

I could not have written this book without the steadfast love and support of my husband, Jim Miller, whose understanding and enthusiasm sustained me throughout this project. And to my wonderful daughters, Alexis and Laura, I thank you for your patience; and now that this book is finished, I promise to take you to the mall!

Introduction

Congratulations! You have made it through eighteen years of parenting and your child is ready to embark on that great personal journey called the college years. You are not alone if you feel a mixture of excitement and dread as you send your child off to college. Few parents really know what to expect from the college years. At best, you may have a slim brochure from the school's admissions office telling you about the academic and social aspects of college life for your child. And you will certainly have heard from the office that collects tuition. But what about your adjustment to the changes about to take place?

As your child grew up, you had plenty of advice about child rearing from books, family members, and friends. You probably noticed that these resources dwindled as your child approached the teen years. Somehow talking about teens and their developmental issues is harder than talking about toilet training and the adjustment to nursery school. Why? Because the issues get scarier and your teenager's need to pull away from the family and create a separate identity can be both troubling and rewarding. You may be confused and even embarrassed by your child's behavior as he experiments with being an adult. This happens most dramatically during the college years.

Parents of our generation have been, and continue to be, more involved in our children's education and development than any generation in American history. We are the parents who took childbirth classes, debated the merits of nursery schools, arranged play dates, carpooled to soccer games, organized violin lessons, and took the grand college tour. We have consumed parenting "how to" books in record numbers. But, until now, there has not been a practical guide that offers concrete advice on how to manage the challenges and changes that accompany our children's college years.

What parent hasn't waited anxiously for a phone call from college and then not received one? What parent hasn't asked, "What is my role now that my child is away from home?" "Why does my child seem so independent one minute but confused and indecisive the next?" "How will I know if my child is in trouble and what should I do about it?" "Who is this person with a new tattoo and an attitude sitting at the Thanksgiving dinner table?" "Why does she seem to reject all of the values we taught her?" "Will my child get a good job after college and have her own health insurance?" "What in the world will he do with a degree in art history?" And what parent hasn't questioned the cost of college and wondered if it was worth it?

Drawing on adolescent development theory and our years of experience with undergraduates and parents, we provide practical advice to parents on these and other questions. Through the use of dialogues and scenarios, this book demonstrates how parents can adjust their expectations to anticipate the inevitable transformation in the parent-child relationship. We encourage parents to adopt a mentor/advisor role, showing, through actual examples, how important it is to relinquish control and instead provide guidance and support. We also offer communication and problem-solving strategies that support the development of a healthy adult-to-adult relationship that will serve you well in the years to come.

Each of us has had more than two decades of experience working with college students and their parents at small liberal arts colleges, state schools, and some of America's most prestigious universities. Our insights result from focus group research with both parents and undergraduates, as well as from years of counseling and program development, including parent-orientation programs, parents weekends, and new student orientations.

Focus groups conducted in seven cities across the country with parents of college students revealed how eager they are for practical information and advice. Parents from Long Island to San Francisco had similar worries about their children's college experience—safety and health, adjustment issues, money concerns, sex and drugs, academic success, and career prospects. Most of all, they were confused about their new role in their children's lives. Our research highlighted the unique challenges that parents encounter as their children become legal adults, but far from independent. We also conducted focus groups with college juniors and found that parents continue to play a significant role in students' decision making, especially when those students were examining their values and beliefs, or facing critical life choices.

Students in Chrissie's course in adolescent development at Cornell University are required to write and analyze an autobiography of their adolescence. Reading more than one hundred autobiographies each year has given her an intimate view of the lives of today's college students. These autobiographies typically include candid descriptions of relationships, sex, drugs, families, emotional problems, and other personal matters.

As director of the Parents' Program at Cornell University, Helen surveyed more than twelve thousand parents from all parts of the country to determine their primary concerns and to find out what information they expected from the university. Helen also corresponded with more than six thousand parents in response to specific problems, and counseled more than two thousand parents by telephone and in person on a variety of issues.

This book will help you cope with the major issues that face parents of college students today. It will show you how to achieve a new relationship with your emerging adult child by understanding the developmental changes that will occur during the college years and by examining and managing the expectations you have for your child.

You have a fascinating job ahead as your child goes off to college. While you will always be your child's parent, the college years signal a change in that relationship—a change this book will help you to understand and even celebrate. You've done the hard work of raising a child capable of going to college and you deserve recognition, consideration, and support. We trust this book will encourage and sustain you during this change.

Chapter 1

Letting Go, but Still Showing That You Care

Laying the Groundwork for a New Kind of Relationship with Your Child

DOONESBURY © 2000 G. B. Trudeau. Reprinted with permission of UNIVERSAL PRESS SYNDICATE. All rights reserved.

When our son called from college, we were confused about what he needed from us. Was he asking for our opinion? Did he want us to make decisions for him? Did he simply want a sounding board? Or did he need us to guide him through a decision-making process? As parents, we've come a long way this year. We've learned to let go and allow him to make mistakes, knowing that our love, support, and guidance are still vital in his life and looking forward to a new and developing adult-to-adult relationship.

One of the most difficult parts of being the parent of a college student is observing from afar as your child makes the often bumpy transition from dependence to independence. After years of being a responsible, caring, and "in control" parent, this change can be frightening, rewarding, and nerve-racking—sometimes all in the same week!

The college years signal the beginning of a long process of letting go. Let's face it—once your child has gone to college, you have very little control. The college or university will treat your child as a legal adult, even though you know your child is far from independent. While you are no longer in a position to regulate, manage, or direct your child's life, you do have a unique opportunity to *influence* your child's decisions and behavior. Your child will experiment with taking on fully adult responsibilities and privileges. What better time for you, too, to try out new ways of relating to and communicating with your child?

The healthiest adult-to-adult relationships we've seen in families with grown children develop when the parents begin to adopt a mentoring/coaching role during the college years. Linda Phillips-Jones, author of *Mentors and Proteges,* states: "I think of good mentoring as analogous to good parenting. Just as a parent brings a child into the world, the mentor is a key figure in bringing a young adult into the world of adults and fostering development so that one can build a life that is meaningful."[1]

Becoming a Mentor: Adding a New Dimension to Your Parenting Role

While it is true that you will always be your child's parent, now is the time to add a new dimension to your parenting role. As your child begins to encounter adult responsibilities and choices, you can become a trusted advisor, assisting your child in making wise decisions and becoming fully independent. The shift to a mentoring style of parenting does not happen overnight, but you will find many occasions where it will be useful during the college years.

You may be familiar with the term *mentor.* It's been around for thousands of years. In ancient Greek mythology a man named Mentor was engaged to guide and protect Odysseus's household during his ten-year odyssey. Mentor became a trusted teacher, advisor, and surrogate father to Odysseus's young son during that time.

Today, the meaning has not changed significantly; formal and informal mentoring programs are found in business, education, social service agencies, and community groups, many of which specialize in working with young people. A mentor acts as an influential person in a protégé(e)'s life, helping the protégé(e) learn and work toward reaching his or her life goals.

Although we strongly believe that parents need to mentor their college-aged children, we recognize that this approach may not fit every situation. You know your child. Trust your instincts. If you sense that your child is in danger or is calling out for help, you may need to intervene. While it is important that you respect and trust your child and encourage independent problem solving, there are times when you need to act. Chapter 9 will help you assess when it's appropriate for you to get involved in the problems and crises that can occur during college.

In typical situations, however, a mentoring approach based on trust, respect, and clear communication between the mentor and protégé(e) will be most effective.

Essential Skills for Mentors

What skills does a mentor use to guide a protégé(e)? A mentor must communicate effectively so that he or she can teach, advise, and challenge in a way that offers support while encouraging the protégé(e) to practice problem-solving and decision-making skills.

Communicating Effectively

Listening, combined with skillful questioning, can help you become an effective mentor to your child.

Listening

The key to mentoring is active and reflective listening. For some of you, this approach will come naturally. For others it may seem awkward and artificial at first. You may be thinking, "Why shouldn't I just tell my child what to do?" "Doesn't my child need to know what I expect?" While you may want to give advice and make your expectations clear, this approach usually stops the process of investigating alternatives and puts your child in the position of either accepting or rejecting your advice. If you start by really listening to your child, the outcome is more likely to satisfy both of you. Effective listening requires that you:

- Make a sincere commitment to listen without evaluating or judging.
- Wait patiently, even if your child struggles to express feelings and thoughts.
- Take notice of verbal and nonverbal behaviors.
- Check your assumptions and responses to make sure they reflect what your child is feeling.
- Listen without trying to "fix" the problem.
- Above all, try not to judge, moralize, manipulate, or "catastrophize" the situation.

Some roadblocks that can hinder effective listening:
- Warning, threatening
- Providing solutions or "shoulds"
- Disagreeing, judging, criticizing, blaming
- Moralizing, preaching
- Interpreting, ridiculing, shaming
- Questioning and probing instead of listening

These roadblocks strengthen the power imbalance between your child and you. Through mentoring, you can empower your child to make decisions and act responsibly. This approach may seem tedious and drawn out, especially for those who like to come up with solutions and get things done. But it is important for parents to acknowledge that it is not their responsibility to solve their child's problems—to do so only weakens the child and makes him or her feel incompetent in managing his or her own life. Your role as mentor is to provide support, encouragement, and information so that your child can solve his or her own problems and explore alternatives.

Closed and Open Questions

A critical component of effective communication is understanding the difference between closed and open questions. Closed questions usually stop the flow of dialogue while open questions encourage continued dialogue. Few parents have escaped the frustration of the following kind of dialogue:

PARENT (noticing your teenager putting on his coat): Where are you going?
CHILD: Out.
PARENT: When will you be back?
CHILD: Later.

This is a good example of asking closed questions. Not much information was shared because closed questions do not call on the responder to think. What if the parent had tried using open questions?

PARENT: Tell me about your plans for tonight.
CHILD: Well, Jason and I are going to the mall and then to a movie.
PARENT: Can you tell me around what time you'll be back?
CHILD: Oh, probably about midnight.

Here are two dialogues, the first using closed questions, the second using open questions.

DAD: How's school going?
JEFF: Good.
DAD: Do you like your classes so far?
JEFF: Yeah.
DAD: Did you get into that biology class you wanted?
JEFF: Yup.
DAD: So do you have a lot of work?
JEFF: Yeah, tons.
DAD: Are you getting enough sleep?
JEFF: Ha! Are you kidding? Nobody sleeps here.
DAD: Are you having any fun?

JEFF: Oh, yeah.

DAD: What did you do last weekend?

JEFF: Just hung out with friends.

DAD: What did you do?

JEFF: Nothing much really, we just hung out.

DAD: Well, it's been great talking to you. I'll call you next week, okay?

JEFF: Okay, Dad, catch ya later.

You can see the difference in the following dialogue using open questions:

DAD: Hi, Jeff. How are you doing?

JEFF: Good, Dad. What's up with you?

DAD: Things are fine here. Is this a good time to talk?

JEFF: Yeah, I guess.

DAD: I was just sitting here wondering about what you were doing right now and how your classes are going. Tell me what your days are like there.

JEFF: Well, today is Tuesday so I dragged myself out of bed around eight-thirty to go to my first class and then I had breakfast at the U Hall and just hung around until my eleven o'clock class. Monday, Wednesday, and Friday I don't have class 'til ten so I get to sleep in. Today, after my eleven o'clock, I came back to my room and crashed until about one-thirty, then tore over to the dining hall to grab a sandwich and get to my two-fifteen class. After that, there's no time to do much, so I just wait around until my three-forty class and that's it for classes. Then I just hang out with my friends until dinnertime, and after that reality hits and I start studying. I usually don't go to bed until pretty late, like two o'clock or so. Last night, though, I had to stay up and finish an English essay.

DAD: It sounds like a pretty busy schedule. Tell me about your English essay.

JEFF: Oh, we had to write about a childhood friend and describe him or her—you know, qualities that made them a good friend. I wrote about Tim.

DAD: Really. It's been a long time since you've seen him, huh? What do you remember most about him?

JEFF: I wrote about how he always came to our house because Mom baked cookies a lot. I remember him covered with flour and eating raw cookie dough. He loved pressing the fork in those peanut butter cookies, making that crisscross design on each cookie and feeling so proud of himself. I also remember feeling kind of jealous 'cause Mom paid so much attention to him.

DAD: How did it feel to think about Tim and being a kid again?

JEFF: Well, I don't know if it was exactly fun, but I got it done.

DAD: So, how do you feel about your classes so far?

JEFF: They're okay. I really like my biology class, and it's a good thing because I spend an awful lot of time with class, sections, and labs.

DAD: What is it that makes biology so interesting?

JEFF: Well, we're doing this really cool unit on environmental hazards to wildlife. Did you know we're adding about ten new species to the endangered list every year? It's really a drag what's happening.

DAD: I just read about that the other day in the paper. What does your professor say about that trend?

JEFF: Well, she says there are ways to stop it, but it means we'd have to change the way we live and stop using up so many natural resources. You know, like cutting down forests and mucking up the rivers with all that industrial pollution and stuff. It's pretty interesting.

DAD: It sounds like it. What about your social life. How was your weekend?

JEFF: It wasn't that much fun. I had a test on Monday so I spent most of the weekend catching up on sleep and studying. I did go to a movie Saturday night with some guys on the floor. Oh, Dad, I gotta go—Dan's waiting for me to go to dinner. Talk to you later.

DAD: Okay, Jeff. Take care.

Open-ended questions help you engage your child in more meaningful conversations. If you want to help your child reflect on his or her experiences and come up with his or her own solutions to problems, open-ended questions are an essential tool. Parents who use open questions feel more a part of their child's life without coming off like the Grand Inquisitor.

Jeff's father started out the conversation by showing respect for Jeff's schedule. He asked if this was a good time to talk. This set the tone for the conversation and invited Jeff to engage in a caring way. It also meant that he could expect a few minutes of Jeff's undivided attention. There is nothing more frustrating than trying to carry on a conversation with your child when he or she is preoccupied or has a roomful of friends unwinding from the day of classes, complete with a CD blaring in the background.

After making sure that this was a good time to talk, Jeff's father proceeded to show genuine interest in his son's experiences by asking a series of open questions. His open questions prompted much more than "yes" or "no" responses from Jeff and helped him get a deeper sense of Jeff's life at school. Moreover, this type of conversation allowed Jeff's father to model useful communication skills. It may be years before Jeff engages his father in a conversation of this type about his father's life, but Jeff will at least have a model for this kind of interaction. Effective mentors are wonderful role models.

Why Questions—Communication Stoppers

You may have noticed that Jeff's father did not use any questions that started with "why." And there were many instances in the conversation when he might have wanted to ask why! "Why don't you get up a little earlier so you have time for breakfast before class?" "Why do you waste so much time during the day between classes?" "Why don't you start studying earlier in the evening so you can get to bed at a decent hour?"

"Why" questions are inherently judgmental and come off sounding critical. Even if you are genuinely curious and concerned about why your child behaves in a certain way, the "why" question will put your child on the defensive, which means that he or she won't be open to sharing his or her experience with you for fear of being judged. Instead of asking "why" questions, you can ask questions about feelings. Jeff's father could have asked him, "How do you feel about your schedule?" or "It must be hard to feel so sleep-deprived."

If your child is struggling with a problem, you can also try asking your child about how he or she would like the situation to be different. For example, let's say your son is someone who needs eight to ten hours of sleep every night in order to feel okay the next day. You're alarmed that he's talking about going to bed at 3:00 A.M. every night and dragging himself out of bed in the morning for class or sleeping through classes because he can't get up. Try putting the ball back in your child's court where it belongs by asking, "If you could wave a magic wand and create the perfect schedule, what would it be like?"

"I" Statements—Beyond Blaming

It's a rare parent who isn't tempted to jump in with solutions to dilemmas, especially when the child's college career or health may be in jeopardy. But usually the parent's response comes in the form of a warning or ultimatum. "You're never going to get through college if you can't get up for class in the morning!" "You'd better figure out a way to get your sleep or you're going to be a wreck when finals come around!"

It's very difficult to express concerns without sliding into "you" messages; such as, "You haven't done your work," "You party too much and therefore you have rotten grades in school." Try to express "I" messages; such as, "I really worry about you when I hear that you are not eating properly or getting enough sleep," or "I'm concerned that you're spending so much time partying during the week." When a parent avoids blaming and expresses sincere and honest concerns through "I" messages, a child is drawn into the conversation in a fundamentally different way. The parent is able to communicate concerns without immediately putting the child on the defensive.

The first year of college, in particular, can be pretty chaotic for students. As they experiment with their new lifestyle, the last thing they want to hear from home is that they're not doing it right. Although they may appear cool and in control, chances are they are as worried as you are about whether they can cope. But they will never admit it if they are confronted with a judging, blaming parent. Although it's frustrating to observe your child going through these adjustments, it's really important to do everything you can to reinforce your faith in your child's ability to manage life at school. At times, this requires a giant leap of faith in your child and a sincere commitment to trust that your child has the resources to deal with the consequences of his or her behavior.

Acting as a Mentor

A mentor teaches, challenges, and supports a protégé(e). Inherent in this relationship is an underlying trust and respect for the protégé(e) as an adult who is capable of learning how to manage his or her own life. The college years are a structured in-between period for most students in which they are treated as quasi-independent adults. Parenting a college student requires that you set aside many of your traditional parenting behaviors in favor of learning ways to mentor, teach, coach, and advise your child through the sometimes rocky transition from child to adult.

This can be done in several ways. Using the communication skills outlined above, you can listen carefully, ask open questions, suggest alternatives, and encourage your child to take responsibility for finding solutions to problems. As a parent, you don't have to have all of the answers for your child. Just by sending your child to college you have exposed your child to one of the most mentor-rich environments available.[2]

Encourage your child to take advantage of the many mentoring relationships that can be developed during college. Professors, staff members, work-study supervisors, coaches, and other students can act as mentors to your child on campus. You can also connect your child to mentors in your professional setting, your social group, or in the wider community at home.

It is ironic that by giving less advice and allowing your child to have ownership of decisions, your child will be more likely to seek your involvement in future decisions. And this, we assume, is your goal: to be involved in your child's life as a loving and helpful parent. In accepting a mentor role, you don't give up your role as a parent, you merely expand it in preparation for an adult-to-adult relationship with your child in the years to come.

The following scenarios further demonstrate ways in which parents can use mentoring skills to lay the groundwork for a new kind of relationship with their college-aged child.

Missing Home

The first few weeks at college have been hard for your daughter Rachel. She calls home often and appears to be having trouble adjusting. She was home for fall break and seemed fine; but a week or so after she returned to school, you received the following call:

MOM: Hello?
RACHEL: Hi, Mom. It's me.
MOM: Oh, hi, Rachel, how are you doing?

RACHEL: Not so great.

MOM: What do you mean?

RACHEL: I just hate it here. I want to come home.

MOM: What's the matter, Honey?

RACHEL: I don't know. I just don't like it here.

MOM: You seemed to be okay when you were home last week. What happened?

RACHEL: Nothing in particular. I just don't feel like I belong here. I'm so lonely and depressed all the time.

MOM: Don't you think you should give it more time? You've only been there two months or so.

RACHEL: I know, but it seems like forever.

MOM: Are you making any friends?

RACHEL: Not really. Everybody seems so gung-ho. It's sickening, really. I can't relate to anybody.

MOM: Your roommate seemed like a nice girl.

RACHEL: Well, she may seem nice to you, but all she cares about is guys and going to frat parties.

MOM: Why don't you go with her?

RACHEL: Mom! I hate frat parties. It's just a bunch of stupid people getting wasted every weekend.

MOM: You mean there's drinking? I thought that was illegal.

RACHEL: Mom, you just don't understand. That's *all* people do here.

MOM: What about your classes?

RACHEL: I don't understand why they make us take all of this introductory stuff— it's so boring.

MOM: What's so boring?

RACHEL: Everything! I just don't like it here, that's all.

MOM: But, Rachel, you were so excited about going to college. What happened?

RACHEL: I just hate it here. Can I come home?

> ### What's on your mind?
> I don't know what to do.
> I wonder if Rachel can make it at college.
> Should I let her come home?

> ### What's on your child's mind?
> I'm miserable.
> I don't fit in here.
> I'm scared about what will happen to me if I quit.

What's going on.

The first few weeks, and often months, of college are a big adjustment for new students. Everything is different, and many students miss the predictability of home and their high school friends. Even for children who are wildly enthusiastic about going to college, the reality of college life can be overwhelming and scary. It's difficult for parents to understand what is really going on with their child when they get a phone call like this one. Your own fears can make it hard to listen to your child's fears and unhappiness. It's tempting to want to fix things for your child when you hear this kind of pain.

What to do.	What to avoid.
• Try to listen to your child's anxieties. • Express your empathy for her situation. • Let her know that you sympathize with the difficulties of adjusting to college. • Express your confidence in and love for her.	• Letting your concern about her situation dominate the conversation. • Judging her ability to deal with college. • Dismissing her fears and telling her everything will be okay if she just sticks it out.

Missing Home: The Replay

Let's look at how this conversation could have gone if the parent had adopted the role of mentor with her child:

MOM: Hello?

RACHEL: Hi, Mom, it's me.

MOM: How are you doing?

RACHEL: I'm feeling awful. I hate it here. I want to come home.

MOM: Oh, Rachel, I'm sorry you're feeling so sad. Tell me what's going on.

RACHEL: I'm just so miserable and lonely.

MOM: You sound really unhappy.

RACHEL: I am. I just don't fit in here.

MOM: So you're feeling pretty out of it, huh? Are you kind of homesick too?

RACHEL: Yeah, I really miss Jen and Chris. I don't have any real friends here.

Mom: It's pretty hard to try to get used to all the things you have to deal with there and meet other kids you can relate to.

Rachel: All the girls on my floor are so into the fraternity scene. All they can think about is going to frat parties on the weekends.

Mom: That must make you feel pretty alone, huh?

Rachel: Yeah, I just feel so out of it.

Mom: You're wondering if you'll ever fit in, I guess.

Rachel: What if I don't? What if this isn't the place for me?

Mom: Well, you can always change your mind and go to college somewhere else, you know.

Rachel: Yeah, I guess I could. But it would be such a hassle to start all over.

Mom: Yes, it might be, but the most important thing is that you feel comfortable and are able to do your work in college.

Rachel: It's hard to feel good about my classes when I'm so depressed. It's really hard to get used to this.

Mom: I know it must be, and I can understand how hard this is for you. Is there anything I could do to be helpful?

Rachel: No, not really. I guess I just have to cope, huh, Mom?

Mom: I think you'll know what to do and I trust that you'll figure it out. You know that your dad and I want to do what we can to help you get through this tough period.

Rachel: I know. Thanks, Mom. I guess I'd better start studying for my test tomorrow. I'll talk to you later. Okay?

Mom: Okay. Do you want me to give you a call tomorrow to see how you're doing?

Rachel: I guess so. Call me after eight though.

Mom: Okay. Well, take care, and good luck on the test.

What's on your mind?

I'm really worried that Rachel is so unhappy.

I wonder what I can do to help.

If she quits college now, what will she do?

What's on your child's mind?

I'm so miserable here.

I really want to quit, but what would I do then?

Maybe I wouldn't be happy anywhere.

What's going on.

Rachel is experiencing normal adjustment issues. She hasn't found a social group that fits her temperament and therefore feels different from everyone. She also feels the stress of the first college-level exams ahead. It's normal for her to want to quit, but she's worried about what she'll do if she does quit. Rachel needs to share her worries with her mom and, once she's done that, she'll probably feel much better about her situation.

What to do.	What to avoid.
• Remember that this is Rachel's life and Rachel's dilemma. • Empathize with her feelings of loneliness and depression. • Let her know that you care and ask if you can be helpful.	• Coming up with solutions ("Why don't you join the Habitat for Humanity group? You loved that in high school.") before you've really listened and responded to her feelings. • Warning, threatening, or moralizing: "If you don't make friends soon, you're really going to feel left out later. All the kids there can't be jerks. You just need to try harder to meet some nice kids."

What you need to know.

We know how hard (and time-consuming) it can be simply to listen to your children and allow them to feel what they're feeling without jumping in with solutions or "shoulds." In the second dialogue, Rachel's mother reflected the basic attitude that fosters a mentoring relationship. She listened and resisted the impulse to come up with solutions to Rachel's problems. This can be a particularly difficult shift for both of you if your child has always relied on you to solve her problems. If she has, you need to make this shift with compassion but also with the resolve to help your child mature so that she can manage her daily life without your constant assistance.

Choosing a Major

Thankfully, not all mentoring situations with your child are fraught with worry. Sometimes your child simply needs a rational, practical advisor or coach, such as in the case below:

When your daughter Tanisha was home on vacation in her first year of college, you had the following conversation:

TANISHA: Mom, I'm having a lot of trouble deciding what I should major in. I really like English and art history and I'm getting good grades in both. What do you think I should do?

MOM: I'm not sure just how to advise you. Tell me more about what you're thinking.

TANISHA: Well, I've heard that some people do a double major and I'm wondering if I should do that.

MOM: What are the advantages and disadvantages of doing a double major?

TANISHA: I guess if I chose to double major, I wouldn't have to make this hard decision between the two, but I might have to stay an extra semester to get in all of the requirements for both majors. And if I double major, I won't have time to take any electives, like the photography course I've been wanting to take.

MOM: It sounds like you might have to give up quite a bit just to avoid making a hard decision, huh?

TANISHA: I guess.

MOM: Have you looked at the upper-level courses in art history and English? Do they seem as interesting as the courses you're taking now?

What's on your mind?

I don't see that there's much difference between art history and English for Tanisha.

I can see it's hard for her to make this decision. I hope I can be helpful.

I wish the professors would do more to help Tanisha make this decision.

What's on your child's mind?

I'm really confused.

I have to decide soon.

What if I make the wrong decision?

TANISHA: I haven't really checked that out. Maybe I should. I do know that there are fewer requirements for an art history major than there are for an English major.

MOM: Maybe if you decided to major in art history, then, you'd have spaces in your schedule for quite a few English courses too. Have you talked to your advisor about this?

TANISHA: No, not yet. I just felt kind of funny about it because my advisor is an English professor. She might be mad if I tell her I like art history better.

MOM: What about talking to an art history professor?

TANISHA: Yeah, I guess I could. My art history professor from last semester was really cool and easy to talk to. I had to meet with him about my final paper and he was really helpful.

MOM: Having a good advisor in your major seems important. Have you talked to other students who are majoring in art history or English? Maybe they could give you some good advice.

TANISHA: Yeah, I know a couple of kids. But what about a job after college? Do you think it matters what I major in?

MOM: Well, from everything I've heard, your major doesn't really matter if you're doing a liberal arts degree. What matters is if you like it and do well in it.

TANISHA: I guess it's not like deciding between painting and premed, is it?

MOM: No, but I know it's a big decision for you anyway.

TANISHA: I think I'll talk to some more kids at school and maybe talk to the art history professor again.

MOM: That sounds like a good plan. I know you'll do well, whatever you decide.

What's going on.

Deciding on a college major is a big decision for most college students, one that many struggle with during their first two years. It's not uncommon for a student to change majors several times before settling on one course of study.

What to do.	What to avoid.
• Encourage your child to seek all of the advice available by talking to academic advisors, faculty members in departments, other students, and staff members in academic- and career-counseling offices. • Listen carefully to your child's concerns about this choice and ask open questions such as, "What are the advantages and disadvantages of each major?" • Remember that this is a time of great exploration and change and that your child's behavior is common.	• Trying to talk your child into a certain major because of its alleged career potential. • Worrying that your child is hopelessly confused and unable to make a good decision. • Dismissing this as a trivial decision, especially if your child is deciding between relatively similar majors.

What you need to know.

You have been an important advisor in your child's life and this remains true during the college years. Tanisha's mother did an excellent job of helping Tanisha move closer to making a difficult decision. She did this by asking open questions and reinforcing Tanisha's ability to research her options and make a choice. So often, what your child needs is a sounding board for her ideas and thoughts and reassurance that you have confidence in her.

Changing Majors

Your son Scott has expressed some doubts about his computer science major and now, in his second semester of college, he calls with an unsettling announcement:

SCOTT: Hi, Dad, how're things?
DAD: Good, Scott, how are you?

What's on your mind?

What's going on with Scott? He seems so confused.

I worry about him changing majors.

What will he do with a major in history?

What's on your child's mind?

I feel like such a failure.

What are my parents going to think if I change majors?

I hate my computer science courses.

SCOTT: Well, pretty good, but I'm really freaking out about declaring a major. I have to decide by April and I'm so confused.

DAD: I thought you were going to major in computer science. What's the problem?

SCOTT: Well, I don't think that computer science is right for me, and I'm not doing that well in my CS classes. But I'm doing really well in history. I love my history class. The professor is so smart and funny. Maybe I should major in history.

DAD: History? I don't understand. You've been so sure about computer science. You loved everything about computers in high school. Maybe you're just taking the wrong computer science classes. And why aren't you doing well? Maybe you're not putting in the time it takes to get good grades.

SCOTT: Dad, that's not it. I try, but it's just so hard and it's not very interesting. I didn't expect computer science to be like this.

DAD: You know there are a lot of great jobs for computer science majors. I can't understand why suddenly you're so discouraged. You seemed happy about your classes when you were home for break in December.

SCOTT: Dad, you just don't understand. Computer science is really hard, and it's not very interesting either. It's almost impossible to get good grades. Do you want me to flunk out?

DAD: No, I certainly don't want you to flunk out. I just want to understand why you're so undecided and why you're changing what you always said you wanted to study. Maybe you should try to get some help with your courses. Isn't there anyone who can tutor you and help you to do well?

SCOTT: I don't know, but that's not the point, Dad. I just don't like computer science anymore.

DAD: But what will you do if you major in history? I'm not too happy about spending all of this money for you to be unemployed when you graduate!

SCOTT: I'm sure I can get a job if that's what you're so worried about!

DAD: Yeah, like what? There are a lot of history majors flipping burgers, I bet. I think you should just stick with computer science and work a little harder. I know you can do it if you try.

What's going on.

Scott's father finds it difficult to deal with the changes that Scott is considering. Instead of listening to Scott, he is dominating the conversation with his own concerns. Neither Scott nor his father are really listening to the other person's point of view, hence the conversation ends up being a series of accusations, judgments, and threats. Scott's father has legitimate concerns about how changing majors could affect Scott's future and whether Scott is really making an effort. He may also believe that he has a right to control Scott's choice of major because he's footing the bill for college. He may convince Scott to remain a computer science major, but in doing so, he will take away Scott's power to make decisions about his own life. It's tempting for parents to jump into the void and take responsibility for decisions when their children are confused.

What to do.	What to avoid.
• Listen to your child's worries. Empathize with his confusion.	• Letting your concerns be most important.
• Ask for information and respond to feelings before telling your child what you think about the situation.	• Criticizing your son for being so indecisive.
• Ask questions that will help your child come to his own conclusions.	• Warning him about the dire future consequences of his decision.
	• Forcing your child to stick with a major that you think is more sensible.

Changing Majors: The Replay

Now, see the difference in the same phone call when Dad communicates as a mentor:

SCOTT: Hi, Dad, how's it going?
DAD: Fine, Scott, how are you?

SCOTT: Well, I'm kinda freaked out right now. I'm not sure I want to be a computer science major any more.

DAD: Really? What changed your mind?

SCOTT: I'm just not doing well in my computer science classes and I have a history class that I really like. It's so much more interesting than computer science.

DAD: What is it that you like about your history class?

SCOTT: I'm learning so much about what happened in the Second World War—it's amazing. This is what Grandpa used to talk about, and now I'm beginning to understand what really happened. It's about people's lives, not just numbers.

DAD: So you're disillusioned with crunching numbers and learning about programming machines, huh?

SCOTT: Yeah, it's just so boring and it's hard too. No one in my computer science classes is doing well.

DAD: Is it the difficulty of the work or the fact that it's not interesting that disturbs you the most?

SCOTT: I guess it's both. I just don't think I'd be happy doing this kind of work forever.

DAD: And the history course seems interesting and fun right now.

SCOTT: Yeah, my professor is great. He's an amazing lecturer and has a way of making the information interesting. I wrote a paper on Pearl Harbor and I got an A on it.

DAD: That's terrific, Scott. It sounds like history interests you.

SCOTT: But maybe I'm wimping out because CS is so hard.

DAD: Do you think that you're going to be a failure if you don't study computer science?

SCOTT: Well, sort of. I mean that's what I came here to study.

DAD: Maybe it would help if you had an idea of what kind of jobs people with computer science and history degrees have after they finish college.

SCOTT: Well, I guess CS majors just sit in a cubicle somewhere and program computers all day. I don't know what history majors do.

What's on your mind?

Scott seems confused about his major and that worries me.

This is a good opportunity for Scott to explore his interests.

I hope I can be helpful to Scott as he sorts this out.

What's on your child's mind?

I don't want to disappoint my parents, but I hate computer science.

Maybe I'm just not willing to invest the time to do well in computer science.

I wonder what I really want to study in college. History is so much more interesting.

DAD: It seems like you're a little worried because you're not doing so well in your CS classes and you also feel the pressure of having to declare a major this term. Is that true?

SCOTT: Yeah, I'm pretty sure I don't want to be a CS major, but I don't know what to do. I've always thought I'd be a computer jockey.

DAD: And you wonder if you should declare a history major after having taken only one course in history.

SCOTT: I don't know what to do. I can't believe I have to declare a major in a month.

DAD: What would you like to do?

SCOTT: Well, I'd like to have more time to decide, but if I *had* to decide today, I wouldn't be a computer science major. What do you think I should do?

DAD: It's not my decision, but I'd be happy to try and help you make a choice. When you come home in a couple of weeks for spring break, would you be interested in spending a day or two with John Warner, my friend who has the small computer business? Maybe if you saw first hand what computer science folks do at work it would help you make a decision. Or you could talk to a professor in computer science and one in history and ask them what their graduates are doing now. I think your mom knows someone at the bank who majored in history in college. She could introduce you to her when you're home.

SCOTT: Well, I guess I could do that. I don't have to make a final decision until April.

DAD: Would you like John's number? You can call him to see if he'd let you stop by and observe for a day or two over break.

SCOTT: Okay, I'll give him a call, but I'm not sure it will change my mind.

DAD: Maybe just having more information will help you make your decision. I have faith in your ability to choose what is right for you.

SCOTT: Thanks, Dad. I'll call him tomorrow.

What's going on.

Parents' expectations can get dashed as college students explore courses of study and seem confused about their direction. It's not unusual for students to change majors—even several times. Scott's father gave him the greatest gift a mentor can give—to help his son believe in his own ability to make decisions. Communicating and caring in this way sets the stage for a more satisfying and respectful dialogue that will carry Scott and his father through many changes throughout the college years.

What to do?

- Listen to your child's dilemma openly.
- Check your assumptions by repeating your child's concerns and asking if you're hearing correctly.
- Suggest ways that your child can get more information to solve his problem.
- Remind your child that you have confidence in his ability to make decisions and choices.

What to avoid?

- Criticizing your child for being confused and indecisive.
- Threatening dire consequences if he changes majors.
- Making your expectations more important than his exploration.

What you need to know.

In our experience, students who feel they must take their parents' advice and direction are ultimately less successful than students who strive to reach their own goals. This doesn't mean that you can't share your feelings about decisions or that you can't take the lead in asking questions, laying out alternatives, and providing suggestions. You do, however, want your son or daughter to take ownership for developing solutions to problems.

While you can't convince your child to approach every decision as you would, you can guide him or her through a process that will help in addressing problems and making difficult decisions. Letting your child know that you're willing to examine alternatives, try on other points of view, and experiment with your own attitudes and beliefs, teaches your child a decision-making process that will be useful throughout his or her life.

Fall Trip

Your daughter Haley decided to go on a camping trip with her new boyfriend over fall break. She calls you from a pay phone in the Smoky Mountains at 11:00 P.M. on Saturday night and announces that she hates camping *and* her boyfriend and wants you to come and get her because she still has three days left of fall break to spend at home.

What's going on.

Haley is miserable and really wishes that her mother would bail her out of this unpleasant situation. She made a decision to go on this trip without knowing Justin very well. Now she's stuck for a whole weekend with him alone in the woods and she's finding out that she doesn't like him very much after all.

What's on your mind?

What's really going on?
Is Haley in danger?
Should I rescue her or let her deal with this?

What's on your child's mind?

I hate it here. It's cold and there's nothing to do.
Boy, was I stupid to come on this trip with Justin.
I just want to go home.

What to do.

- Find out if she is safe.
- Ask her, "What changed your mind about this trip?" and "What are your thoughts about getting out of this situation? How would you like me to help?"
- Be frank with her about what you're willing to do to help her once you've determined that she's not in danger.
- Help her brainstorm her options: She could ask Justin to drive her home, she could ask him to get her to the nearest bus station, or she could decide to stick it out.

What to avoid.

- Jumping in the car and going to get her.
- Feeling that it's your job, as her parent, to get her out of this situation.
- Criticizing her for going on the trip in the first place.
- Blaming her for ruining your weekend and making you worry.

What you need to know.

Once you've determined that Haley isn't in danger, you can be an effective advisor, helping her to brainstorm solutions to her dilemma. In asking her how she would like to resolve her problem, you reinforce her ability to evaluate her situation and take action. It's not appropriate, or helpful, for you to simply approve or disapprove; it *is* your role to listen and support your child in examining her options and recognizing the consequences of her behavior.

While fall break may be ruined, she will also have learned something about herself—that even though she made a poor choice, she is in charge of her behavior and decisions. Parents who rob their children of the consequences of their actions deprive them of their dignity and impede their progress toward responsible adulthood. Better a wasted fall break than a child who learns that someone else has to take responsibility for his or her actions and choices.

Even though mentoring often seems like an inefficient exercise, it's helpful to remember that mentoring is like teaching and coaching. No one is born with these skills fully developed. As you try out these new mentoring skills, you need to be patient with your child who is also confronting new situations that demand he or she take on adult responsibilities.

Academic Probation

You're visiting campus for a special spring weekend and your son Brian seems nervous and preoccupied. You finally ask what's wrong:

BRIAN: Well, it's bad news. I was put on academic probation. I failed a course last semester and didn't do too well in my other courses either.

DAD: When did you find out? Why didn't you tell us?

BRIAN: I just got the letter from the dean this week. I thought I could do better this semester.

DAD: Well, are you doing better?

BRIAN: Not that much.

DAD: What do you mean, "Not that much?"

BRIAN: Well, I'm having trouble with chemistry, and I'm getting way behind in a couple of my other courses too.

DAD: I can't believe this. Do you know how much money it's costing me to put you through college? I know you have the ability. Why aren't you applying yourself?

BRIAN: I am, Dad, it's just so hard.

DAD: Of course it's hard. What did you think it would be? You have to work hard in college. It sounds like you've just been goofing off. Doing well in college takes discipline. You better straighten out your priorities and get off of probation.

BRIAN: I'm not sure I can. I'm already so far behind and my midterm grades haven't been so hot.

DAD: What do you mean you're not sure if you can? Of course, you can. You need to try harder. You better get busy and improve those grades. You were such a good student in high school. What is going on here?

BRIAN: I don't know, Dad. I guess I'm just a loser.

DAD: You *will* be, if that's your attitude.

What's on your mind?

I can't believe how hard I'm working to keep Brian in college and he's just screwing off.

I'm really mad at him. He's just not willing to try.

I'm so disappointed in Brian and his attitude stinks.

He better not be partying all the time.

What's on your child's mind?

I feel lousy. Maybe I can't handle college work.

My dad is really mad at me, but he doesn't understand how hard this is.

What if I flunk out? What will I do?

What's going on.

It's not unusual for the first year of college to present real challenges and disappointments to students and parents alike. Even students who have done well in high school may find college overwhelming, especially when they have to be in charge of every aspect of their life away from home. Parents are usually shocked when their child is put on academic probation and angry that their tuition money is being wasted.

What to do.	What to avoid.
• Try to put your feelings on hold and listen to your child.	• Blaming him for being in this mess. He knows he's screwed up.
• Tell him that while you're disappointed in his performance, you have confidence in his ability to do the work.	• Warning him that you're going to cut off financial support.
• Ask if he's thought of any ways he might salvage this semester's work.	• Moralizing and preaching about what he could have done better—the point is, he didn't!
• Suggest that he get help, either by asking his professors, going to the learning skills center, or getting a tutor to get him through this semester.	• Issuing ultimatums: You'd better get it together, or else!

Academic Probation: The Replay

Your mentoring skills will come in handy when your child faces a serious situation and you're a bit baffled about what to do. In this replay, Brian's dad demonstrates an ideal mentoring response, which we realize is hard to do in such an emotionally charged situation:

BRIAN: Well, it's bad news. I was put on academic probation. I failed a course last semester and didn't do too well in my other courses either.

DAD: What does academic probation mean?

BRIAN: It means that I'm outta here if I don't get at least a 2.5 GPA this semester, and it doesn't look too good right now.

DAD: When did you find this out? We had no idea you weren't doing well.

BRIAN: I just got the letter this week. I guess I should have told you, but I thought this semester would be better. It's just that the work here is so hard. I had no idea it would be this hard.

DAD: I've been wondering why you seemed so edgy. You must be feeling pretty rotten about this.

BRIAN: Yeah, I guess I'm just not college material, huh?

DAD: Is that what you really feel?

BRIAN: Well, what am I supposed to feel? I'm flunking out of school! I just don't know what happened. I guess last semester I fell too far behind and couldn't catch up when finals came around. But I was sure that I could do better this semester. I didn't party as much and I really tried to study, but I just couldn't concentrate. Maybe I should just take a year off like they suggested and try to figure out what to do next.

DAD: Tell me more about what you've been thinking.

BRIAN: I've been feeling like a loser. You and Mom must be really upset with me. I don't know. Maybe I need to go home and work for a while and take some courses at the community college. I'm sure I could do okay there. It's not that hard, I've heard. At least it's not so competitive.

DAD: Have you decided what you'll do for the rest of the semester here?

BRIAN: I don't know. What do you think I should do?

DAD: What I think isn't really important. *You* need to decide what you're going to do.

BRIAN: You *always* say that! Sometimes I just wish you'd yell at me and tell me what to do.

DAD: Well, I could yell at you to work harder and get better grades. Would that make it happen?

BRIAN: I guess not.

DAD: Your mom and I aren't around every day to make sure you study. It's your responsibility now. You need to figure it out. We'll be disappointed if you don't try, but we can't *make* you do what it takes from home.

BRIAN: I know. It's just so hard.

DAD: Having to pull yourself out of this hole seems pretty overwhelming, huh?

BRIAN: Yeah. I've been trying, but it's just so hard; there's so much to learn in such a short time.

DAD: So it may not be possible, but it sounds like you want to stay and try to finish. Is that right?

BRIAN: I guess I should. After all, you and Mom have spent so much money on this year, it's depressing to waste all of that. Maybe I could leave with a few credits anyway.

What's on your mind?

Brian is in a lot of trouble.
I wish we had known about his failing grades.
I'm not sure he has the resilience to get through this.

What's on your child's mind?

Boy, are my parents going to be pissed at me.
I can't believe this has happened to me.
Maybe I'm not smart enough for college.

DAD: Do you see any way that your mother or I can help you right now?

BRIAN: Well, I should have done it before, but I could hire a tutor if you guys want to spring for it. Especially for my chem class. I've heard that there are some pretty good tutors here, but I'd have to pay them.

DAD: I think that would be a good investment. I'd be willing to pay for it if you think it will help.

BRIAN: Yeah, I think it would. If I could just get chem under control, I might have more time to work on my other classes too.

DAD: Have you given any thought to getting some study skills help? I think I remember reading that they have a pretty good learning center here on campus.

BRIAN: Yeah, I guess I could check that out too.

DAD: Struggling with this worry must have been really hard for you. I know you came to school with lots of hopes and enthusiasm.

BRIAN: Well, I didn't have a clue, I guess.

DAD: It's hard to know what's coming when it's such a new experience. You've had to spend so much energy getting used to a whole new living situation.

BRIAN: Yeah, that's the sad part. I would really like it here, if it weren't so hard. It would be really depressing to leave all of my new friends.

DAD: It must be hard to think about leaving all of this behind and starting over.

BRIAN: I guess I just need to try to get it together and see what happens.

DAD: That sounds like a good plan. I have a lot of confidence in your abilities. You'll know what's right for you. And you know we'll love you no matter what, don't you?

BRIAN: Yeah, Dad. Thanks.

What's going on.

Students learn a lot about themselves during the first year of college, and not all of the lessons are easy ones. Many are asked to take time off to reassess their goals when they are failing courses or are unable to maintain an acceptable grade point average. Some students need extra time to mature into the responsibilities of college life. If Brian had been assertive and taken the initiative to get help in his first semester, he may not have been asked to take a leave. This may seem like the end of the world for your child or for you, but it can also serve as a wake-up call that your child needs extra help in handling college work.

What to do.	What to avoid.
• Listen to your child's feelings. • Empathize with his experience and try to keep your own ego out of it. You may find it's easier to do this if you can imagine advising the son or daughter of a friend. • Ask for clarification when needed. Ask for his point of view and then listen, without evaluating it. • Reinforce your confidence in his ability to manage this difficult situation. • Help him problem solve, encouraging him to make short-term and long-term decisions when he is ready.	• Coming up with hasty solutions that will make you feel better. • Dwelling on how upset you are. • Punishing him: Having to leave school will be punishment enough. He'll learn more from the real consequences of his behavior.

What you need to know.

In this replay, Brian's father exhibited superior mentoring skills in a difficult situation. Becoming this skillful at mentoring your child doesn't happen overnight and this response may not feel comfortable for you in the beginning. You will be on the way to being an effective mentor, however, just by taking the first steps: trying to focus on your child rather than on your own feelings of anger and disappointment, and recognizing that your role is to help your child solve his or her problem, not to solve it for your child.

As parents, we have little control over what happens to our children in college, but we do have control over how we respond to the situation. Keep your eye on the end goal—the issue here is to get through this crisis and help your child land on his or her feet again. This doesn't mean that you can't express your fears and desires to your child. It's just that this isn't the time to do it. This situation calls for empathy and reasoned response, not panic. It might be helpful, however, if you share a story from your life in which you felt like a failure and describe how you felt and what you did about the situation. Children need to know that their parents have weathered storms in the past and that these experiences were tough but ultimately manageable.

If you feel, after some time has elapsed, that your child is still floundering and not able to be productive, it may be the time to express your concerns. Remember, though, that you should avoid using "you" messages, such as, "You haven't done your work," "You're just lying around all day when you should be studying," "You party too much and therefore you have rotten grades." Try to express "I" messages, such as, "I really worry about you when I see you are neglecting your studies," "I don't feel I can continue to support your education if you're not willing to put in the time to get decent grades," "I'm concerned that you're not motivated right now to do college work."

When students fail at something, they are the first to recognize that failure. It's not necessary to criticize or blame. Doing so doesn't change the failure into a success; it only serves to make a child feel more helpless. An effective mentor sees a problem or crisis and responds like Brian's dad did—listening, reflecting, empathizing, suggesting, and supporting. This takes time and patience, but it is well worth the effort on your part.

One of the greatest joys of parenting is witnessing your child take on the responsibilities, rewards, and challenges of fully independent adulthood. The college years present a unique opportunity for you, as a parent, to begin to relate to your child as an emerging adult and adopt behaviors that will serve you well in the years to come.

Want to Know More?

Newman, Barbara, and Philip Newman. *When Kids Go to College: A Parent's Guide to Changing Relationships.* Columbus: Ohio State University Press, 1992.
Tice, Lou, and Joyce Quick. *Personal Coaching for Results: How to Mentor and Inspire Others to Amazing Growth.* Nashville: Thomas Nelson, 1997.

Huang, Chungliang A., and Jerry Lynch. *Mentoring: The Tao of Giving and Receiving Wisdom*. San Francisco: HarperCollins, 1995.

Shea, Gordon F. *Making the Most of Being Mentored: How to Grow from a Mentoring Partnership*. Menlo Park: Crisp Publications, 1999.

1. Linda Phillips-Jones, *Mentors and Proteges* (New York: Arbor House Publishing, 1982), 49.
2. The concept of a mentor-rich environment comes from Marc Freedman, *The Kindness of Strangers: Adult Mentors, Urban Youth, and the New Voluntarism* (Cambridge, UK: Cambridge University Press, 1999), xxvi.

Chapter 2

Getting Them Off to College

Preparing Yourself and Your Child for the Transition

> *I never understood the meaning of the word inevitability until I was wheeled into the delivery room to give birth to my first child. The responsibility of caring for a helpless child was awesome indeed. Then, about two minutes later, he was eighteen years old and we were packing the car to take him to college. Again the word inevitability came to mind, but in a different way. This time I knew in my heart of hearts that he would never really come home again.*

With the flurry of activity surrounding the college choice and admissions process, you haven't had much time to think about how *your* life is going to change when your child actually leaves home for college. This chapter will help you deal with many of the logistical and emotional challenges you'll face in the weeks leading up to his or her departure. You may be surprised by the intensity of your feelings about having your child (whether he or she's the first or the fifth!) go off to college.

Before You Leave Home

What can you do to prepare yourself (and your child) for this major change? First, you can take pride in the job you have done as a parent. The years of caring, chauffeuring, nursing, listening, empathizing, supporting, and, yes, sometimes just coping with your child are nearly over. The last year of high school is usually a challenging one. High school seniors typically are more than ready to move away from the family, and they have a way of making that clear. After the stresses of applications, test taking, and acceptance decisions are over, most high school seniors find themselves in an ambivalent place—still at home but ready to move on. Parents complain that their high school seniors are hard to recognize as the children they've known and loved. Some feel this is nature's way of preparing you to say good-bye. In fact, at some points, you can't wait to say good-bye!

Getting Organized

As the excitement of anticipating college acceptance letters and the relief of having made the choice wears off, you'll notice a gradual shift in your child's behavior, which usually intensifies in the weeks just before he or she leaves for college. Just as parents are ambivalent about this event, their children are often experiencing conflicting emotions too. They are nervous, excited, sad, and confused, all at the same time. And this can make for some intense family interactions.

It's two weeks before you make the car trip to deliver Ashley to college. She has finished up her summer job and is doing an impressive imitation of a young woman without a care in the world. At the dinner table one night, you finally confront her:

MOM: Do you realize that in just two weeks from today we're driving you down to school?

ASHLEY: Yeah, I guess so.

MOM: When are you going to start getting ready to leave? You have a million things to do.

ASHLEY: Mom, chill. I have plenty of time. I just finished my job and I want to veg out for a while.

MOM: But, Ashley, you can't wait until the last minute to get it together.

ASHLEY: I just have to pack up my clothes and stuff.

MOM: Speaking of stuff, what do you plan to take? Are you taking your CD player? Have you read the packet of information from school on what you should bring? Have you talked to your roommate yet about what she's bringing?

ASHLEY: MOM, stop it! I'm not a baby. I can handle getting ready to go to school.

MOM: I just don't want to deal with the last-minute panic that I see coming if you don't get organized now.

ASHLEY: Yeah, well, I gotta run. I promised Jess I'd meet her at the mall at seven o'clock. See ya!

What's on your mind?

Ashley is driving me crazy. She can't seem to do anything but sleep and hang out.

I'm going to get stuck with getting her ready for school at the last minute.

She seems so lukewarm about going to college now—she was so excited a couple of months ago.

What's on your child's mind?

I wish Mom would stop bugging me about getting ready to go to school. She acts like I'm twelve and going to summer camp.

I can't wait to get away from here, but I'm really going to miss Jess and Carol.

I wonder what my roommate is like? Maybe I should call her, but I don't want to look weird or anything. I hope she's not a loser. I hope she doesn't think *I'm* a loser.

What's going on.

You're surprised that Ashley appears so disinterested in preparing to go to school. You wonder if she's having second thoughts about going at all. Ashley seems to be withdrawing from the family scene but not getting ready for college either. This behavior is natural for a student entering college. As the day draws closer to leaving for school, the "what if" fears and thoughts begin for both parents and children. You may find yourself arguing with your child over seemingly trivial things, a common occurrence before a separation. You're most likely trying to deal with this situation on two levels at once—logistical and emotional.

What to do *logistically.*

- Recognize that this is normal precollege jitters on your child's part and that it is important for her to spend time with her high school friends in order to make the break with them.
- Ask if there is something you can do to be helpful (while not taking on the whole project yourself). For example, you might be able to help by comparing prices so that she has the information to make a decision about buying a computer.
- Ask Ashley to set aside a couple of hours on a specific day to go out for lunch with you to talk about plans for the move. Make a list of things that you feel need to be addressed, and ask Ashley to do the same.

What to avoid *logistically.*

- Taking on the packing and organizing yourself.
- Giving her the third degree or nagging her every day about getting ready.

What to do *emotionally.*

- Take care of yourself. Recognize that you may be expressing your own precollege jitters in trying to be hyperorganized when what you really need to do is deal with your feelings about your daughter leaving home. Commiserate with a friend who's in the same situation.
- Ask Ashley, "What are your hopes, fears, and expectations about being a college student?" Then simply LISTEN without judging or dismissing anything she says.
- Let her know *your* hopes, fears, and expectations. You may be most concerned about safety, grades, drinking, drugs, the social scene, eating habits, and basic adjustment. It will be interesting for you to hear your child's concerns. Warning: Your child may not be eager to do this. That's okay. Expressing some of your feelings will make *you* feel better.
- Remind your child that she may be on an emotional roller coaster for a while, but that you are confident that she is ready for this new life away from home.
- Reassure her that she can always call on you for support.

What to avoid *emotionally.*

- Ignoring your own feelings or projecting them onto your child.
- Taking on your daughter's tasks and emotions as your own. This will only make you feel frustrated and angry.

Helping Your Child Decide What to Bring

Most colleges send entering students a list of things they will need to set up their rooms, including personal items. Ask your child to review this list with you. We have suggested some of the most common items to consider.

Electronic Equipment/Appliances/Furniture

College students often arrive on campus with a room-clogging array of electronic equipment in addition to mini-refrigerators, microwave ovens, and even furniture! Most dormitory rooms cannot accommodate all of this stuff. It's a good idea for roommates to discuss what they're planning to bring to avoid having two or three of everything in a small room. Dormitory rooms typically have the basics: a bed, desk, dresser, and a closet. Things like TVs, VCRs, CD players, speakers, telephone answering machines, phones, small refrigerators, coffee/tea makers, toaster ovens/microwaves, irons, extra bookshelves, laundry hampers, drying racks, fans, and wastebaskets can take up a lot of room. Most residence halls have television lounges and group kitchen facilities, so many of these things are not necessary in each individual room. Moreover, local merchants usually rent small refrigerators and sell residence hall–sized rugs and other room furnishings to incoming college students.

Decorating the Room

We've noted a remarkable difference between males and females in approaches to "decorating" dorm rooms. Girls often want to coordinate bedspreads, rugs, curtains, and wall decorations, and boys usually don't. Your daughter may want to wait to decorate her room until she confers with her roommate so that their things will match. Your son will probably take very little interest in things like room furnishings and will not want to coordinate with a roommate. Either way, you and your child can decide whether to purchase these items before leaving home or to take extra cash to buy them at school. It's a good idea to remember that many residence hall mattresses are not high quality. The beds are often extra long and regular fitted sheets may not work. You may want to bring extra mattress padding or even a piece of plywood to help firm up the mattress.

Computers

Although most campuses include extensive computer lab facilities for students' use, your son or daughter may have or want to purchase a personal computer. Many colleges have good deals on computers because of educational discounts, and they'll be eager to sell you computer equipment. If you decide to purchase a computer beforehand, make sure that the computer's software will be compatible with networking systems on campus and in the residence halls. Most colleges are trying to wire residence halls for Internet use because students, administrators, and faculty are increasingly using E-mail to communicate with one another.

Cars on Campus

Many colleges do not allow students to bring cars to campus during the first year. Some discourage having a car at all. Find out the school's policy before you agree to allow your child to have a car. Most campuses have limited parking space and will charge your child a hefty fee for parking. In general, it's not a good idea to have your child bring a car to campus during the first year. It adds a level of complexity to a new student's life that is easily avoided. If your child is going to bring a car to campus, check on the regulations beforehand. It's also a good idea to review basic car maintenance and service needs with your child beforehand. Simple things like checking the oil or adding antifreeze and coolant may need to be covered, especially if you have taken responsibility for those things in the past.

Bicycles

Bicycles can be a terrific, inexpensive way for your child to navigate the campus and get some exercise as well. Check ahead of time to ensure adequate, safe storage for the bicycle in the residence hall. Few rooms can accommodate a bicycle, unless you install special hooks to hang it from the wall or ceiling. It's important to have a high-quality lock to discourage theft—bicycles in college towns are often stolen.

Money

Have a frank conversation with your child about finances before he or she leaves for college. For most people, talking about money is somewhat difficult, but being open with your child about what resources you have (or don't have!) to commit to his or her college expenses helps your child understand and appreciate your point of view. It's important to try to do this in a straightforward way—you don't want your child to feel guilty if you are making great sacrifices to send him or her to college, but you also don't want your child to expect support that you aren't able or willing to provide. Don't apologize, just describe what you are willing and unwilling to do. Discussing money openly with your child may be awkward, but it will seriously reduce tension and problems later.

Initial Costs

Room furnishing and setup costs can be considerable. The first textbook bill can also come as a surprise. It is not unusual for a student's textbooks to cost around five hundred dollars for a semester or term. If the student is an architecture, engineering, or art major, the additional cost of supplies can be significant. Check with your home or apartment owner's insurance carrier ahead of time to ensure that your child's expensive electronic equipment (including computer) is covered under your policy. Consider getting replacement value insurance coverage, which usually adds very little cost to your policy. It ensures that you will be able to replace this expensive equipment instead of only getting reimbursed for a used computer, which will be considerably less than you'd have to pay for a replacement.

Spending Money

Many parents expect their children to earn spending money through a summer job or a job on campus. If you agree that your child must earn spending money, make it clear that you will not send more unless there is an emergency. If you're planning to provide spending money, discuss a reasonable amount. If you have a limit, make it clear. You may agree to renegotiate this amount at Thanksgiving break when the actual costs are clearer.

The amount of spending money your child will need varies a great deal, depending on several factors, such as the school's location and its general social culture. If it's an urban school, opportunities to spend money on entertainment and expensive diversions will be greater; if it's a rural school, more time may be spent on campus taking part in college activities and cultural events that are free or relatively inexpensive. It will depend mostly on what kind of social life your child wants. If fraternities and sororities are the main social activity and your child decides to pledge, it can be costly. If your child has an active social life, his or her need for spending money may be greater than those who spend their time studying and eating pizza with friends in the dorm or going to a movie occasionally. The availability of E-mail has dramatically decreased the amount of money most students spend on long-distance phone bills, but it is a good idea to have an understanding of who will pay phone bills. You may choose to contribute to your child's phone calls home or give the child a special calling card that only allows him or her to call certain agreed-upon numbers. Encourage your child to discuss payment of the phone bill with the roommate as well, if they share a phone number.

If you have a high-maintenance child who spends a lot of money on personal care products, try to buy these things in quantity at home. College stores tend to respond to their captive consumer audience by charging more for basics, such as shampoo, toothpaste, soap, tissues, aspirin, cosmetics, and so on. Cleaning supplies for the room will also be necessary, as most residence halls have cleaning services only for public areas and communal bathrooms.

Credit Cards/Checking Accounts

Many college-bound students already have credit cards and checking accounts. You may want your child to have a credit card (or access to yours) for emergencies. Talk about what constitutes an emergency (running out of pizza on Friday night isn't one!). Credit card companies feel that college students are a good risk due to their future earning potential, and they will provide your child with applications as soon as they arrive on campus. Students can sign up for multiple credit cards during their first year in college and can get into serious credit card debt if they are not aware of the pitfalls. Talk to your child about how to choose a credit card, and discuss the various deals offered on interest rates, annual fees, and so on.

Many colleges offer credit cardlike charging privileges at the campus store with the student ID card. Be clear about what you will pay for if your child uses a commercial or college credit card. You may approve charging textbooks and school supplies but not CDs and clothing.

It's a good idea for your child to have a local checking account and an ATM card that will be easily accepted and accessed on campus. This may mean having a cashier's check prepared before leaving home with funds from an existing account to start the new one. Have enough cash in the account to last for a couple of weeks after arrival until your child finds out about check-cashing policies on campus and in the new community.

Health Insurance

Make sure that your child will continue to be covered under the family health insurance plan. Many insurance companies will cover children if they are full-time students, but you usually need to notify your insurance carrier as to that status. Most colleges and universities offer a health insurance plan for students if your policy will not cover your child. Check it out in time to make the change if necessary.

Extras

If special trips or expensive events come up, talk about who will foot the bill. This will avoid the frantic calls home for more money at the last minute to attend a concert or athletic event out of town. It will also encourage your child to think ahead about which extras are important to them, instead of simply going along with the gang on spur-of-the-moment adventures that may be very costly. This may be the first time your child encounters other students who are much wealthier or much more financially limited. Clear up expectations for "extras" ahead of time, as peer pressure will undoubtedly kick in to attend special events.

Dealing with Special Needs

An increasing number of young people come to college with special issues, challenges, and needs. Some students need regular medications, psychological counseling, and/or help in coping with academics due to a learning disability. If your child has special issues such as these, it is useful to discuss how these needs will be met at college. For example, if your child has an eating disorder, it can be especially frightening to "let go" of monitoring his or her eating behavior. What can you do? Talk to your child about the challenges he or she will face at college. While it's not appropriate to enlist the aid of a roommate in getting your child to eat properly, it is useful, with your child's consent, to inform the resident advisor that this is an issue for your child. You might also, with your child's knowledge and consent, help arrange an initial consultation with the campus health service or counseling group.

If your child needs special help with a learning disability, check with the college to ensure the necessary support services are available. Encourage your child to take advantage of these services.

Planning to Stay in Touch

Parents who are proactive initially in helping their children get the support they need in college can relax and work on relinquishing control. It's appropriate to tell your child that, while you have confidence in his or her ability to manage the adjustment to college, you would like to agree on a mutually acceptable form of keeping in touch for your own reassurance.

Phone Calls/Letters/E-mail, and Care Packages

Your child will be involved in a dizzying array of activities during the first few weeks of college. Days will fly by as he or she meets new people and grows accustomed to an entirely new living environment. Calling or writing home may get lost in the shuffle. It's best to let your child decide on how he or she wants to accommodate your need for information and updates, but you may have to take the initiative in making an agreement—before you leave home.

- Set a day and time for your child to call home for the first time.
- Make your expectations clear—if you expect to hear from your child every week, set a day and time for weekly calls.
- If you would rather hear by letter or E-mail, talk about those options.

Be prepared to do most of the keeping in touch yourself. Don't expect your child to take the initiative in writing or calling. It is extremely important, though, that your child hears from you often, especially during the first few weeks of college. Make your messages light—short notes with news from home, E-mails, care packages, or phone calls are appreciated and comforting. Even if you E-mail your child often, you may also want to drop a note from time to time. It's sad, particularly for a first-year student, to go to the mailbox every day and find it empty. They especially feel grateful for the occasional care package from home. Most students won't admit it, but they really do want to hear from you and generally want reassurance that everything at home has stayed the same.

I (Helen) remember a call from my younger son about two weeks into his first year at college. The first call was a short message on our answering machine. "Hi, Mom and Dad. Where are you? This is Ben. I'm just calling to say hi. Well, I guess I'll try later." A couple of days later, another message sounded a little indignant. "Hi, guys. Well, I guess you're out again. Call me." When we managed to connect with Ben, he was incredulous that we hadn't been hovering around the phone waiting for his call! How dare we have a life without him? For a young man who couldn't wait to escape from home, he was clearly anxious to be reassured and a little shocked that we could actually amuse ourselves without him. Of course, he had totally forgotten that we had left five messages on his answering machine before he got around to giving us a call.

Visiting Your Child

It's good to wait at least a couple of months before you visit your child at school. Many schools have an organized parents' weekend in the first semester when you can visit. Whether you're planning to attend parents' weekend or making your own informal visit to campus, always call your child first to make sure that it's a good time to come. This can be especially tricky if you live close to the college and are tempted to drop in on your child to see how things are going. This is never a good idea! Just as you wouldn't barge into your child's room at home without knocking, you need to respect his or her new space and privacy.

Orientation/Send-off Parties

Many colleges and universities include a component for parents in their orientation program. If so, it's a good way to have many of your questions answered and meet other parents as well. If you can't attend, or the institution doesn't offer a parents' orientation, call the office of the dean of students on campus and ask for orientation materials to be sent to you. Even materials prepared specifically for students will help you become more familiar with life at college.

In some cities, alumni groups give send-off parties for new students and their families in the summer before the college year begins. These can introduce you to other parents of new students. There are also parents' programs at many colleges through which you can receive information and possibly a listing of parents in your area. Sharing this experience with other parents can help, particularly in the first few months of adjustment for you and your child.

The Dreaded Drop-off

Whether you say good-bye to your new college student at the residence hall or at the airport, you've anticipated this moment and perhaps dreaded it for months. For years we have witnessed that most poignant of scenes—arrival day for students with their parents in tow. Families wandering around campus looking confused and concerned. New students trying to distance themselves from their parents and younger brothers and sisters. Families standing around feeling useless after the last box has been carted to the room and the roommate has appeared for the obligatory handshake.

Saying Good-bye

Parents who plan for this unceremonious leave-taking can avoid interactions like the following:

MOM: So, Josh, do you want me to make up your bed before we leave?
JOSH: No, Mom, I can handle it.
MOM: Well, maybe we should unpack some of these boxes and throw the empty boxes out.

What's on Mom's mind?

I don't want to leave yet. I'm not ready for this!

Josh is acting like he doesn't even care that we're leaving.

I wish we could just spend the day together.

What's on Dad's mind?

I think it's time to clear out.

Josh seems pretty anxious to get rid of us and get to know his roommate.

What's on Josh's mind?

I wish they'd just go. They're driving me crazy!

I want to get unpacked and hang out with my room-mate.

I know my mom is going to cry and make me feel stupid.

JOSH: It's okay. I can do it later.

DAD: Well, let's go get some lunch.

JOSH: I'm supposed to go to a hall meeting in an hour. I think I'll just stay here and hang with Jim. His parents have left already.

MOM: Oh, okay. Well, where will we meet you later?

JOSH: I'm not really sure—there's a lot to do here and there's a party later on in the quad for new students.

AMY (JOSH'S LITTLE SISTER): Can we leave now? I'm so bored. There's nothing to do here.

MOM: I told you, Amy, that we were going to stay until tonight and go to some of the parents' activities.

DAD: Let's go get some lunch and then we can go to the new parents meeting. It's at two o'clock in McAlister Hall. I've got a map. We can find it. We'll see you later, Son.

MOM: When?

JOSH: Uh, I don't know, Mom. Maybe we could meet back here at around five before I go to dinner.

MOM: Aren't you going to go out to dinner with us before we leave?

DAD: Maybe we should just say good-bye now and then Josh can get settled.

AMY: Mom, Dad, I'm bored! Can't we do something?

DAD: Well, Josh, have a great time and study hard. Let us know how you're doing, okay?

MOM (hugging Josh with tears in her eyes): Bye, Hon. Are you sure you're going to be okay? Call us if you need anything. We should be home by ten o'clock tonight.

AMY: Bye, Josh. Have fun!

What's going on.

Everyone's caught in an emotional bind. The parents' expectations for a last, meaningful good-bye are not going to be met, and Josh fears the worst—a tearful scene with his mom that will make him look ridiculous. The family needs to make a quick, dignified separation and allow Josh to begin the process of settling in. The first few hours and days of college are critical for the new student to share the "blending in" with the other new students. If Josh spends the day with his family, he'll miss those crucial first hours of getting to know other students and participating in planned activities. At this point, he's eager to get on with his new life and is totally focused on himself, and your feelings will probably make him extremely uncomfortable. It's the rare student, indeed, who clings to parents, wishing they would stay a bit longer.

What to do.	What to avoid.
• Have the meaningful conversation and tearful good-bye before you leave home. • Make a rapid, graceful exit! A quick hug, preferably when no one else is around, and you should be on your way. • Tour the campus and attend parents' events on your own. • Do something fun with the rest of your family.	• A drawn-out leave-taking. It will only make you and your college student miserable. • Don't be tempted to come back for just one more good-bye before you leave town. It's guaranteed to be an unsatisfying experience for all of you.

Returning Home

As the car pulls away from the dorm parking lot, Josh's dad seems happy to get on the road for home:

DAD: What a great day! Josh's roommate seemed like a good guy, huh?

MOM (HER EYES MOIST WITH TEARS): Yes, he does. I just wonder if Josh will get his bed made and if there's room in that tiny closet for all of his stuff.

DAD: I'm sure he'll be fine. Honey, why are you crying? He's only four hours away. Just think of how peaceful it's going to be at home. Ah, just the thought of being first in line for the shower and finding the car in the driveway makes me smile. Seriously, though, aren't you glad he's at such a good school? I was

What's on Mom's mind?

Will I ever get used to Josh being gone?

It's going to feel so strange not having him around the house anymore.

Am I the only one who's going to miss him?

Is he going to be okay?

What's on Dad's mind?

It's great to have this whole getting into college hassle over.

All I have to worry about now is paying that tuition bill.

I think Josh is going to love it here. What a great place to go to college.

He's a smart kid. I'm really proud of him.

really impressed with the facilities, and the people we met seemed really nice. He's going to be just fine, I'm sure. How about you?

MOM: I feel like I've lost my son. I knew this was coming, but I guess I wasn't ready to say good-bye.

DAD: But just think of all the extra time we'll have together now.

MOM: I know, but what if he doesn't like it, or the classes are too difficult, or he doesn't make any friends? He might be really lonely. It's much worse than when he went to kindergarten because we're not there to help him.

DAD: Hey, honey, be realistic. He hasn't needed, or wanted, us around much for quite a while. He's probably going to love the independence. He never had trouble making friends before, so why should he now?

MOM (SNIFFLING): I guess the truth is that I'm the only one who's upset. I mean, he didn't even seem sad to see us leave.

DAD: He wasn't! I'm sure he's already on his way to some orientation party. He's been waiting a long time to get to college and be on his own. I'm sure he'll miss us, but he's got an exciting year ahead.

MOM: I can't believe you're so happy. It's almost like you're glad to be rid of him!

What's going on.

As you begin to contemplate life back at home without your child, your feelings may differ from those of your spouse, partner, or other family members. When students go to college, the family changes. Some parents feel guilty that it's great to be rid of their kids and look forward to some peace and quiet at home. Some feel devastated and dread going home. Or they may feel like one parent at orientation who shouted with glee, "This is my last child to go to college. As soon as the dog dies, I'm free!" You may have all of these feelings at different times or all at once. Not everyone experiences major changes in the same way—and this kind of change usually includes feelings of loss as well.

I (Helen) have vivid memories of crying nearly all the way home from dropping our first son at college. My husband kept stealing sidelong glances at me, genuinely perplexed at the flood of tears. He seemed to accept this transition as natural and logical; I could only feel the sadness and the loss. He thought about the pride he felt in his son beginning college at a prestigious university and about how much more freedom we'd have. I worried about whether he'd be safe and happy and wondered if this "pit of the stomach" feeling of emptiness would ever go away. I was grieving, while my husband was rejoicing.

What to do.	What to avoid.
• Ask your spouse about his or her hopes, fears, and expectations as you leave your child at college.	• Accusing your spouse of being unfeeling or too emotional.
• Try to listen, without judgment, to your partner's feelings, even though yours may differ.	• Expecting your partner to react the same way you do.
• Realize that change, even though it's essentially positive, can leave you with feelings of loss.	• Burdening your new college student with your feelings of loss and sadness.

Going It Alone

We were surprised by our friend Susan's account of her husband Dan's experience taking their daughter to college. He set off on the trip with enthusiasm, the van loaded to the ceiling with Jennifer's belongings. Later that day, he called home to talk to his wife:

DAN: Hi, Hon, how are things at home?
SUSAN: Fine. How did it go? Is Jennifer all set up in her room?
DAN: Yeah, she's fine, but I feel lousy!
SUSAN: What happened?

What's on Dad's mind?

I can't figure out if I'm mad at Jennifer for being so rude or sad to see her go.

She didn't even say thanks or really say good-bye.

I don't think she realizes how hard we've worked to get her to this point and how much its costing us.

This seems like such an anti-climax.

What's on Mom's mind?

I wish I could have been there to see Jennifer's new room.

I feel guilty that Dan had to do this alone, even though he knows I couldn't change my work schedule.

I wonder if Dan would have felt this way if I had been there.

DAN: I don't know, I just felt like I was a "fifth wheel" and cramping her style all day. I really wish you had been here. Jennifer acted like I was an embarrassment and basically ignored me most of the time. Then, after we'd unloaded all of her stuff, she just took off with her roommate for some new students' barbecue and barely said good-bye to me. She acted like she couldn't wait to get rid of me, so I just left, went into town alone, and found a place for dinner.

SUSAN: I'm sorry that you're all alone. Actually, though, I'm not surprised at Jennifer's behavior. She's acted like we were pretty annoying all summer.

DAN: Well, I guess I just expected her to want to spend some time with me. After all, I'm not going to see her again for a while.

SUSAN: I know it would have been easier for you if I had been there. When will you be getting home?

DAN: I guess I'll start out now. Nothing to do here.

What's going on.

Parents who make the trip to college alone with a child often feel the separation more intensely, without a partner to share the experience. If Susan had been along on this trip, she might have absorbed the feelings of rejection that Dan felt, and he might have been the one to remind her that Jennifer was just acting like most new college students.

When we surveyed more than ten thousand parents of new college students, the responses to the question, "How did you feel when your son or daughter went off to college?" all came from mothers. Even though fathers certainly miss their children and care deeply about them, the mothers tended to be more openly expressive about their feelings of loss and sadness. Mothers may, over time, find that the so-called "empty nest" syndrome frees them to do some things that child rearing has put on hold. Fathers can find the "empty den" tougher to deal with. Many fathers have spent a major portion of their child's growing-up years trying to establish a career and respond to a growing family's need for increased income. Because of this, the transition to college can bring strong feelings of loss and guilt for fathers. Single parents who have had to fulfill multiple roles in the family often feel this separation intensely and have to cope with these feelings alone.

What to do.	What to avoid.
• Remember that each person experiences change and loss in his or her unique way. No one way is right or wrong. • Try to respect your spouse's feelings, even if they are unexpected and uncomfortable for you. • Listen to the feelings without judging them. • Talk to a friend who has gone through or is going through the same experience.	• Blaming, "I told you so" responses. • Confronting your daughter about how she treated her father. • Taking on your spouse's reaction and getting in between your daughter and him.

What you need to know.

Whether you are a single parent, a divorced parent, or part of a blended or traditional family, you will surely feel the loss of one of your family members. If this is your last child to go to college, you may miss the presence of children in your life. If that's the case, you may want to volunteer to work with teens in your community to help fill that void.

When leaving their child at college, most parents are concerned about safety, adjustment, and what the college culture may do to change their child. Parents who themselves experienced college in a different era may long for the good old days of *in loco parentis* when the college and its staff acted as surrogate parents, setting rules and enforcing them instead of treating students as quasiadults and providing free condoms. Today's college campuses reflect the problems of the larger culture—including drugs, sexually transmitted diseases, and crime. College is no longer a cloistered youth ghetto, safely isolated from the larger world. To parents of new college students, there seem to be so many things to worry about, so many things that could go wrong for their child.

It's important to remember, however, that you've laid the groundwork for this change through years of instilling values in your child. Our experience (supported by research on adolescent development) shows that most students finish their college years with most of their family's core values intact. This doesn't mean that they won't try out other values and ideas during the college years—they will. But you can rest assured that the foundation you've provided will remain strong, although you may have to struggle through some disconcerting experimentation with new "looks," taste in music, religious questioning, and lifestyle adventures.

As the columnist Ellen Goodman wrote, going to college is for families "a part of the great American balancing act between independence and connection. And at the end of this long process, if it goes well, parents and children are adults, connected by choice as well as history."[1] In chapter 5 we will explore, in greater depth, the changes in the family when a child goes to college.

Want to Know More?

Borden, Marian Edelman, Mary Anne Burlinson, and Elise R. Kearns. *In Addition to Tuition: The Parents' Survival Guide to Freshman Year of College.* New York: Facts on File, 1995.
Barkin, Carol. *When Your Kid Goes to College: A Parents' Survival Guide.* New York: Avon Books, 1999.

---

1. Ellen Goodman. "Parental Connections," *The [Syracuse] Post-Standard,* 19 September 1997.

Chapter 3

Roommates, Fraternity Parties, All-nighters, Changing Majors, and Hanging Out

Adjustment During the First Year

Doonesbury

BY GARRY TRUDEAU

I was so naive when my daughter went off to college. Of course, I had read everything in the newspapers about teenage drinking, sex, and drug use, but I still didn't think college could be so different today from when I was an undergraduate. After all, my generation had started the sexual revolution—sex, drugs, and rock and roll, and all that. Wow, was I surprised! When I was in college, if girls had sex at all, it was only with their boyfriends. We had the pill and we didn't have to worry about AIDS. Now it seems that casual sex is much more common. What are these kids thinking? In some ways kids today are much more knowledgeable and sophisticated than I was, but they're faced with decisions that I never had to consider. And the risks are so much higher. I read that the marijuana is much more potent now too. My daughter never really partied in high school. She definitely wasn't ready for all the choices she faced in college—and I wasn't ready to talk to her about them.

An exciting, if somewhat disconcerting, process has begun. You wonder how your child will handle the increased academic and social pressures of college. You worry about his or her safety, underage drinking, living habits, roommate problems, and whether he or she is happy. You'd like to know what's going on, even as you realize that your parental role is beginning to change. This chapter will help you understand what to expect during your child's first year of college.

Adjustment Issues

As students begin college, they will be adjusting to taking care of themselves, making new friends, finding a place in the social scene, and handling increased academic expectations. The following scenarios will help you to anticipate the adjustment challenges that face your child.

What's on your mind?

I miss her.

How is she doing?

Is she making friends?

Why is she staying out so late on a school night?

What's on your child's mind?

There are so many great people here.

I'm glad I have a good roommate.

I've never been to so many great parties.

I wonder if that cute guy I met last night will be in any of my classes.

Staying in Touch

In the first few days and weeks after Megan left for college, your home felt empty and you found yourself lingering at her bedroom door, marveling at its neatness. You've actually missed the CDs playing at ninety decibels and wonder if she will call home, as promised, on Sunday night. When Sunday evening passes with no phone call, you phone the residence hall at 11:00 P.M. and get the answering machine. You leave a cheery message and go to bed, tossing and turning while wondering just where she is at 11:00 P.M. on a Sunday night. You're a little worried and a little irked.

Finally, on Monday night at 11:30 P.M., the phone rings:

MOM: Hello?

MEGAN: Hi, Mom.

MOM: Oh, Megan, it's you! I'm so glad you called. I was worried when you didn't call last night.

MEGAN: Oh, yeah, I'm sorry. I forgot. You see, there was this really cool party and I didn't get back until late.

MOM: How late?

MEGAN: Oh, I don't know. Late. Anyway, I met the neatest people from all over and it was really fun. They had a great band and then we went to this fraternity house afterward. Look, I gotta run. I promised the kids down the hall that I'd come over for pizza later and I have to take a shower.

MOM: But Megan, I want to know how you're doing. Did you get your classes all scheduled? Did you see your advisor? Did you eat breakfast?

MEGAN: Mom, I'm all set. Everything's cool. Look, I'll call you later, okay? Give my love to Dad and Joey. Bye.

MOM: (to herself as she's hanging up): Well, at least I know she's alive.

What's going on.

You're looking for a connection and reassurance; your child is so involved in this new life that you are irrelevant (for now!). You need information at this point, and your college student needs to deal with the overwhelming "newness." It's hard to believe that less than a week ago, this same child was sitting at the kitchen table asking your advice about what to pack for college.

What to do.	What to avoid.
• Keep in mind that your child is getting used to a totally new place—it's appropriate that social adjustment is consuming a great deal of time.	• Grilling your child for detailed information: "Have you seen your advisor?" "How is your class schedule?"
• Realize that your child is going to be self-absorbed during this period.	• Making your child feel guilty: "Why didn't you call when you said you would?"
• Be open with your child about your need to be in touch. Simply say, "I need to hear from you because I care about you and what's happening."	• Making demands for attention and reassurance. Your child can't be expected to meet your needs now.
• Stay in touch—send notes and news from home—but don't expect many responses.	

What's on your mind?

I'd like to know what Megan's day is like.

I'm a little worried about the late hours and lack of sleep.

Why isn't she ever in her room?

Is she taking care of herself—sleeping enough, eating properly, doing her laundry?

What's on your child's mind?

College is awesome! I already have so many new friends.

I hope I can do the work—it's going to be a lot harder than high school.

I'm so busy, I wonder if I'll ever get a full night's sleep again.

A few days later, Mom catches Megan at her dorm:

MEGAN: Hello?

MOM: Hi, Megan, I'm so glad I caught you in your room. How is everything going?

MEGAN: Great, I love my classes and my roommate is really fun. Did I tell you she's an art major? She's been all over the world with her parents and she's got the best clothes. Oh, that reminds me, can you send my winter coat? It's really cold here already.

MOM: Sure, I'll get it off in the mail tomorrow. So, tell me about your classes.

MEGAN: Well, my German professor is young and really tough. I mean, he makes us do homework every night, which isn't so easy with my other classes. I'm already so far behind. It sure is different from high school. There's so much time during the day when I don't have class but I don't get any studying done. So I stay up late every night and then have to drag myself out of bed. I never make it to breakfast. I just don't have time.

MOM: Well, maybe you could try to study a bit during the day and then you could get to bed at a decent hour.

MEGAN: Even if I did study during the day, there's no way I can go to bed early. Everyone's up 'til two or three A.M. every night. After dinner, everyone just hangs out and talks and then we start studying around eleven o'clock when things quiet down on the floor.

MOM: That sounds a little crazy.

MEGAN: No, everything's cool, Mom. So, what's happening there?

MOM: Not much, just the usual. Joey made the JV soccer team.

MEGAN: That's great. How's Dad?

MOM: He's fine; he sends his love. Listen, there's something I wanted to talk to you about. Dad and I miss you and want to talk to you once a week at least. Is there a time that's good for you to call home each week, or a time that you know you'll be in your room so that we could call you?

MEGAN: Yeah, well, Sunday nights are good. I usually don't go out until later. I'll try to call you around eight o'clock on Sunday night, okay?

MOM: That sounds good.

MEGAN: Well, I have to run. My English essay is due tomorrow and I haven't even started it yet.

MOM: What are you writing about?

MEGAN: Oh, just something about Elizabethan England. So I'll call you next Sunday, okay?

MOM: That's good. Have a good week and try to get some sleep.

MEGAN: Okay. Bye.

What's going on.

Although this conversation gives the parent more information, the child is still "high" on the new experiences, talking a mile a minute and not really connecting on a personal level with the parent. Megan is beginning to focus on the academics. The parent accomplished her goal for staying in touch by setting a phone-call time each week.

What to do.	What to avoid.
• Try to listen, without judgment. • Remember that your child's behavior is natural. • Suggest a mutually convenient time to talk each week. • Get an E-mail connection—it's the easiest way to stay in touch with your child. • Write letters—you may not get many in return, but your child will love getting news from home, and it may help you to write to her when you miss her.	• Giving orders: "Megan, you need to get yourself on a schedule or you're going to be overwhelmed by all the work." • Setting unreasonable expectations: "Make sure you get eight hours of sleep and eat breakfast." • Asking your child to write you once a week.

What you need to know.

Many college students are rarely in their rooms in the evenings. They may be visiting with friends down the hall, studying in a lounge or at the library until quite late at night. It's hard for parents, who are usually home at 11:00 P.M., to imagine why their child isn't. Setting a time that is mutually convenient for a phone call once a week can make staying in touch less of a frustration for both of you.

Academic Adjustment

Given Megan's carefree attitude in the last two calls, the parents are surprised to get an unexpected phone call from her a week later around midnight:

DAD: Hello?

MEGAN: Hi, Dad.

DAD: Megan, is that you?

What's on your mind?

I'm worried that she's in over her head.

Can she cope?

Should I do something to help?

What's on your child's mind?

I'm overwhelmed—this college stuff is harder than I thought it would be.

Maybe everyone else is smarter than me.

What if I fail?

MEGAN: Of course it's me. Who did you think it was?

DAD: I don't know. I was just surprised to hear your voice. Are you okay?

MEGAN: Well, not really. I got my English essay back today and I got a C. I couldn't believe it. I worked so hard on it and she gave me a C. I haven't had a C since seventh grade! Everyone in the class got horrible grades. I think she's just trying to prove that she's some tough professor or something. Most of the class got Cs and Ds. Can you believe it? Everyone here is so smart and they're getting terrible grades.

DAD: Well, have you talked to her about your grade? Maybe she could help you learn about what she wants in an essay.

MEGAN: Dad, there's no way I'm talking to her. She's so intimidating, you wouldn't believe it.

DAD: But that's her job to teach English and help you learn how to write better, isn't it? We're paying a lot of money for you to learn these things.

MEGAN: Dad, you just don't understand. Look, I gotta go. I have this test in bio tomorrow and I have to memorize insane numbers of organs and stuff. Did Mom send my coat?

DAD: I think so. Do you want to ask her?

MEGAN: No, that's okay. I hope it gets here tomorrow though 'cause it's really freezing here.

DAD: Well, honey, get some sleep and you'll feel better. Okay?

MEGAN: Okay, Dad. Bye.

What's going on.

Within a few weeks of classes, students can become somewhat overwhelmed and wonder if they can meet the challenges of college work. This is alarming for them. You may receive late-night calls and worry about your child's ability to cope. What you may not realize is that these calls are an early alert that college kids send out when they feel overwhelmed by the work and have yet to settle into a reasonable study schedule. For many college students their first C comes in their first semester at college and it shakes their confidence in their abilities. What do they do? Call home, of course. Your child still sees home as a haven in a scary new world, although he or she will rarely want advice on how to manage studies more efficiently. Students really want reassurance that they are loved, regardless of how well they do in college.

What to do.	What to avoid.
• Reassure your child that you have confidence in him or her: "This must be really upsetting for you, but I know you've tackled tough situations before and managed to figure out what you need to do."	• Solving the problem for your child.
	• Getting into an argument about whether the professor really stinks.
• Ask "leading" questions that help him or her come up with a solution: "Have you thought about what you could do to learn to write an essay that is closer to what your professor is looking for?"	• Offering advice before you have finished listening to the emotional issues.
	• Letting yourself be alarmed by a relatively insignificant issue.
• Ask if a follow-up call would be helpful in a day or so.	
• Remind yourself that this is transitory, a natural part of the adjustment process.	
• Have faith in your child's ability to cope.	
• Call a friend with a college-aged child and commiserate. Talk to someone who is going through the same experience.	

Academic Adjustment: The Replay

Let's see how Dad could have helped Megan through this crisis of confidence in her academic ability:

DAD: Hello?

MEGAN: Hi, Dad, it's me.

DAD: Hi, Megan. How are you doing?

MEGAN: I had a horrible day. I got a C on my English essay.

DAD: I'm sorry. You sound really upset. I can't remember you ever getting a C before. What happened? Tell me about it.

MEGAN: Well, everyone in the class got terrible grades. We were all just freaked out. I think the professor really stinks. How could she give everyone horrible grades like that? There were only like two As in the whole class.

DAD: That must have been pretty upsetting to get a grade like that. You're so used to being a top student.

MEGAN: I don't know. Maybe I'm not smart enough to be here. What if I flunk out?

DAD: You sound pretty worried.

MEGAN: I'm behind all the time and everyone else is so smart.

DAD: So you're feeling pretty overwhelmed by the workload, huh?

MEGAN: Yeah, it's just so hard. I can't believe it. There isn't any time to do all the stuff they want us to do. I wish I hadn't come here to begin with. Or I wish I had been a fine arts major like my roommate. All she does is go to the studio and hang out with her art friends and paint things.

DAD: She has it pretty easy, huh?

MEGAN: I don't know. It just seems to hard, Dad. What do you think I should do?

DAD: Well, that's really up to you, Honey. We have a lot of confidence in you and know that you can do the work.

MEGAN: Why? I'm already failing. I just can't keep up.

DAD: Is there someone there you could talk to? Like an advisor or someone?

MEGAN: No, there isn't anyone like that. Look, Dad, I gotta go and get something done on my project for tomorrow.

DAD: Okay, Honey, but maybe we could talk tomorrow and see how you're doing then?

MEGAN: Okay. Bye.

What you need to know.

Chances are that minutes after Megan hung up the phone she felt better. She unloaded her frustrations on you and you reassured her that she was smart and capable. You, however, don't feel so great. If you could have a hidden camera in her residence hall, you'd know that she was fine. A little shaken, but fine. She touched base with you, gave you the reality check that she might not come home with all As her first semester in college, and was reassured that you understood her anxiety and believed in her abilities.

It's a good bet that if you had called her the next day to find out how she was, you would be greeted with a cheery response: "Hey, everything's okay." You may have lost a night's sleep, but Megan now feels fine. Her anxieties of last night are ancient history and she may be a little embarrassed that she blew her cool with you on the phone.

Roommates and Residence Hall Living

What's on your mind?

My daughter's roommate is taking advantage of her.
Why can't she learn about lending her things to others?
What is this going to cost?

You find out when your daughter comes home for break that her roommate borrowed one of her favorite sweaters and lost it at a party. The roommate has also put off paying her part of the phone bill, and now the phone company has threatened to cut off their service. The phone service is in your daughter's name, and she's not sure what to do.

What's on your child's mind?

I'm really bummed that she lost my favorite sweater.
Should I confront my roommate, and if I do, will she hate me?

What's going on.

Residence halls are living and learning laboratories in which students learn to get along with people who are very different from them and negotiate touchy situations. Many college students have never had to share a room or possessions. It's important that they learn to be both assertive and respectful of other people's space and things. At the same time, it's really important to them to be liked and not appear selfish or immature.

What to do.

- Remember that this *is* a big adjustment for your daughter.
- Ask your child if she feels comfortable negotiating solutions; if not, suggest getting the residence hall director or advisor involved.
- Be firm in reinforcing that she needs to deal with these issues.

What to avoid.

- Replacing her sweater or paying the phone bill for the roommate.
- Blaming the roommate: "I told you I thought she would be trouble. Don't let her wear your stuff anymore."
- Calling a college staff member yourself to complain.

What you need to know.

Residence hall staff are there to offer support in situations like this. They will not solve the problem for your daughter, but they will help her find the solution. She may want to meet with a staff member before confronting her roommate and to get some advice on how to handle the problems. In the end, however, it's up to her to take the initiative.

About two months into the first semester, you get a call from your son.:

ANDY: Hi, Mom, what's happening?

MOM: Oh, not much. How are you?

ANDY: Okay.

MOM: Just okay? You sound a little down. What's going on?

ANDY: My roommate is being a pain in the butt.

MOM: What do you mean?

ANDY: Well, for starters, he has these really disgusting lizards that he loves, and he keeps them in a couple of cages under his bed.

MOM: Isn't that against the rules? I thought pets weren't allowed.

ANDY: Yeah, well he's not the only one who has some kind of animal, but the thing that really bugs me is that his girlfriend is here all the time. They just found out they both have mono—not a big surprise—and so now they just lie around all day and it's driving me crazy. I think she's really rude and I can't even walk around in my underwear because she's always here. I spend most of my time down the hall in Ben's room, but they are really becoming annoying.

MOM: That's terrible! Can't you get the dorm director to do something about this?

ANDY: Nah, I don't want to go tattle on them. I just wish he'd get rid of her at least. The animals aren't so bad, but I feel like I don't have a room anymore. Oh, well, maybe they'll decide they don't like each other and she'll go back to living in her own room.

What's on your mind?

I'm really upset. I'm paying for a room for my son, not a shack-up place for some other kid with no manners or morals.

Andy will probably get sick too.

Aren't there rules in these residence halls, and shouldn't the director be enforcing them?

What's on your child's mind?

I can handle this, but it's a real drag.

I don't have any privacy—my roommate's a jerk.

If I complain to the RA, I'll look stupid.

I wish this would just go away.

MOM: Andy, I think you should do something about this. Do you want me to call the director?

ANDY: No, it'll be all right. Look, I gotta get to work. I have a paper due Friday and I haven't started it yet. So I'll see you soon. I'll be home for Thanksgiving in a couple of weeks. I can't wait to get home and do nothing but eat and sleep. Talk to you later.

What's going on.

For most students, having a roommate is a new and challenging experience. Many college students have never had to share a bedroom with a brother or sister, let alone a virtual stranger. Mom and Dad may have mediated bedroom-sharing struggles at home, and few students are prepared for skillfully negotiating a reasonable living situation at school.

What to do.	What to avoid.
• Listen and empathize with this unfortunate situation. • Remind your son of his entitlement to half a room with one other person and his right to request a room change. • Instead of sharing your alarm and anger, ask your son, "Have you talked to your roommate about this and asked him to remove his girlfriend?" or "What do you want to do about this situation?" • Suggest that he ask his residence hall director for advice about the situation.	• Calling the director and demanding that he fix the problem. This action should be reserved for times when you feel there is a real safety or health threat to your child. • Imposing your cleanliness or basic living standards on the situation. This is your son's home; you can't dictate living standards for him or his roommate. They need to work it out.

What you need to know.

Residence hall staff members are there to help with these situations. They handle these kinds of roommate problems and negotiations all the time. Your child can request a room change if the situation is unworkable. It may be that 90 percent of the time your child is content with the roommate and just needed to blow off steam.

One of the most common complaints in residence halls is the roommate who brings home a boyfriend or girlfriend on a regular basis. It's totally reasonable for your son to insist that the roommate move his girlfriend out of their room, but he needs to do that himself or with the help of the director, who can assist through mediation.

Stress and Pressure

You are really looking forward to having Lisa come home for Thanksgiving break. She arrives laden with books and announces that she has two midterms next week and a paper to write while she is home. She looks exhausted, but immediately gets on the phone, calls her old high school friends, and makes plans to go out later. You next see Lisa when she drags herself out of bed the next day at noon and begins complaining about how tired she is and how much work she has to do. Later that afternoon, she makes plans to go out with her friends again. By Sunday, when it's time for Lisa to return to college, she hasn't cracked a book or spent much time with the family, but she's still obsessing about her work and how far behind she is.

What's on your mind?

If she had buckled down and done some work, she wouldn't be in this position.

What if she's really in over her head with school work?

She didn't seem happy to see us or to be at home.

What's going on.

Thanksgiving break is often a crisis point in the first semester at college. Early feedback on school work may not look good and papers and exams are looming ahead. Your daughter is exhausted from the personal adjustments she's making to college life, but when she's home, she wants to forget college pressures and see old friends and have fun. She also wants to let you know just how hard this is.

What's on your child's mind?

Panic: I'll never get all of this work done.

I should have spent the whole holiday working.

Why are my parents on my case when I'm so stressed?

What to do.	What to avoid.
• Try to be sympathetic. Let her know that you understand how difficult the adjustment to college can be. • Remember this is your child's problem, not yours. • Reinforce that you have faith in her ability to complete her work. • Relate stories from your own life—perhaps a tough challenge and how you handled your fear about accomplishing it. • Ask, "Have you thought at all about what you might do to cope with all of this work hanging over you? What gets in the way of your doing your work? Is there a way for you to get some help with managing your workload?" • Make it clear to her what level of involvement you expect from her in the family's holiday plans: "We are all having Thanksgiving dinner together, and I expect you to be a part of our celebration from three until about seven o'clock."	• Taking on her problem and trying to fix it yourself. • Telling your child what to do: "If you'd stay home and study for your exams or work on your paper instead of going out every night, you wouldn't be in this jam." • Reorganizing your holiday weekend around your child's erratic schedule or nagging her about being involved with the family. This will only make you feel exasperated and resentful, and probably won't get your daughter to change her behavior.

What you need to know.

Your child may need to come home and recover from the stress and pressure she is under at school. She's still learning to manage her schedule and handle the much more challenging academic work at college. Just the volume of reading alone can be a big shock to new students. There are resources on campus to help students who are willing to take advantage of them. Most colleges and universities have learning-skills centers, time-management workshops, peer-tutoring programs, and other support services to help new students adjust to college-level work. The first semester at college demands personal and academic adjustments that will test your child's confidence and force him or her to accept the consequences of his or her actions (or inaction!). This is not a lesson you can teach Lisa; she has to learn it herself by trial and error.

Making the Transition from High School and Home

When you visited your daughter at school for a football weekend, you were surprised that she complained about her lack of social life at school. She talked about how much she missed her high school friends. Although she was a bit shy in middle school, she had several close friends by the time she graduated from high school. She doesn't know anyone other than her roommate at college and feels pretty lonely.

What's going on.

Social adjustment the first few months of college can be hard, especially if your child is a bit shy. It's difficult for some students to leave behind close high school friends and start all over. For many new college students, the social group consists of roommates and others living in their residence hall. It's challenging to find new friends while students are trying to adjust to so many changes, especially when they feel homesick for old friends.

> ### What's on your mind?
> I'm worried that she spends so much time alone.
> I wonder if she's too shy to get out and meet people.
> There must be social activities that would appeal to her.

> ### What's on your child's mind?
> I miss my high school friends.
> No one here seems like me.
> I don't feel comfortable going to fraternity parties.
> I wonder if I'll ever fit in.

What to do.	What to avoid.
• Listen to your daughter's feelings and let her know you sympathize with her loneliness. • Show that you understand how difficult it is for her to make new friends. • Remind her of how she survived the middle-school years, while empathizing with how hard that was for her. • Suggest that she look into joining a club or activity so that she can meet other students with similar interests.	• Suggesting that she have her old high school friends visit her at college. • Letting her know you're really worried about her. • Trying to fix it for her by suggesting she come home for weekends more often.

What you need to know.

Even the most socially skilled students go through adjustments when they arrive at college and have to make new friends. Many students who appear well adjusted socially actually have a hard time fitting into the college social scene. Although social adjustment is one of the biggest challenges for new students, most find a niche for themselves eventually. On campuses where fraternities and sororities dominate social life, it can be more difficult for students to find a social group who aren't the sorority or fraternity type. There are many ways to fit in at college, but students have to be assertive in seeking out alternative avenues for social life: for example, joining clubs, getting involved in volunteer work, signing up for an intramural team, working on the school newspaper, or going to movies or concerts with hall mates.

It's common for students to feel as if everyone else is happy and well-adjusted socially, while they feel awkward and out of place. This usually changes within a few weeks or months. Going through this part of the adjustment process is hard, but it's important to let this evolve naturally. There are few students indeed who haven't made good friends at the end of the first year of college.

Finding a Social Niche

Ever since you talked with your son on the phone last week, you've been worried about his social life at college. He doesn't seem to be making friends. He spends most of his time studying, sleeping, and talking on the phone to his girlfriend at home, who is a senior in high school.

What's going on.

It's hard for some students to leave high school behind when they go to college. The social scene can be intimidating at first, and if your son doesn't get involved in social life in the beginning, it gets harder to break in later in the semester. Joining an organization, or having one good friend who will get your son involved in something, often begins the process of acclimating to college and letting go of high school.

What's on your mind?

I wonder if he'll ever make friends at college.

I think he's hanging on to her because he's afraid to try to make new friends.

What on your child's mind?

I'm glad I have a girlfriend or I'd really feel out of it.

Why should I go out when I'm not interested in meeting girls?

What to do.

- Try to be patient and understanding of your son's need to cling to a high school sweetheart.
- Suggest that he join a club or organization that is not completely social in nature.

What to avoid.

- Trying to split up the relationship. It almost always backfires.
- Telling him he can't come home so much.

What you need to know.

It's not unusual for your son to hold onto the security of this relationship. If you are patient with his need to hang on to his high school girlfriend, he'll probably grow out of that relationship in time. Many high school relationships don't last beyond the first semester, when one person goes off to college. As long as you see some evidence that your son is slowly beginning to get more involved in college life, you don't need to worry.

The Freshman 10—Weight Issues

When your daughter Ellen was home for winter break, you noticed how much weight she had gained during her first semester in college. You've always struggled with weight and you're worried that Ellen is getting fat.

What's going on.

Gaining the "freshman 10" is a common experience for new college students. This may be the first time they have control (or lack of it!) over what they eat, and it may take some time for them to settle into a sensible and healthy eating pattern. Most colleges offer cafeteria-style dining and some even offer "continuous dining" around the clock. Students can eat whatever and whenever they want, and their days often end with a pizza party.

What's on your mind?

Ellen was so slim and attractive when she went off to college.

Her clothes look terrible on her.

If she keeps gaining weight at this rate, she'll be a blimp.

What's on your child's mind?

I can tell my mother thinks I'm fat.

What's the big deal? Everyone gains weight their freshman year.

What to do.	What to avoid.
• Listen to your daughter's anxiety about her weight, without preaching. • Reinforce that her weight and body type do not define her as a person. • Discuss the cultural pressures related to body image and let her know that your love for her is not based on her looks or her weight. • Ask if she would like to talk about how to eat sensibly and suggest that getting some exercise might help her maintain a weight that is reasonable for her.	• Making this a big deal and trying to shame her into dieting. • Leaping to the conclusion that she's on the road to obesity. • Overreacting, thereby emphasizing weight issues over other developmental concerns, such as learning healthy eating patterns. • Imposing your attitudes about weight and body image.

What you need to know.

The freshman 10, 15, or 20 is a common phenomenon for new students. In trying to adjust to so many lifestyle changes away from home and parental supervision, many students gain weight, and it may take a couple of semesters for them to settle into a normal eating pattern. Some students get carried away with the freedom of being able to eat whatever they want and some find food a comfort in a new and stressful environment.

Parents need to be very careful about overreacting to this situation. You don't want your child to begin to obsess about food. Try to keep your perspective on this and avoid making it a big issue. Although you can no longer control what and when your child eats, you can influence how she views this weight gain and offer helpful advice on maintaining a healthy lifestyle. If you are worried about your child's eating habits and suspect that she may have an eating disorder, you may want to take the advice we offer in chapter 9.

Greek Life

Your daughter called home last night in tears. She's just been through rush and did not receive a bid from a sorority. Her two best friends were pledged, and she is devastated.

What's going on.

The Greek system, like many other selective systems, is inherently unfair. Choices made on appearances and personality traits are often subjective, confusing, and hurtful. It's a lesson in life that you don't want your child to have to learn.

What's on your mind?

I feel so sorry for her.
What can I do to make her feel better?

What's on your child's mind?

Why didn't they like me?
I'm so embarrassed and hurt.
I'm going to miss out on all of the fun.

What to do.	What to avoid.
• Listen to your daughter's feelings. • Sympathize with her pain and tell her you're sorry she's so sad. • Keep in touch with her, write her notes, and generally reinforce that she's an attractive and likable person.	• Trying to make her feel better by telling her you think sororities are silly or not important. • Getting involved by calling the dean of Greek life.

What you need to know.

The campus culture determines the role that sororities and fraternities play in student life and how much interaction there is between students who are in or out of the Greek system. On some campuses, fraternities and sororities provide most of the social life; on others, Greek life is one of several social systems. Even if students don't join a fraternity or sorority, chances are that they will be able to attend Greek parties, especially if they have good friends in a house. If your daughter still wants to be a member of a sorority, there are often opportunities to join early in the sophomore year.

What's on your mind?

Will my son be safe?
I've heard so many frightening stories about fraternity hazing.

Your son calls from school to tell you he's decided to pledge a fraternity. You've always been anti-Greek and you're not sure you approve.

What's going on.

What's on your child's mind?

Initiation was so awesome; everybody was completely out of control.
I'm in the best house here.

It's reasonable to be concerned about fraternity initiation activities and fraternity life. Drinking is often involved in fraternity activities, and it can get out of control. You're worried, but your son seems so happy to be included and to be a part of this selective group.

What to do.	What to avoid.
• Congratulate your son on getting into a fraternity. • Ask your son what he likes best about the fraternity. • Try to remember how important it was to be liked and included when you were eighteen years old. • If you're concerned, ask your son about his fraternity brothers' attitudes on hazing and express your concerns. • Have a frank talk about money and who will pay for fraternity fees. • Plan to visit the house when you're on campus and meet some of his fraternity brothers.	• Generalizing about fraternities and their "animal house" reputation. Your son's house may be very different. • Recounting all the horror stories you've heard. • Forbidding him to join.

What you need to know.

All fraternities and sororities have strong policies prohibiting hazing and most colleges have strict rules governing Greek life on campus. Still, fraternity life, in particular, can be pretty crazy and out of control. Excessive drinking is a problem, and too often fraternity parties are the sites of accidents, injuries, and illegal, underage drinking. (We deal with this issue in more detail in the upcoming section: "The Big Three: Drinking, Drugs, and Sex.") Greek life can also be a very positive experience, giving your son a close group of male friends, a feeling of belonging, and an opportunity to learn about leadership. Most fraternities also have a charter that mandates public service and charitable work in the community.

What's on your mind?

I'm afraid she can't handle work and school.

I'm feeling badly that I don't have more money to help out. Should we get another loan?

She'll lose all she's worked for if she flunks out.

What's on your child's mind?

I'm just overwhelmed with the workload.

I don't know what I'm supposed to do. There are only so many hours in the day.

My parents have to help me or I have to work these hours at my job.

Time Management and Working on Campus

You thought things were going along well with your daughter until you phoned her last night.

MING: Hi, Mom, how're you doing?

MOM: Things are fine here. How are you?

MING: I'm freaked out—I have so much to do and no time. I think I'm failing two of my courses.

MOM: Oh, honey, that's not good. What's the problem?

MING: I *told* you. I have no time to do any work. I get up, go to class, go to my job for three hours, go to classes all afternoon, eat dinner, and then try to study starting at about ten o'clock. I try to stay up and work, but I'm so tired and I have an eight o'clock class in the morning. I'm so behind, I don't know if I'll ever catch up.

MOM: Are you working at your job three hours every day? That seems like a lot.

MING: I have to. I need the money. I really should work more hours, but I can't because of my class schedule.

MOM: I thought your financial aid package included only ten hours of work a week.

MING: Well, at financial aid they don't seem to know how much it costs to live here. I have extra lab fees this semester, and the books cost more than I thought they would.

MOM: I wish I could send you some more money, but we're just not able to right now.

MING: I know, Mom, it's okay. I just didn't think it would be so hard to keep up with everything.

MOM: You know the important thing is that you get your school work done. Do you really think you're going to flunk those courses?

MING: I don't know, but my midterms were horrible. Look, I gotta run to the computer lab and get my assignment done for tomorrow. I'll talk to you later, okay?

MOM: Okay, Ming, take care.

What's going on.

Your daughter may be at a critical time in the semester when midterms, finals, and papers loom on the horizon. It also may be that she *is* working too many hours and needs to cut back until she can get her studies under control. Or she may be in a tight spot financially because she has made some unwise spending decisions.

What to do.	What to avoid.
• Listen to her feelings of panic. • Ask questions: "Could you work fewer hours just this week? Can you think of any ways to solve this dilemma? Can you get by with less money for a while? Could you cut back your hours for now and see how you manage for a couple of weeks during exams? Can you talk to your supervisor about flexible hours for the rest of the semester? • Tell her how much you respect her for working and going to school at the same time; recognize that this is admirable but also difficult to manage.	• Telling her she has to quit her job or cut her hours dramatically. • Lecturing that she has to get organized or she will flunk out and lose everything she's worked for. • Jumping to the conclusion that she will *never* be able to work on campus and contribute to her education.

What you need to know.

Most colleges and universities have guidelines that govern how much a student should work, particularly during the first year. The recommended commitment is usually ten to twelve hours per week. Most students have trouble managing anymore than that.

Students often find the balance of work, social life, and academics difficult at first. Many students, however, actually enjoy their jobs on campus and find that work offers a welcome change from classes and studying. In fact, students can benefit from developing a relationship with an adult supervisor who is supportive and able to offer advice and nurturing. Most supervisors of college student employees recognize that studies come first and are willing to negotiate flexible hours throughout the semester.

Time management often is at the root of problems balancing work and study. Most campuses have programs to help students learn to manage competing demands. Some students thrive when they are busy; others need more downtime in order to cope with the pressures of college. Staff members in the Financial Aid Office can review a student's package to make sure that the work commitment is not too heavy and that the student has sufficient time for academic work.

Sports/Athletics

Playing soccer has been a significant part of your daughter Erica's life since third grade when she started playing in the community soccer program. She was a letter winner in high school and was actively recruited to play soccer in college. But a phone call from Erica has left you concerned:

DAD: Hello?

ERICA: Hi, Dad. How are things?

DAD: Just fine, sweetheart. How about you?

ERICA: I'm exhausted! I can't believe how tired I am all the time.

DAD: What's going on? Are you partying every night?

ERICA: No, Dad. It's just that there's no time for sleep. I have so much school work, and soccer practice is three hours every day. It's so much more of a commitment than in high school, and I don't even know if I'll get to play. There are so many great players here.

DAD: Well, you probably won't get to play a lot your first year. It's understandable that the upperclasswomen have more experience and will play more often.

ERICA: But what if I can't keep up with both my classes and soccer? Pretty soon we have to start traveling to games, and that takes up even more time.

DAD: I know it's a big change, but you seemed to be able to do sports, schoolwork, and lots of other activities in high school. Maybe you're not making the best use of your time. You really have to be disciplined to play a college sport.

ERICA: Dad, it doesn't matter how disciplined I am—there are still only twenty-four hours in a day, and college is much harder than high school. I just can't believe how far behind I am already in my classes.

DAD: Well, maybe you should talk to your coach.

ERICA: That won't help. She just tells us we have to set goals and work hard. I know that!

DAD: Do you think you should quit soccer?

ERICA: But, Dad, I love playing! If only practices weren't so long every day. I get back to the dorm after practice and it's all I can do to stay awake after dinner and study.

DAD: I know it must be hard. Maybe I could talk to the coach.

ERICA: No! Promise me you won't call the coach. I can handle this myself.

DAD: Well, I just worry about you handling everything your first semester.

ERICA: I just can't wait to come home at Thanksgiving and sleep! Well, I'd better go. I have an essay to write for Spanish tomorrow that I haven't even started yet.

DAD: I hope you get it done and get some sleep, Honey. Take care and call if you need anything, okay?

ERICA: Okay, Dad. Bye.

What's on your mind?

Maybe she shouldn't have tried to play soccer her first year.

I worry about her handling the pressure of sports and academics.

She's not in class that much. I wonder what she does with her time.

What's on your child's mind?

I am really stressed out.

The coach is so unreasonable with her demands. This is nothing like playing sports in high school.

I wonder if I even want to play soccer anymore, not that I'm getting to play anyway.

I like the other girls on the team, but they are all so much better than me.

What's going on.

You are pleased that Erica's done well in sports in the past but are concerned about the time commitment that college athletics require. You know it's a lot for her to handle her first year in school, and you certainly don't want her to flunk out because she's playing soccer. You worry that she will get overwhelmed and give up on everything. Erica is struggling with the general adjustment issues of the first year in college. She's also trying to balance seemingly unlimited social life, late hours, long team practices, a heavy academic workload, and still managing to do her laundry.

What to do.	What to avoid.
• Listen to Erica's fears and anxieties. • Sympathize with her struggles and show that you understand how hard she is working to try to stay on top of things. • Reinforce that you have confidence in her and will love her no matter what she decides to do about playing soccer. • Remind her of another time when she was stressed out and ask her how she handled that situation.	• Lecturing her on time management. • Telling her you think she should quit the team and concentrate on her school work. • Offering to call the coach and plead her case.

What you need to know.

Adjusting to playing sports at the college level is a tough challenge for most new students. College teams do require a serious commitment of time and energy, and not every student will continue playing because of that. It's also disheartening for a star player in high school to face the fact that he or she may not get to play much for the first couple of years on a college team. The competition is usually intense for the starting positions, and it's discouraging to be on the bench most of the time.

It's also true that sports can be a positive and rewarding part of college life. The team provides a ready-made group, easing the social adjustment for students. Coaches are usually very interested and involved in their players' development, both on and off the playing field, providing the support and encouragement that many new students need. Moreover, the commitment to a practice schedule can help students manage their time more effectively.

Many students receive the same benefits of sports in college by playing on intramural teams. This may be an option if your child wants to play but can't afford the extraordinary time and energy that a varsity team requires.

Top Parent Concerns

Our focus group research with parents of college students revealed a number of areas of concern. Being informed, dealing with issues of safety, health, and basic security, as well as coping with sex, drugs, and alcohol emerged as the top parent concerns.

Staying Informed

Your son tells you that the faculty has decided to reinstitute a foreign language requirement in his intended major. He's upset that if he has to take a foreign language, he won't be able to take other courses that he wanted to take instead.

What's going on.

It's common for students to get anxious when they hear about changes in the curriculum that may affect their course of study in a negative way. Often they will call you to vent their frustration before they investigate the facts of the situation. Like many other momentary "crises," this too will probably be over before you've stopped worrying about it. Parents feel cut off when these issues arise; they really don't know what's going on.

What's on your mind?

I don't understand this. Can they change the requirements now?

How can I find out more about this?

What's on your child's mind?

How can they do this to me? I'm terrible at languages. This will really screw up my GPA.

What to do.

- Ask your son to check with his faculty advisor or the department office to see if this is rumor or truth and if the change will affect him.

What to avoid.

- Being alarmed before you fully understand the situation.
- Telling your son you think he'll do just fine with a foreign language.

What you need to know.

When students start college, the requirements for degrees remain constant until graduation. Any changes that are made to curricular requirements after they have started school do not apply to them—they may apply to the next incoming class.

Lots of events occur on campuses and many of them will affect your child in some way. Whether it is a campus demonstration about a political issue or a change in academic or student life policy that is important to your child, you will want to be informed. You may not get the information you want from your child or the university administration. Most parents feel frustrated that they receive only the tuition bills from the university and are left out of the loop when important events and changes occur.

If you want to know what is happening on campus, there are ways to find out. You may want to subscribe to the student newspaper (many colleges now have their student newspaper on the web) or talk to alumni or other parents. Many alumni associations host informational events for parents. Most colleges and universities have a parents' program office that can provide you with information about campus activities and they may be able to connect you with other parents living in your area.

Safety

What's on your mind?

Is my daughter safe walking around alone at night?
Who would be there if she was in trouble?

What's on your child's mind?

My mom is such a worrier.
I've never known anyone to get attacked here.
I have to go to the library and the computer lab at night.

You are worried because your daughter goes to the computer labs or library late at night and walks back to her residence hall as late as midnight or 1:00 A.M. You've heard that rapes and assaults are becoming more common on campuses and wonder if your daughter is safe.

What's going on.

Most parents list safety as a top concern when their children leave for college. Campuses, unfortunately, are not much different from the rest of the world today. There was a time when campuses were more like ivory towers and relatively immune to real-world problems. No more. It is appropriate to be concerned about your child's safety and reasonable to ask your child to be careful in situations that could be dangerous.

What to do.	What to avoid.
• Ask your daughter to have a friend walk with her to the library or lab late at night or inquire about a campus escort or bus service. She can find out what's available by calling the campus security office. • Acknowledge that your daughter is an adult and capable of taking care of herself but remind her that everyone today has to exercise caution to be safe.	• Trying to scare your daughter into taking extra precautions. • Giving her the message that you don't trust her judgment and ability to take care of herself.

What you need to know.

College campuses are no safer than any other environment today. In 1990, Congress passed the Student Right to Know and Campus Security Acts (the latter is now known as the Jeanne Clery Disclosure of Campus Security Policy and Campus Crime Act), both of which were enacted to require colleges to make crime statistics available to students. A recent book on campus crime urges that colleges provide students with information on campus police, escort services, emergency phones, and education on crime prevention tactics.[1]

Awareness is the key to prevention and is the most powerful defense that a student can take to school. Many students come to college naïve and trusting and need to develop a healthy paranoia. Most colleges acknowledge this fact and have taken measures (such as keeping residence halls locked twenty-four hours a day and changing locks annually) to ensure that their students are as safe as possible. If you are concerned about your child's safety, you can contact the campus security office and receive information on crime and prevention programs.

Health

When Laura's mom phoned campus one evening to chat with her daughter, the following conversation took place:

What's on your mind?

Something terrible has happened to my daughter.

I've got to find out what's wrong.

Why didn't she tell me? What could it be?

What's on your child's mind?

I feel awful. Thank goodness I'm in the infirmary where someone will take care of me.

I'm going to get so far behind in my classes.

What if I'm so sick I have to drop out of college?

JULIE: Hello?

MOM: Hi, Julie. May I speak with Laurie?

JULIE: Oh, hi, Mrs. Thomas. Uh, Laurie's not here right now.

MOM: Do you know when she'll be back?

JULIE: Well, I'm not sure.

MOM: Where is she?

JULIE: Oh, gosh, I'm not sure, but I'll have her call you when she gets back.

MOM: Do you think it will be late?

JULIE: I don't really know. Maybe she could just call you tomorrow?

MOM: Well, I really need to talk to her tonight. Something's come up that I need to tell her about. Just have her call, no matter what time she gets in.

JULIE: Well, uh, Laurie left a note telling me not to worry, but that she's in the health center. She said probably just for overnight.

MOM: What? Julie, what's wrong with Laurie? You must tell me. I'm her mother!

JULIE: Well, I don't know. I'm sorry, I'm sure she'll be okay. She looked fine when I saw her last night.

MOM: Julie, just give me the number of the health center and I'll find out myself.

What's going on.

Students tend to be in their own world of classes, social life, and activities and don't always think to let their parents know right away if they are sick or injured. Their concern is with their own recovery not their parents' worries, at least initially. College students also tend to believe they are immortal, and that if they are sick or get hurt they will get better and everything will be fine. They also may be afraid to tell you if they have an embarrassing or frightening condition, such as a sexually transmitted disease. The same child who wanted you to bring her chicken soup when she was sick at home over fall break may not want you to know that she is in the infirmary because she is vomiting all the time and suspects she may be pregnant.

What to do.	What to avoid.
• Call the health center and try to talk to your daughter. • Find out if she's okay before you start grilling her on what's wrong. • Give her a chance to tell you what's wrong; if she doesn't want to talk about it, just remind her that you care about her and love her. • See if there is any way that you can be helpful. • Ask her for permission to talk to her doctor. If she says no, tell her you respect her right to privacy but that you're worried and need some reassurance that she's going to be okay. • Try to keep the lines of communication open. Tell her you'd like to call her again tomorrow just to see how she's doing.	• Leaping to the worst-case scenario before you know what's happening. • Letting your panic and anger take over. Yelling at your daughter for not telling you she is in the hospital. • Showing your hurt if she says she just didn't think to call you.

What you need to know.

This is one of the worst nightmares any parent can imagine. Your child is sick or hurt in some way and you're not there. You're upset and anxious. You want to know what's going on and if he or she will be okay. You're also angry that no one informed you that your child was in the hospital. It's very difficult for most parents to accept the fact that their eighteen year old is a legal adult and that the hospital is bound to protect the doctor-patient confidentiality that is the right of every adult. This means that the health center will not call you when they admit your child unless it is a life or death situation. If the condition warrants a stay in the hospital, most health center staff members will ask students if they have notified their parents and may even encourage them to do so. However, doctors and nurses are not entitled to call the parents if a student refuses, or just forgets, to make the call.

The Big Three: Drinking, Drugs, and Sex

You probably have dealt with these three issues during your child's high school years by talking, sharing your values, and monitoring your child's behavior. In fact, the majority of college students today have had sex and experimented with drinking and sometimes even drugs before they left high school. Nevertheless, when your child goes to college, these issues seem to take on new meaning. There are new freedoms and responsibilities that come with living away from home; your child will be facing a vast array of choices in college out from under your watchful eye. Although it is true that your child will likely graduate from college with most of your core values intact, it is also true that most college students experiment with drinking, drugs, and sex.

This experimentation can cause you a fair amount of worry, even though you recognize that your ability to control your child's behavior is slipping away. It doesn't mean, however, that you have lost your influence on your child. Most college students are too cool to admit it, but they still want your approval and often value your opinions on these issues. Most likely, you will need to initiate a continuing discussion on these issues if you want to influence your child; this can be tough because you are removed from the context of the behavior. For example, you may be concerned about what you consider to be excessive drinking because your son talks about going to fraternity parties every time you speak to him. You're not sure if he's at a party four nights a week or once a week. It's a good idea to ask about the context of the behavior if you have concerns: "Do you go to frat parties often?" And it's also a good idea to make your expectations clear: "I can understand you want to party with your friends, but I worry that your social life is going to affect your studies and your health. I hope your partying isn't getting out of control."

While it's important for you to be able to let go of control (you don't really have it anyway!) and trust your child to make reasonable, independent decisions, responsible parenting also includes making your expectations clear. This is easier said than done when contact with your child is minimal. It is difficult to let your child deal with consequences, especially when the consequences can be serious. Indeed, there may be times when you need to act, especially if you sense your child is in danger. We'll address those instances in chapter 9.

For now, however, your task is to give your child the opportunity to test his or her own values and to provide support during this period of exploration and experimentation. This is the beginning of a new kind of relationship, not the end of your influence as an important role model and guide.

The following examples will help you clarify your response to these three critical issues.

Drinking

It seems as if every time you call your son at school, he is either going out to a party or hungover from one. You begin to wonder if his drinking is out of control and where he's getting the alcohol. All the literature from the school says that underage drinking is not allowed on campus. Your son talks about drinking as though it's the only way to unwind and handle the academic pressure.

What's going on.

Although the legal drinking age is twenty-one in most states, drinking is common on college campuses. In fact many students have had their first drink in high school and come to college with a fake ID or find out quickly where to get one. While it's true that most colleges have rules about drinking on campus, those rules are broken with regularity. It is almost impossible for campus security staff to enforce the underage drinking laws because students are drinking in private spaces, such as their dorm rooms or apartments.

What's on your mind?

I'm worried about all this drinking going on.

Is it possible he could become an alcoholic?

Why doesn't the college crack down on these parties?

I thought liquor wasn't allowed in the residence halls.

What's on your child's mind?

My mom is so clueless—she thinks we're all loser alcoholics.

Everyone drinks a lot—I actually drink less than my friends.

I need to unwind after working so hard on exams and papers.

What to do.	What to avoid.
• Talk to your son about the larger issue of drinking on campus and ask questions about the social culture. Ask him what he thinks of the parties he goes to. • Talk about responsible drinking and what that means to you, acknowledging that he is in control of how he behaves and that you trust he acts responsibly. • Remind him of the possible consequences of breaking the law and/or drinking too much. He could get arrested and have a record that would keep him from some options later. He could consume too much and risk alcohol poisoning. • Be aware of signs that may indicate your son is abusing alcohol. Don't be afraid to bring up the subject if you are concerned about alcohol abuse. Just start by saying, "I'm concerned about how much you are drinking. Are you?"	• Moralizing and lecturing about drinking. • Being unrealistic: "You know drinking is against the law. I want you to stop going to parties where they serve alcohol to minors." • Encouraging the behavior by bragging about your son's ability to hold his liquor and joking about what a party animal he is. • Supplying him with liquor when you're visiting campus and drinking a lot yourself. • Glossing it over with "kids will be kids" remarks and denying that there may be a problem with excessive drinking.

What you need to know.

There is great concern about the amount of binge drinking on most American college campuses today. It is troubling to recognize the extent to which students binge on work and then follow that with binge drinking. Many campuses have organizations that promote responsible drinking behavior among college students. There are staff members who can answer your questions as well. If you are concerned about this issue, you can contact the college's Dean of Students' Office or health center. Binge drinking can have grave consequences for your child. Many serious offenses and accidents on campus are the direct result of excessive drinking, including date rape, alcohol poisoning, and other injuries. Most students end up handling alcohol responsibly, but they may be greatly influenced by peers to engage in excessive drinking, particularly during the first year of adjustment to college.

Drugs

Your daughter is home for fall break and you notice a small plastic bag that has fallen out of her shirt in the pile of dirty clothes next to the washer and dryer. It looks like marijuana.

What's going on.

Even though you may know your child tried drugs in high school, it's more worrisome now because you don't have the advantage of being able to monitor your child's behavior on a daily basis and notice changes that may be due to drug use or abuse. It's easy to leap to the conclusion that your child has a serious drug problem. Depending on your values and experiences, you may feel it's hypocritical to insist that your child behave differently than you did when you were in college, but you also worry that drug use now seems more dangerous. You may feel strongly that no one should ever use drugs and be proud of the fact that you have never experimented with them. Or you may feel very little concern because you have great confidence in your child's ability to handle this experimentation responsibly.

> ## What's on your mind?
>
> My daughter is doing drugs, and that worries me. Should I confront her with it? I wonder how much she's involved in this?

> ## What's on your child's mind?
>
> So I smoke pot with my friends once in a while. What's the big deal? I know my parents wouldn't like it, but they probably did it in college too.

What to do.	What to avoid.
• Tell your child that you found the marijuana.	• Reacting with anger and an ultimatum: "If you ever use drugs again, I'll make you leave school and come home where I can keep an eye on you."
• Without blaming her, let her know your concerns.	
• Be honest if you have used drugs. Describe the context within which you experimented with drugs and share how you feel about it now.	• Moralizing and preaching: moralizing and preaching rarely change behavior, but they almost always shut down the communication.
• Be clear about your expectations and attitudes about drug use: "I am not so worried about a bit of experimentation with drugs, but I worry about the variety of serious drugs that might be available to you and how you would handle that," or "I am worried that any experimentation with drugs will be bad for you and I feel strongly that you shouldn't be using drugs at all."	• Trying to make her feel guilty or ashamed. This tactic may just make your child a more defiant and committed user.
• Ask her how she feels about those expectations and attitudes. Keep the lines of nonjudgmental communication open.	

What you need to know.

Although illegal, experimentation with drugs is common on most college campuses. This doesn't make your child's experimentation any less troubling. While students try out new lifestyles and values, they can be very dependent upon peer relationships and acceptance. Most students will do what their friends do. Some students choose not to experiment with drugs either because they and their friends have committed themselves to being drug free or because they are afraid of parental and/or societal repercussions.

Research shows that whether a person experiments with, abstains from, or abuses drugs is largely dependent on individual personality, much of which is formed early in life. These are not just college-age students' issues; many of these behaviors began in high school or earlier. One study has shown that experimenters in college actually have a healthier psychological profile than either abusers or abstainers.[2] Experimentation can be a healthy behavior when a young person is striving to form an individual identity and make choices about values and life-styles. This doesn't mean that the experimenter is committed to those choices forever.

Parents can have significant influence on their children's drug use by continuing to talk about this issue. They need to make it clear where they draw the line on drug use. Some parents may feel that moderate marijuana use is harmless, but that cocaine, crack, heroin, and other drugs are completely unacceptable. Other parents would draw the line at any experimentation with drugs, including alcohol. Many parents can tolerate a bit of experimentation with drugs and alcohol, but worry that too much experimentation can lead to dependency, abuse, and addiction. Because alcohol is considered by many to be a socially acceptable drug, discussion of drinking may come up naturally; however, few students will volunteer information about other drug use. It's your responsibility, as a parent, to initiate discussions about drugs and to continue to make your values and expectations clear to your college student.

What's on your mind?

Matt is sleeping with his girlfriend. I'm not sure how I feel about that.

I don't even know this girl.

Sexuality—Your Son

Your son has announced that he's bringing his new girlfriend home for spring break and has asked you to put away his high school girlfriend's picture and put the new flannel sheets on his bed.

What's going on.

You must now confront the fact that your son is sleeping with his girlfriend. You may feel shocked, you may feel pleased that he is open with you, you may worry about whether he is

What's on your child's mind?

It's going to be great to bring Ann home.

Mom didn't sound happy about Ann staying in my room.

I hope my parents will be cool about this.

having safe sex, and you may feel that he has a lot of nerve to expect that he can bring this girl home and share his bedroom with her.

What to do.	What to avoid.
• Be honest with yourself about your feelings about your son sleeping with his girlfriend in your home. • Talk with him. Don't be afraid to tell him that you're uncomfortable with this arrangement if that's the way you feel. • Acknowledge that he can disagree with you on the issue of premarital sex, but let him know that your feelings need to be respected when he's in your home. • Take this opportunity to start a dialogue exploring values about sexuality. Share your thoughts about responsible sexual behavior with your child. For example, you may feel premarital sex within a mutually respectful relationship is okay, but that a series of one-night stands with casual acquaintances is not okay. • Find out if your son has shared the proposed sleeping arrangements with his girlfriend. She may not be comfortable sleeping with him in your home. • Make sure he has information about practicing safe sex and understands the consequences of unprotected sex, even if you had the same discussion when he was younger.	• Judging his behavior. • Judging his girlfriend's behavior or character before you've met her. • Giving him a lecture on the dangers or immorality of premarital sex. • Overreacting and assuming that this will be his lifelong relationship.

What you need to know.

In addition to exploring new freedoms, lifestyles, surroundings, and activities, students are also discovering new friendships and creating new intimate relationships. This can take the form of dating a number of people, having one steady partner, or even engaging in casual sex. This experimentation can also mean forming intimate relationships with partners who come from different backgrounds, lifestyles, and value systems.

Sexuality—Your Daughter

It's winter break and you overhear your daughter Amy and some of her old high school friends regaling each other with stories of guys they have "hooked up" with during fall semester at college.

What's going on.

You find this behavior shocking, but you're not sure what you can or should do about it. Although you're relieved that Amy is on the pill, you are very concerned that, if she's sleeping with many different guys, she is at risk of contracting a sexually transmitted disease of some kind. You also wonder how she can feel good about sleeping around and how she's handling this emotionally.

What's on your mind?

I know Amy's on the pill, but I still worry about her safety.

How many guys has she slept with?

I'm worried that she'll get hurt.

And what, exactly, does "hooking up" mean?

What's on your child's mind?

I'm sure glad I'm on the pill.

I wonder what my parents would think if they knew how many guys I'd slept with this semester?

What to do.	What to avoid.
• Keep in mind that Amy may just be trying to impress her high school friends with her sophistication.	• Jumping to the conclusion that Amy is sleeping with a different guy every night.
• Tell Amy that you overheard the discussion and tell her you want to talk about it.	• Preaching and moralizing about "easy" girls and their ruined reputations.
• Let her know that you respect her right to privacy, but that you have concerns if she is sleeping with many different guys.	• Warning or threatening her about the consequences of her behavior.
• Share your values and attitudes regarding sex, and ask her what she thinks of your point of view.	• Shaming her in the hope that she'll stop having sex.
• Tell her if you feel uncomfortable with her behavior, but reinforce that you love her and care about her.	
• Be prepared to honor her feelings if Amy tells you that her sex life is none of your business. You can still share your expectations without discussing her sexual behavior.	

What you need to know.

There is no doubt that the sexual climate on campus is dramatically different than it was when you were eighteen to twenty-two years of age, and it's hard to find out what's really going on. We have found that your child's particular group of friends in college will have a great influence on sexual behavior. You may find the social culture disturbing; for example, casual sex or "hooking up" is common on many campuses, even in light of the epidemic of sexually transmitted diseases and AIDS. If your child's friends condone and engage in casual sex, it is likely that he or she will too.

Many new college students see only the two extreme ends of the range of choices: not having sex at all or having casual sex with lots of partners. You need to be clear with your child about what kind of sexual conduct you feel is responsible and healthy. Parents, while often not aware of the intimate details of their child's sexual experiences, can play a critical role in modeling trusting and respectful intimate relationships and talking about sexual values and expectations. Undoubtedly, you will have to initiate these discussions, while taking care to respect your child's privacy.

In our culture, there is a lingering double standard for young men and women when it comes to sex. Particularly in the first year of college, some young men and women engage in unhealthy sexual activities, especially when alcohol and drugs are involved. But young women are more likely to find themselves in exploitive and dangerous situations. The aftermath of these experiences can leave them feeling anxious and guilty or pregnant. Moreover, the physical and emotional consequences of this behavior can be much more serious for young women than for young men. For both, however, this experimentation with sexual freedom is usually short-lived, and most students end up settling down and behaving more responsibly before serious consequences result.

Your Adjustment Issues

Although you may be most concerned about how your child is adjusting to college life, it's good to keep in mind that this is a transition period for you as well. Many parents feel like check-writing spectators as their children cope with the changes that are part of college life. You may have been involved in each phase of your child's development and education to date, and now you are faced with parenting from afar with little direct interaction with your child.

You are also adjusting to the culture of the college or university. Whether your child chose a large state university, a small private college, a prestigious Ivy League institution, or a nearby community college, your role in your child's education will be very different from now on. You may feel that you don't know much about the college, and you will probably not get to know other parents as you did in elementary, middle, and high school. You won't know much about the students your child is hanging out with, and they may come from different backgrounds.

You're cut off from your child's daily experiences for the first time and that means your role as parent is changing dramatically. In dealing with many of these adjustment issues, you may want to refer again to the first chapter where we explored the changing nature of your relationship with your college child.

Want to Know More?

College Parents of America (CPA) is a new, national membership association dedicated to helping parents prepare for and put their children through college. CPA advises parents on the opportunities and challenges they will encounter during their child's college years and serves as an advocate on Capitol Hill, in state capitals, and on the nation's campuses. You can find out more about CPA by visiting their web site at www.collegeparents.org or calling their toll-free number 1-888-256-4627.

Coburn, Karen Levin, and Madge Lawrence Treeger. *Letting Go: A Parents' Guide to Understanding the College Years.* New York: HarperPerennial, 1997.
Grayson, Paul A., and Philip W. Meilman. *Beating the College Blues.* 2nd ed. New York: Checkmark Books, 1999.

---

1. Curtis Ostrander and Joseph Schwartz, *Crime at College* (Ithaca: New Strategist Publications, 1994).
2. J. Shedler and J. Block, "Adolescent Drug Use and Psychological Health: A Longitudinal Inquiry," *American Psychologist* 45 (1990): 612–30.

Chapter 4

Is Your Child Confident, Confused, or Coasting?

The Search for Identity and Autonomy

Doonesbury   BY GARRY TRUDEAU

> *When Dan came home for semester break last week, I hardly recognized him! He had grown his hair and looked like he had rolled out of a dirty laundry bag. I could live with his appearance, but then he started expounding about how the Republicans were responsible for all of the country's problems and that he no longer wanted to study economics and support what he called the "conservative agenda." I snapped! I started yelling, "Who do you think you are?" He was rejecting everything we stood for, everything we'd worked for, and everything we'd taught him.*

This chapter will help you understand the puzzling things that your college student may do while on the quest for identity and autonomy. Just remember two things:

- It's necessary for your child to be on this quest; in fact, it would be troubling if he or she weren't!
- It's also natural if your child's behavior drives you crazy and you begin to wonder, "Where did I go wrong?"

Identity

"Who am I?" is a question your child will ask during the college years. Who am I as a distinct person, who am I in relation to others, and who will I be in the future? Grappling with these questions is an essential part of becoming an independent adult. Most parents have no trouble with these questions—they have trouble with the behavior and lifestyle experimentation that accompanies them.

The search for identity is a lifelong process, but late adolescence and the college years are a particularly intense period because, for the first time, your child has the physical, intellectual, and social maturity that makes this quest possible. Drawing on our years of experience working with college students and our background in adolescent development, we will show why this search is a natural process in the transition from child to adult. Many facets of your child's life will reflect this search for identity, as illustrated in the examples that follow.

Appearance

What's on your mind?

Why is he doing this?
What will people think of me as a parent?
Is this permanent?
Where will this lead?

What's on your child's mind?

What's the big deal?
Why is my mom so hyper about my hair?
My family is so boring.

You eagerly looked forward to Doug's arrival home for Thanksgiving break. But when he walked in the door, you barely recognized him with his green-tinted Mohawk haircut left over from fraternity initiation and a small hoop earring hanging from his right ear. You can't imagine what your relatives are going to think when they arrive for Thanksgiving dinner.

What's going on.

Parents who are excited about having their child come home for a holiday may be shocked to see such dramatic changes in their child's appearance. Parents assume those changes are profound and lasting; they probably aren't. While the student will maintain a "no big deal" attitude toward these changes, they are symbolic of the need to differentiate from parents and to begin to create a new and separate identity.

What to do.	What to avoid.
• Keep in mind the important priorities. Will this matter a year or five years from now? Pick your battles, decide what really matters; tell your son if this bothers you, but listen to his ideas as well.	• Fighting the small fights over issues that don't matter much to you. How important is the hair issue really?
• Remember, this is a healthy process for your child. It doesn't have to do with the quality of your parenting.	• Judging and criticizing: "I can't believe you let the fraternity do that to your hair. It looks ridiculous."
• Remember, this too shall pass. Next time it may be a buzz cut.	• Generalizing beyond the issue at hand: "Is this the beginning of a slide into crazy behavior?"

What you need to know.

Most experts on human development point to late adolescence as a particularly important time in an individual's identity formation. Erik Erikson, one of the most well-known human development experts, argued that, ideally, adolescents need a period of moratorium. This moratorium (a kind of accountability "time out") gives teenagers the opportunity, removed from the burdens and responsibilities of adulthood, to explore their identities and to learn critical lessons about who they are in the world.[1] College presents the ideal setting for late adolescents to "try on" new identities.

As the parent of a college student experimenting with a new identity, you need to decide which battles to wage. Most students will experiment a bit with new looks and personal appearance. Remember the late sixties and early seventies when families engaged in raging battles about hair length and rock music? A lot of damage was done over relatively trivial issues in those days. Today we are faced with tattoos, body piercing, and even stranger tastes in music and entertainment.

These aspects of popular culture are important to adolescents. For example, take a walk in the mall and notice how you can categorize young people. You can tell the jocks from the nerds, the alternatives from the popular crowd, simply by the way they dress. When your son or daughter became a teenager, you probably noticed how they all looked alike and spent a lot of time talking to friends about what kind of music and what musical groups they liked. Music, appearance, and other somewhat superficial aspects of popular culture define social groups for adolescents, much as neighborhoods, profession, church affiliation, and political and community involvement define social groups for adults. For adolescents, these social groups provide a temporary group identity while they search for their own individual identity.

Friends

Your daughter Alexis calls to tell you that she wants to go home with her roommate for fall break:

What's on your mind?

Why doesn't she want to come home? I miss her.

She sees her roommate all the time; why can't she spend some time with her own family?

Will she be safe in New York City?

What's on your child's mind?

My roommate's family is so much cooler than mine.

I'm dying to go to New York City.

What's the big deal? It's just a long weekend.

ALEXIS: Hi, Mom. What's up?

MOM: Oh, hi, hon. Not much new here. What's up with you?

ALEXIS: I just wanted to call to tell you that Claire invited me to visit her family in New York City over fall break. Isn't that cool? Can I go?

MOM: Well, I don't know. I was really looking forward to seeing you for the long weekend. Don't you want to come home?

ALEXIS: Well, yeah, but I've never been to New York and it would be so much fun to see the city.

MOM: Where do Claire's parents live?

ALEXIS: Some place in Brooklyn, I think. Anyway, we could ride the subway into the city, and she's promised to show me all the sights.

MOM: But we don't know anything about her family. Does she live in a safe place?

ALEXIS: Mom! She's my roommate, remember? I know I'll have a good time. Her older brother is going to take us to some really cool clubs.

MOM: What kind of clubs?

ALEXIS: You know, dance clubs and stuff.

MOM: I don't know, Alexis, I feel a little nervous about you being in the city all alone.

ALEXIS: I won't be alone. Her whole family will be there. I think her dad's a cop. How much safer could I be?

MOM: Well, I guess it's okay. But be sure to give me the phone number where you'll be.

ALEXIS: Okay, Mom. Thanks. This is going to be so much fun. I can't wait. Talk to you later.

What's going on.

Part of trying on new identities in college is interacting with people from different backgrounds and geographical areas. This doesn't mean that your daughter is rejecting you. She's excited about exploring a whole new city and culture and finding out about how her roommate's family lives.

What to do.	What to avoid.
• Try to give your child permission to experiment and learn about other ways of living.	• Being overly disappointed that she won't be home for break.
• Remember that she is not rejecting you and your family; she is merely trying to create her own identity separate from you.	• Saying "no" just for the sake of saying "no."
• Ask her to give you the phone number in New York in case you need to get in touch with her.	• Trying to make her afraid of her adventure.
• Remind her that she needs to be more aware of her personal safety in the city and ask her how she thinks she can do that.	

What you need to know.

Friends are very important to college students. When your child was young, being a friend meant being a playmate, able to share and interact in play. When your child reached adolescence, however, the nature of friendships changed. Your teenager needed to develop a complex set of skills in order to have close friendships—these included the ability to share intimate feelings, provide emotional support to friends, and trust friends to be open and honest in return. These skills help adolescents form intimate attachments and build self-esteem. Most students have transferred their primary attention from parents to peers by the time they enroll in college. This doesn't mean that you are no longer important in their lives. It does mean that they are exploring who they are in other relationships, a necessary step in eventually forming the intimate attachments central to independent adulthood.

Opposites Attract

What's on your mind?

This young man just isn't right for Kelly.

We didn't send her to college to fall in love with someone with so few future prospects.

She seems to spend all her time with him.

What's on your child's mind?

I'm really in love with Mike. He's so special and so mature. I don't think my parents like him. They're so conservative and narrow-minded.

Your daughter's phone calls home consist of gushing on and on about her new boyfriend. You met him when you were on campus for parents' weekend and are concerned about her interest in him. He's so different from anyone your daughter dated in high school, and you wonder how she could be so infatuated with someone from such a different background. You hate to admit it, but you're worried that she's falling in love with this young man who was raised in the projects in a big city.

What's going on.

Kelly's behavior is typical of many college students who have grown up in relatively sheltered environments with few opportunities to meet different types of people. This difference is attractive, and having an intimate relationship with someone like Michael helps Kelly understand other life experiences and begin to explore her own values and background.

What to do.	What to avoid.
• Try to understand why Kelly finds Michael so attractive. • Ask her what characteristics he has that appeal to her. • Let her know your feelings without assaulting Michael's background. You could say, "I know that Michael's motivation to put himself through college attracts you and that is impressive, but I worry about your falling in love with someone from such a different background. Do you think that's a problem?" • Listen to her response and let her know that you trust her to make good decisions.	• Telling Kelly that you think Michael is wrong for her and that you wish she'd stop seeing him. • Warning that couples from such different backgrounds have many problems to deal with later. • Jumping to the conclusion that this will be Kelly's lifelong mate.

What you need to know.

Some experts believe that intimate relationships can come only after an individual has established a stable identity. However, other researchers have found that girls tend to discover who they are through forming intimate relationships and emotional bonds.[2] Boys may be more likely to discover who they are before they form intimate relationships. Either way, relationships help adolescents explore their identity.

Intimate Relationships

You were surprised when your daughter Cassie came home from college over semester break and announced that she was in love and wanted to spend part of her holiday with her new boyfriend who lives in another city.

> **What's on your mind?**
>
> She's in love after knowing this boy for only two months? I can't believe how much time she's spent talking with him on the phone.

What's going on.

Intimate relationships tend to develop with great speed and intensity during the college years. It's alarming to parents when their child forms such a passionate relationship so quickly. The main difference in dating between high school and college is that college students have twenty-four hours a day to spend with each other if they choose; hence, the relationships and friendships are usually more intense in a shorter period of time.

## What to do.	## What to avoid.
• Recognize that this is a natural and predictable stage in your daughter's development. • Honor her feelings. • Ask her to tell you about her new boyfriend. • Share your values about intimacy and sexuality, while recognizing that she may have different values and needs to explore these values within the context of this new relationship.	• Telling her that this can't be real love. • Warning her about making such quick judgments. • Asking her to slow down this relationship. • Refusing to allow her to see her boyfriend over the holiday.

What you need to know.

The ability to form intimate attachments with both friends and romantic partners is a major task of adolescent development. In high school, peers become an important source of emotional support; in college, many students begin to rely on romantic partners. College students are more likely to disclose intimate information to romantic partners than to friends or parents.[3] Although romantic partners can become the primary source of emotional support in college, do not underestimate how important it is to your son or daughter to know that you will always be there to provide emotional support.

Career Choices and Majors

When Sam when to college, everyone marveled at his maturity. You were proud of his focus on becoming a research scientist and his determination to tackle a demanding course of study. You are surprised when, during spring break at home, he sits down at the kitchen table and says:

SAM: Mom, I've been thinking lately about changing my major to English.
MOM: You have? I thought you always wanted to be an environmental scientist.
SAM: I know. I really liked science in high school, but it's so different in college.
MOM: How?
SAM: It just seems so dry. And if I major in chemistry, I'll be taking almost all science courses from now on.
MOM: But you used to love your science courses.
SAM: I did, but before I always got to take English, history, and art too. I'm taking this English criticism course right now that I really love. We're analyzing all of this great literature and it's fascinating. I think I want to major in English.
MOM: But what would you do with a major in English?
SAM: Well, some of the kids in my English classes are talking about being teachers or going into advertising or publishing. That sounds kind of cool.
MOM: Oh, Sam. I don't know what to say. Do you really think you want to be a teacher?
SAM: I don't know for sure, but I'm doing some volunteer tutoring with the local high school kids and it's really fun. I think I could be a good teacher.
MOM: This is kind of hard to believe. You always seemed so sure that science was your interest.
SAM: I know, Mom, but I'm not sure anymore. Are you upset with me?
MOM: No, I'm just surprised and confused.

What's on your mind?

Sam has always wanted to be a environmental scientist. What happened?

I'm worried about how vague his plans seem now.

We're sacrificing a lot to keep him in school and now he's not taking advantage of this great science program.

What's on your child's mind?

I'm so confused and worried about my future.

I really don't like science any more, but English is really interesting.

My parents seem so disappointed in me.

What's going on.

Sam, like many other college students, is discovering that what he always thought he wanted to do doesn't fit his interests anymore. This discovery often happens in the sophomore year when it becomes necessary for most students to declare a major course of study. Parents who have sent a focused and confident child off to college may wonder what has happened and feel concerned about his or her future prospects. In fact, it is common for this questioning to occur more than once during the college years.

What to do.	What to avoid.
• Open up the discussion and listen to Sam's interests, concerns, and fears. • Give him permission to be confused and to explore. • Let him know if you're worried and be specific about why. For example, "I am concerned about your dropping your science major and what that may mean for your future job prospects. Tell me more about how you feel about your decision." • Reinforce that this is his decision. Remind him that you love him regardless of his major and future career choices.	• Trying to convince him to change his mind and continue with science. • "You" messages: "But, Sam, you always wanted to be a scientist. What's happened to you?" • Blaming him for being so confused and indecisive.

Confident, Confused, or Coasting

In our work with students, we have found that they tend to fall into one of three types—confident, confused, or coasting—when it comes to exploring who they are and making decisions about their lives. A confident student has solid goals in mind and sticks to them; a confused student actively tries out alternatives and questions everything; a coasting student goes with the flow, seemingly unconcerned about taking action and making decisions. Parents have difficulty with the shifting that goes on between these three states during the college years. Few students stick to one type throughout college; in fact, most move in and out of these states frequently as they face new situations. Although this behavior can frustrate parents, going through these states is a critical exercise in identity formation for your child.

A student can be confident in one arena (certain of which fraternity or sorority to pledge) and confused in another (unable to choose a major). He or she may coast for a semester (not worrying about a major), be confused for a semester (exploring two or three different majors), and be confident a year later (finally choosing a particular major).

Let's look at Sam's situation from the previous dialogue and see how he fits these types. He began college confident that he would be a scientist. A year later, he was confused and began exploring alternatives, but he still was not ready to make a commitment. After his conversation with Mom, Sam may return to school and coast for a while, afraid to explore different majors and upset his Mom. In time, he may acknowledge his confusion again, and actively examine alternatives. After investigating options, he may be able to make a commitment and become confident again. This pattern is common as college students make decisions and explore who they are.

An Identity Formation Model

Our experience in working with college students follows a model of identity formation developed by James Marcia.[4] Marcia's model offers another way of understanding your child's behavior as he or she struggles with achieving a unique identity. The chart shows Marcia's four statuses of identity—identity achievement, identity moratorium, identity foreclosure, and identity diffusion. According to Marcia, the degree to which an adolescent either explores or commits to a course of action results in that child being (at that moment) identity diffused, identity foreclosed, in identity moratorium, or identity achieved.

FOUR STATUSES OF IDENTITY

		Exploration	
		High	Low
Commitment	High	Identity Achieved	Identity Foreclosed
	Low	Identity Moratorium	Identity Diffused

   Let's look again at Sam's situation and try to understand his behavior using this model. When Sam was in high school, he was confident that he would be a scientist—he was low on exploring alternatives and high on his commitment to science and, therefore, identity foreclosed. He committed to study science in college without exploring alternatives. During college, he actively began to pursue other courses of study. When he spoke to his Mom he had entered a moratorium stage—exploring other options and low on a commitment to science. Simply put, he is confused. Over time, after exploring English and teaching, Sam may develop a firm commitment to an English major and to a career as a teacher. At this point, Marcia would say he had achieved his vocational identity—he had sufficiently explored other options and then made a commitment. Sam, however, could have decided that he really didn't want to think about this big decision anymore. At this stage, according to Marcia, he is identity diffused (coasting)—he has ceased exploring alternatives and yet isn't making a firm commitment to one course of study either.

   While we have characterized students as simply "confident," Marcia maintains that there are two distinct categories of "confident"—identity foreclosed or identity achieved. A student who enrolls in college with a premed focus, for example, without having explored other vocational interests, is confident and identity foreclosed. He has decided to be a doctor based on little exploration. Ultimately, he may end up being a doctor and happy with his choice, but problems can arise when a student hasn't explored other paths. If an "identity foreclosed" student begins to question his commitment to medicine, it can upset his sense of himself and confuse his parents. In order to truly be confident and "identity achieved," however, it may be necessary for him to experience other phases of Marcia's model. This could take the form of coasting for a while, being confused about alternatives, or choosing to go back to being confident in the "identity foreclosed" manner and forge ahead with his decision to study medicine. Or, he may explore other majors and decide, finally, to make a commitment to medicine—at that point he would be confident and identity achieved.

It's good to keep in mind that throughout their life span, people usually move back and forth many times between these states. In fact, one of the ironies of this stage of adolescent development is that it can be quite similar to adults in midlife. Parents may be asking similar identity questions during the time their children are in college. Although careers and vocations do not necessarily define a person's identity, they express change in identity formation throughout life.

Values/Lifestyle

Your son Paul seems thrilled with his new friends at college, all of whom come from wealthy families and have lots of money for expensive vacations, clothes, alcohol, and, you're afraid, recreational drugs. He's been asked to a friend's vacation home in Florida over spring break and wants extra money to buy some new clothes for the trip.

What's going on.

Paul is exploring how he fits into the peer culture of college. This is a vital part of his ability to form a unique identity in the world. During this period, his peers will have a definite impact on his desires and expectations. This can be intimidating for parents, but these experiences help adolescents formulate their own value system by observing other families' values.

> ### What's on your mind?
> Paul is pretty infatuated with all of that money.
> We can't afford to support his adventures with this crowd.
> I'm concerned about the drinking and possible drugs.

> ### What's on your child's mind?
> I am so psyched about going to Florida for spring break.
> These guys are so much fun.
> I wish my parents had more money.

What to do.	What to avoid.
• Let your son know that you're pleased he has this opportunity for a nice vacation.	• Reminding him that you're not made of money.
• Be honest about what you can afford to do to support this adventure. If you can't afford to give him extra money for clothes, tell him.	• Questioning the values of his friends and their families.
• Help him figure out if he should try to earn some extra money and how he could find a temporary job.	• Saying no because you're not sure about his new friends.
• Ask him what he likes most about his new friends.	

What you need to know.

As we've said before, the vast majority of college students eventually adopt most of their parents' values. Not all of them do, however. Liberal, socially conscious parents who work for egalitarian values in the culture may have difficulty accepting a child who wants to be an investment banker and have tons of money to live what he or she considers "the good life." Just as you no longer can choose the environment in which your child lives and makes friends, you no longer can control his or her values and lifestyle choices. However, if your parenting style shows respect for your child's individuality, you will have a better chance to sustain an intimate and satisfying relationship as he or she finds his or her own niche and moves into the adult world.

Values/Religion

Your family has always had a strong religious background. Most of your activities have revolved around the church, and you feel that religion is an important part of life and central to your family's value system. The following phone call with your son John has you wondering what is going on at that university:

DAD: Hi, John, how're you doing?

JOHN: Pretty good, Dad. I got an A on my philosophy paper.

DAD: That's great. What did you write about?

JOHN: Well, you're not going to like this, but we've been reading and talking about world religious beliefs and I'm seriously rethinking whether Jesus was all that everyone thinks. I mean, who knows how his ideas were interpreted over the years?

DAD: You're right, I don't like your attitude. Don't you remember anything you learned in church?

JOHN: Yeah, but I'm not sure I really believe it anymore. I mean, if Jesus is the only Son of God, where does that leave Buddha?

DAD: But you're not a Buddhist!

JOHN: Well, I know you won't be happy with this either, but I'm not going to church anymore. It just doesn't seem all that relevant here, and I like to sleep in on Sunday morning.

DAD: You're not going to church?

JOHN: Well, no, I haven't been going lately.

DAD: I can't believe you're throwing away years of being involved in the church because you want to sleep in on Sunday.

JOHN: Dad, chill. It's not like I'm a heathen or something. I just don't see why this is so important to you. I mean, I know it's important to you, but it's just not that important to me right now.

What's on your mind?

I'm really upset that John is rejecting his religious training.

Religion has an important place in our family.

I wonder what they're teaching him up there. To reject Christianity?

What's on your child's mind?

My dad is so rigid about religion.

I wish he'd get off my back about it.

I wonder what I really do believe.

What's going on.

Students tend to question many of the values with which they've been raised. A family with a strong religious tradition may feel shocked to find that their child is rejecting all of that training; even more upsetting may be their child's questioning of basic religious beliefs that the family holds sacred.

What to do.	What to avoid.
• Engage your child in a discussion about religion. Use this as an opportunity to talk openly about different religious belief systems. • Share your beliefs, but recognize your child's right to choose whether he practices your religion. • Ask what he is learning about himself and explain how you came to believe in your Christian values. • Remember that the values you have instilled in your child are powerful and lasting, even though he is questioning them at this point.	• Trying to make your child feel guilty for not going to church. • Berating his philosophy professor for filling his mind with crazy notions. • Cutting off the discussion; trying to force him to adopt your beliefs and refusing to listen to his.

What you need to know.

When they enter college, most students have a dualistic way of approaching intellectual and ethical problems, according to William Perry.[5] By dualistic, Perry means having a narrow understanding of right and wrong and good versus bad. When tackling intellectual and ethical dilemmas, students who think dualistically tend to believe in an absolute right and wrong, and that authority figures always know the right answer. Throughout the college years, most students move from being dualistic to relativistic in their thinking.

John came to school believing in the Christian values he had learned through church and family. He believed that Christianity was right and other religions were wrong. But when he enrolled in his first philosophy class he began to question the absolute "rightness" of "Jesus as the only Son of God" and began to explore the truths expressed in other religious ideologies. He began to see that religious questions may have multiple right answers and that the authority he once accepted without question had only one of the possible right answers. At this point, he believes that all religions have equal value. And he believes that "everyone is entitled to his or her own opinion."

In this dialogue, Dad assumes that John has rejected his Christian values, while John is simply thinking that there is not one absolute right or wrong; that is, Buddhism's ideology is just as valid as Christianity's. Parents may interpret this type of thinking as intellectual curiosity, confusion, rebellion, or just plain wishy-washyness. But to John's dad, it signaled that John had taken the first step on that slippery slope to rejecting his Christian heritage and values. But the chances are good that John, after this period of relativistic thinking in which he explores other ideologies and value systems, will return to a belief in Christianity and have a stronger belief for having questioned it. Before he went to college, John was committed to the family's values; now he is exploring *his* personal religious beliefs. It's possible that he'll eventually make a personal commitment to Christianity; it's also possible that he'll make a commitment to another religious belief, such as Buddhism.

Many parents feel alarmed when they realize they have sent a child with cherished values and ideals to college only to find that their child is questioning and, at least temporarily, rejecting them. As students explore their role and identity in the world, they may also question ideas that are a part of their value system. This intellectual and ethical questioning forms an important part of John's identity development. While you can't dictate your child's personal beliefs, you can have an influence on his or her thinking through continuing to discuss this topic openly.

Values/Politics

As a card-carrying liberal Democrat, you were disturbed when your daughter called to tell you she was going to a Right to Life rally over the weekend:

MOM: Hello?

CAROLINE: Hi, Mom. How are you?

MOM: Good, honey. What's up?

CAROLINE: Not too much, other than that I've just decided to attend the Right to Life March on Washington this weekend.

MOM: You are? Did you say "Right to Life"?

What's on your mind?

What is the matter with her?
Doesn't she realize how hard women have fought for the right to choose?
I can't believe I have a Republican daughter. No one in our family is a Republican.

What's on your child's mind?

I've been brainwashed by my liberal parents.
I don't believe all the Republican ideals, but I'm not a liberal either.
My parents are so "sixties." They don't know what's really going on now.

CAROLINE: Yes, I've decided that I'm against abortion and I'm going to do something about it.

MOM: Caroline, no one is *for* abortion. No one would want to have to make that choice, but don't you think women should be able to decide? After all, these are our bodies.

CAROLINE: Mom, that's just such a liberal cop-out. Abortion is killing and that's wrong. How can you be against the death penalty and pro-abortion?

MOM: I'm not pro-abortion. I just told you I'm pro-choice. And I support Planned Parenthood to help ensure that abortion doesn't have to be the only choice.

CAROLINE: I'm happy that Planned Parenthood is working to increase contraceptive use, but I think it's wrong that they kill babies. So many families want babies and can't have them. And besides, how can you condone killing defenseless babies? It's just wrong.

MOM: Oh, Caroline, it's such a complex issue. Maybe we should talk about it when we have more time.

CAROLINE: It doesn't seem too complicated to me—you either kill babies or you don't. I'll tell you, I'm really beginning to change my mind about a lot of issues. So many of my friends here are in the Young Republicans Club on campus. I went to a meeting last week and I've decided to join. For example, do you know how much we're spending on welfare each year? It's unbelievable, we give all this money to people who just don't feel like getting up and going to work. If we don't stop this now, my generation will have nothing.

MOM: You're joining the Young Republicans? I can't believe it.

What's going on.

Politics, like religion, is an expression of personal values and attitudes. Students often question these basic values during college when confronted with different points of view. Peers, and the general political climate on campus, will undoubtedly influence this exploration of political and social values.

What to do.	What to avoid.
• Engage your child in an open discussion of her political beliefs. • Ask her what is appealing about the Republican point of view. • Challenge her to think through her opinions on social issues: "I'm curious about why you feel abortion rights should be limited. I'd like to know what you're thinking about this issue."	• Insisting that she rethink her political views. • Dismissing her opinions. "You're just not thinking about this in the right way." • Telling her you're disappointed that she's rejecting everything you've tried to teach her.

What you need to know.

Caroline, like John in the previous example, may have come to college committed to the political principles with which she was raised. Opening up to new people and ideas in college, she is now questioning some pretty fundamental political and social policy values. She has moved from dualistic thinking ("Democrats are right; Republicans are wrong") to relativism. She questions her democratic beliefs and begins to see that some of the republican beliefs she's been exposed to at college are valid and true as well. It's easy for parents to overreact to these intellectual and ethical developmental changes and try to persuade their child to return to an earlier point of view. It may be helpful for parents to remember their own young adulthood and recall instances in which they may have moved from dualistic to relativistic thinking before making a commitment to their current values.

Parents who became more liberal than their own parents when they were in college may be surprised when their children are attracted to conservative political views. Your child's values may become more liberal or more conservative than yours, often depending on the beliefs of friends and the political climate of the school he or she attends. Showing a genuine interest in your child's new ideas and continuing to discuss your own values with your child will help ensure that you maintain a strong relationship.

Values/Character Issues

What's on your mind?

I can't believe Chad did this. I'm so ashamed and embarrassed. Where did I go wrong as a parent?

What's on your child's mind?

I guess I really blew it. A lot of kids do this when they get in a pinch. I'm really scared that I'll get kicked out of school.

Your son Chad turned in a research paper that one of his fraternity brothers wrote last year. The professor figured it out and has brought your son up on academic integrity charges before a review board.

What's going on.

Colleges and universities take the issue of academic integrity very seriously and often impose stiff consequences if they find a student has plagiarized work without attribution, stolen other people's work, or in any way cheated on an examination or paper. Many schools have an honor code that they expect students to adhere to and have judicial boards to address violations of this code. This can, and should, be a very sobering experience for students who violate academic integrity rules.

What to do.

- Above all, try to keep in mind that this is Chad's problem.
- Try to empathize with his fears and ignore his "excuses."
- Ask him how he plans to deal with this crisis and to keep you informed as to his actions.
- Focus on what he is learning from this situation.
- Tell him that you are disappointed in his behavior but that you still love him.

What to avoid.

- Yelling at him for being dishonest. It will only make him defensive.
- Threatening to disown him, take him out of school, or remove your support.
- Focusing on how embarrassed and ashamed you are.
- Offering to call the school and try to "fix" the situation.

What you need to know.

College students are learning critical lessons about who they are in the world as individuals. This is a time of considerable privilege for a child who has the benefit of the learning environment that college presents, both academically and personally. Erik Erikson posits that students in this time period may engage in what he calls "transitory delinquency," which may mean breaking laws or at least exploring antisocial or immoral behavior.[6] While this alarms parents, it is almost always short-lived and, indeed, may be a key part of the search for identity and adult maturity, both of which require that an individual take personal responsibility for his or her actions. Of course, a continuing pattern of illegal or antisocial behavior demands a strong response. See chapter 9 for how to determine if a situation is a crisis and calls for immediate action.

Special Identity Issues for College Women

During the college years, young women begin to face choices about the future and are often confused about balancing relationships and careers. Although our culture has come a long way toward supporting young women, there are still special questions and challenges for daughters in college.

Confused and Unsure

When your daughter Audrey was home for midyear break, the following conversation took place:

MOM: What are you planning to do over the summer, honey?
AUDREY: I'm not sure. One of my professors at school told me that I should apply for an internship at Arnold, Jamison, and Cutter, the big accounting firm.
MOM: Really? That sounds interesting.
AUDREY: Yeah, but it's really competitive and I probably won't get it. If I did, it would be really intense with all those math geniuses all summer.

> **What's on your mind?**
> What's wrong with Audrey? She actually seems scared to apply for this internship. Why is she dragging her heels on this?

> **What's on your child's mind?**
> I don't know what to do this summer. Everyone's pressuring me to take this internship.
> I don't want to be away from my friends all summer.
> I bet I don't know enough about accounting for this internship.

MOM: But, Audrey, you're hoping to become a CPA some day. Wouldn't this be good experience?

AUDREY: I guess so. My professor says that Arnold, Jamison usually hires the people that have done summer internships with them.

MOM: Wow, you might even get a job offer before you graduate from school!

AUDREY: Mom, don't get so excited. I probably don't have a chance at this internship anyway and I'm not so sure I really want to be away from home and from all my friends for the whole summer.

MOM: But, Audrey, it sounds like such a great opportunity. Your professor wouldn't have asked you to apply if she didn't think you were qualified.

AUDREY: Okay, okay. I'll apply for it, but I'm not sure I want to do it.

What's going on.

It's great that Audrey's professor (not surprisingly, a woman herself) has taken an interest in Audrey and is encouraging her to compete to achieve her career goals. We've found that college women especially need mentoring by important people in their lives (their parents, friends, relatives, teachers, and professors) in order to achieve their potential. Daughters need parents and other adults to support their emotional, intellectual, and career development during the college years. Even the brightest and most motivated college women can find themselves losing confidence in themselves and confused about their goals. Young women like Audrey can appear confused when they anticipate a future in corporate America, which typically rewards competitiveness and individual achievement over relationships and collaboration.

What to do.	What to avoid.
• Ask your daughter what has caused her confusion.	• Blaming her for her lack of decisiveness and focus.
• Try to sympathize with the difficult choices she's facing.	• Asking her why her friends are more important than this great career opportunity.
• Reinforce how proud of her achievements you are and how much you admire her hard work.	• Reminding her of how lucky she is to have so many choices.

What you need to know.

Carol Gilligan, a psychologist who has studied girls' development, found that self-confident young girls often become confused when they reach the teen years, and that confusion continues to plague college women as well.[7] Gilligan and other scholars have found that girls flourish in collaborative learning and working environments and that self-esteem can actually decrease during the college years as young women struggle with the conflicting interests of personal choice, relationship demands, and family and career aspirations.[8]

A Chilly Climate for Women

Your daughter Hillary has always been an outstanding science student and won numerous awards and scholarships when she graduated from high school. She's now in her sophomore year at the university and she has become disillusioned about going on for a graduate degree in science. Her faculty advisor has told her it can be really tough for women in science when they get to graduate school. She's wondering if she should reconsider her major in physics and her plans to get a Ph.D.

What's on your mind?

What has happened to Hillary? She went there feeling so confident in what she wanted.

Why didn't her faculty advisor encourage her?

Is it still so tough for women in science today?

What's going on.

Hillary is taking her advisor's comment to heart. She's not sure if she can get into graduate school or if she really wants to make that commitment of time and energy. She may not know any women who have become professors in physics, and it's hard for her to see herself as an accomplished scientist if she hasn't seen or known a woman who has taken this path.

What's on your child's mind?

I'm so confused.

Do I want to commit six or seven years to get a Ph.D?

My faculty advisor doesn't seem to think I can do it.

What if I *do* want to have a family too?

What to do.	What to avoid.
• Encourage her to seek out women faculty members in science and ask them for advice. • Remind her that she can switch academic advisors if her current advisor is not actively supporting her plans. • Let her know that you have confidence in her ability to make choices about her major and her future course of study.	• Reinforcing her image as a star science student and discounting her current dilemma. • Pushing her into going to graduate school or readily accepting her fears. • Encouraging her to make a quick decision.

What you need to know.

At most colleges and universities there are very few, if any, women physical science professors to act as mentors or role models for young women. Even faculty members who recognize the unfairness of gender bias in teaching and advising have difficulty changing their behavior toward and expectations of women students. Recent research has shown that male and female students are treated differently by professors even when their capabilities and achievements are equal.[9]

Having It All

The following phone call from your daughter Sara in her junior year at college has you troubled:

SARAH: Hi, Dad.

DAD: Hi, Sara, how are you?

SARA: Pretty good.

DAD: Just pretty good? You don't sound too happy.

SARA: I'm just worried because I'm not sure I want to go to law school anymore.

DAD: What? I thought you'd just taken the LSAT and were on your way.

SARA: Yeah, I took it, but now I'm not sure where to apply or even if I want to go.

DAD: What's going on? Tell me about it.

SARA: There are so many things I don't know. Where I should go, if I want to go through three more years of school right now, and, of course, the Jake question.

DAD: What do you mean, "the Jake question"?

SARA: Well, he's applying to law school too, and I really want to be with him. Even if I apply to the same schools he's applying to, we may not get into the same one. Then what will I do?

DAD: Is this about Jake or about law school?

SARA: No, I really want to go, well I think I do, but I also really want to be with Jake.

DAD: Honey, it sounds like you need to decide what *you* want to do. I know Jake is important to you, but after all it's just for law school. You can still have Jake as your boyfriend if you're not at the same school.

SARA: But, Dad, it would be so hard. I don't know. I'm just so torn.

DAD: But, Sara, you can't plan your whole life around Jake.

SARA: But I love him and I want to be with him. Maybe I'll just put off law school for a few years.

DAD: Is that what you really want to do?

SARA: I don't know! Why do you keep pushing me on this?

DAD: Sorry, honey, I was just trying to help.

SARA: I know. I'm sorry.

What's on your mind?

I thought Sara was set on going to law school. What happened?

This can't be just about Jake. I hope not.

I wonder how I can help her.

What's on your child's mind?

What am I going to do about law school? I have to make a decision soon.

I don't want to follow Jake around, but I don't want to be separated either.

Why is this so hard?

What's going on.

Sara is experiencing a rather typical conflict. In college, young women usually come face-to-face with the dilemma of playing dual roles in their lives. This is especially true for women who want to have a career, an intimate relationship, and perhaps a family someday. Chances are Jake is not agonizing over these choices.

Unfortunately, the gender roles still in place for young men and women present women with tough choices. Even though many college graduates today put off marriage and family until their late twenties or early thirties, young women still have these competing roles and demands to consider when making career and graduate school decisions.

What to do.	What to avoid.
• Empathize with Sara's confusion and indecision. • Ask her if she has discussed this dilemma with Jake. • Remind her that she is a capable, smart young woman who has worked hard for the opportunity she has now. • Let her know that you appreciate how torn she is in making this decision.	• Telling her she can't throw away law school for Jake. • Reminding her that this relationship may not last anyway. • Trying to talk her into going to law school regardless of her feelings.

What you need to know.

Many young women tend to form their identity in terms of relationships and emotional bonds. When Carol Gilligan studied identity formation in girls, she found that many form their identity in the context of intimate relationships. This poses a formidable dilemma for young women when looking at their future prospects. Moreover, many college women have not had the benefit of the mentoring from faculty that young men receive in formulating future plans. Fathers, in particular, can have a significant impact on how their daughters approach career and vocational decisions. But fathers can also find it disturbing that their daughters are so focused on personal relationships, seemingly at the expense of their career advancement.

Because intimate attachments and relationships are so central to many young women's identity development, keep these factors in mind when trying to understand your child's decision-making process. There are no easy or generally applicable solutions, but parents can be sensitive to this dilemma and try to help their daughters sort through the conflicting expectations and demands.

Identity Issues for Ethnic and Racial Minority Students

Although we are rapidly becoming a nation of a majority of minorities, young people who are not members of the dominant white culture still face special identity issues during the college years. The following scenarios will help you understand and respond effectively to these challenges.

Exploring Racial Identity

Your son Eric is home for fall break and the following conversation takes place:

MOM: Eric, what's this with the dreadlocks?

ERIC: All the brothers at school have dreads, Mom. My college friends are so cool; they're so much more mature than my high school friends were.

MOM: How so?

ERIC: Well, you know, in high school all my friends wanted to be so "white" and do everything the white kids did. Now, at college, I hang with the black kids. I haven't even met many white kids there.

MOM: Really?

ERIC: Yeah, my friends at school really understand what's happening. One of them actually got harassed by campus security for being on the quad late at night. He was just walking home from the library, and this security guy gave him a hard time. When he told us about it, we were really steamed. We decided to go to the dean, tell him what happened, and ask him to do something about it.

MOM: Did you get in trouble with the dean?

ERIC: No, Mom, somebody has to stand up and let people know they can't push us around.

What's on your mind?

Eric seems so angry.

I wonder what's going on with him at school.

He's never been an activist before.

What's on your child's mind?

I'm really angry that black students get harassed.

This never happened in high school.

It's really great to have black friends. They really understand me.

MOM: Well, I just don't want you getting into trouble up there. You need to tend to your studies.

ERIC: I am, Mom, but I'm just sick of our crowd always being suspect. It's not right and you know it too.

MOM: You can't fight all those battles yourself, you know.

ERIC: Maybe not, but I'm going to stick up for my black brothers anyway. They're my friends.

What's going on.

Ethnic and racial identity can take on a new dimension when students get to college. Students who have been raised in middle-class African-American families often suddenly realize that they have not really interacted with other members of their racial group, and that their high school was dominated by white values and attitudes.

What to do.	What to avoid.
• Support your child in exploring his racial identity. • Ask him what it is that makes him feel comfortable with his new friends. • Let him know that you are proud of his identification with African-American students. • Tell him about situations in which you have experienced discrimination and what you did about it. • Reinforce that his academic work should be his highest priority, without dismissing his concerns about racial issues.	• Reminding him that he lives in a white culture and that he needs to conform. • Telling him to keep a low profile and stay out of trouble.

What you need to know.

The search for identity can be complex for ethnic and racial minorities. Members of nondominant groups often find that their racial identity comes to the forefront when they get to college, according to William Cross, who has studied identity development in African-American students.[10] His findings, although limited to African Americans, can also be helpful in understanding other minorities' experiences in searching for identity in the dominant culture. Cross found a predictable progression in their ethnic identity development.

If we look at Eric we can see this progression. In high school Eric tried to fit into the dominant culture. The incident in college with his friend and the security guard jolted him out of his acceptance of the dominant culture as he began to encounter racism on a personal level. He began to reject the dominant culture and immerse himself in his own ethnic culture. When Eric came home he had even changed his appearance to more closely identify with his minority group. His friends, for the first time, were mainly African American. He began to feel pride in his cultural heritage.

Cross would predict that Eric would eventually recognize that there are some good things about the dominant culture as well as his own ethnic culture. He would be able to pick and choose which aspects of each culture fit his emerging sense of self and adopt some aspects of each culture. He may eventually become committed to helping others deal with the ethnic identity issues he has been through. For example, he may become a Big Brother to an African-American youngster and help that youngster feel proud of his minority culture, while helping him succeed within the values of the dominant culture.

While not every college student goes through this process of ethnic identity development, Cross's observations can help parents understand their child's experience as a racial minority in what is still a dominantly white culture at most colleges. Moreover, research indicates that minority students who explore their racial identity have higher self-esteem than those who don't.[11]

Finding Comfort in a Shared Background

Your daughter Maria seems pretty unhappy when she makes her weekly call home:

MARIA: Hi, Mama.

MOM: Hi, Maria. How are you?

MARIA: I miss you guys so much. How is everyone?

MOM: Just fine. Victor and Grandpapa are out fishing, and your Papa has just come home from work. Grandmama is helping me fix dinner. Wish you were here.

MARIA: I miss you all so much. I can't wait to come home for Christmas.

MOM: Aren't you happy there?

MARIA: I'm okay, but everyone here is so different from me. My history professor asked me today what it feels like to be a Latino at the university. I was so embarrassed; I didn't know what to say.

MOM: What *did* you say?

MARIA: I just told him that I don't have any friends who aren't Latino. It's hard, though, because the whole class is different from me. There are blacks and Asians, but I'm the only Latina in the whole class. And I don't like to speak up anyway.

MOM: Do you know anyone who isn't Latino?

MARIA: Not really. I just feel so much more comfortable with my Latino friends. We're having a party on Saturday night at the student union.

MOM: That sounds like fun.

MARIA: We got a really cool band, Mama. It should be fun.

MOM: Maybe you should try to get to know some Anglos.

MARIA: Mama!

What's going on.

There are so many other adjustments to be made in college that minority students are often drawn to the security of spending time with others who are like them. All students, minority and majority alike, find comfort in relationships with students who share common experiences and backgrounds, especially during the initial transition to college.

What to do.	What to avoid.
• Sympathize with your daughter's feelings of isolation and homesickness. • Let her know that you understand that these feelings are painful. • Recognize that this is an important part of the process of exploring her identity in the dominant culture.	• Asking her if she wants to come home and go to school nearby where there are many other Latinos. (She may do this anyway, but it needs to be her decision.) • Telling her she'd better get to know some white students or she'll never make it in the "real world." • Reminding her that you knew she'd feel different at that college and that she'd better learn to speak up in class.

What you need to know.

Some students have always lived in an ethnic minority community and have had little contact with other cultures. For students like this, college may be the first time they have to live immersed in the dominant culture. In this environment, many minority students are asked to "speak for their entire ethnic group" in class or become the "token" minority in their residence hall or in college activities. It is not surprising that students, such as Maria, feel more comfortable with other students who share their ethnic background. It's a secure and comfortable place where they can relax and be themselves.

Interracial Dating

Last night you received a phone call from your son David and he asked if he could bring his girlfriend home for spring break:

DAVID: Hi, Mom. How are you and Dad and the girls?

MOM: We're fine. How are you? How are your studies going?

DAVID: Oh, I'm fine and I'm doing pretty well in school. I wanted to talk to you about spring break.

MOM: Okay.

DAVID: Well, I was wondering if I could bring Kristen home with me for break? Her parents live in Chicago and it's too far for her to go home.

MOM: Who is this Kristen? Is she Chinese?

DAVID: No, Mom. I think she's part Swedish or something. I'm not sure. But she's really nice. I know you'd like her. She's a premed student too.

MOM: Aren't there any nice Chinese girls there? I know there must be.

DAVID: Mom! Why do you always ask me that? We're American now and so is Kristen.

MOM: But, David, I don't know how your father will feel about this.

DAVID: I know Dad will like Kristen. She's really smart. In fact, her grandfather is Japanese, but he's lived in California since World War II. Her parents were here for fall weekend and they're nice too.

MOM: Well, I'll talk to your father and we'll see.

DAVID: Okay. And, Mom, if you and Dad say Kristen can come home with me, can we speak English while she's there? You should practice speaking English more anyway.

MOM: We won't say anything. Would that make you happy?

DAVID: Mom, you know what I mean. I like Chinese, but Kristen only knows a few words. She'd feel weird if we spoke Chinese all the time.

MOM: If only you would meet a nice Chinese girl, this wouldn't be a problem. She'd fit in here. What are we going to tell your sisters?

DAVID: I'm sure they'll like Kristen too. Why are you making such a big deal about this? It's only for a week. I'm not marrying Kristen!

MOM: I'll talk to your father and call you back.

DAVID: Thanks, Mom. Say hi to everyone.

What's going on.

David wants to be a typical American college student and feels a little embarrassed that he isn't like everyone else. He can live a completely different life on campus. He accepts the dominant culture and likes the white friends he has made. His parents can no longer control who he meets and are worried that his new girlfriend represents a rejection of his Chinese heritage.

What to do.	What to avoid.
• Try to accept your child's freedom to choose new friends, even though you'd prefer they were all Chinese. • Make it clear to him that you are proud of your Chinese culture. • Ask him to tell you more about Kristen and her family. • Do your part to help Kristen feel welcome by speaking English when she's around.	• Refusing to allow him to bring a new girlfriend home. You are the one who will ultimately lose if you remain inflexible. • Telling him that you'll never accept it if he marries a non-Chinese girl. • Trying to make him feel guilty for rejecting his heritage; refusing to speak English to Kristen.

What you need to know.

David is a typical second-generation child who has adopted the dominant culture's values as his own. He feels a strong desire to be American and may work very hard to "fit in" and be accepted by members of the dominant culture. David may reject his minority culture for years, or he may have an experience that leads him into re-examining the role his ethnic culture plays in his identity. For example, he may join a Chinese students group in protesting treatment of Chinese dissidents and become fascinated with Chinese culture. He may even want to travel to China to study and learn more about his heritage. It's important to remember, though, that he must work through his ethnic identity on his own. Parents can't force a child to embrace his or her heritage before he or she is ready, but they can make this process more comfortable for everyone if they support their child throughout this development, even during times when they disagree with him or her and feel rejected.

Identity Issues for Gay, Lesbian, and Bisexual Students

Campus communities vary in their tolerance and acceptance of gay, lesbian, and bisexual students. If your child has come out before choosing a college, he or she probably assessed the college's climate before enrolling and may have an easier adjustment. However, if your child comes out during college, you will need to be especially aware of and sensitive to the identity issues that will arise.

Coming Out/Your Son

What's on Mom's mind?

What's happened to Jacob? He's always been such a good boy.

I can't believe this is happening to us. We've always tried to be good parents.

What are his grandparents going to think? We can't tell them—or our friends.

What's on Dad's mind?

Jacob's been taken in by some weirdo group up there at the university.

He can't do this to us.

I'm going to get him in that program and fix this before anyone finds out.

When your son arrived home for holiday break, he said he had something important to discuss with you:

JACOB: Mom, Dad, I have something to tell you. . . . I'm gay and, actually, I've known I was gay for quite a long time.

MOM: Oh, Jacob, no. How can you be gay? No one in our family is gay.

DAD: What made you come up with this crazy notion? You've always been a regular guy, good athlete, and everything.

JACOB: I know this is a surprise to you guys, but I wanted to be honest with you. I've never been attracted to girls and I've just fallen in love with a guy at school.

MOM (CRYING): How can you do this to us? Haven't we always been good parents?

DAD: Look what you've done to your mother. No son of mine is gay!

JACOB: Mom, Dad, I'm sorry if you're upset, but I hoped you'd understand.

DAD: Look, let's calm down. I know what we can do. Our minister talked about a group that helps homosexuals recover. I'll call him right now. We'll straighten out this mess.

JACOB: Dad, you don't get it. I'm gay and I don't need to be cured. It's not a disease.

DAD: Well, I think it is, and it's a sin as well. We're going to do something about this NOW!

JACOB: Well, you go right ahead, but I'm going back to school NOW!

What's going on.

Many parents are shocked and hurt when their son announces that he is gay. This admission can go against deeply held values and religious beliefs, and parents can find it difficult to set aside their fears and listen to their child.

Coming Out/Your Son: The Replay

Let's replay this dialogue with Jacob and his parents, and see how it could have gone. We recognize that the conversation below is an ideal one and very few parents could make such a rapid adjustment to the surprising news that their son is gay.

> **What's on Mom's mind?**
>
> I always wondered why Jacob didn't go out with girls. Now I know.
>
> I'm worried about what lies ahead for Jacob.
>
> How am I going to tell the relatives? I hope they'll accept Jacob's homosexuality.

JACOB: Mom, Dad, I have something important to tell you. I'm gay and, actually, I've known I was gay for quite a long time.

MOM: Oh, Jacob! I guess I'm shocked. How do you know?

JACOB: Well, as I said, I think I've known since seventh grade that I wasn't attracted to girls. I just didn't know what to do. I was afraid to tell anyone. When I got to college, I decided to be honest with myself. I went to a meeting of the Coalition for Gay, Lesbian, and Transgender Concerns on campus and I met so many great people. They were so nice and I started to feel much better about myself.

DAD: I'm really sorry that you've been troubled about this for so long. It must have taken a lot of courage for you to tell us.

JACOB: I was worried that you'd be upset, but I wanted you to know. It's important to me.

MOM: Of course it is, Jacob. I'm so glad that you found some support at school.

What's on Dad's mind?

This is a huge shock, but I'm glad that Jacob felt he could tell us.

I wonder what this means about my fathering. Is it nature or nurture?

This is hard to accept and understand, but we have to. He's going to have a difficult enough time without us giving him grief.

What's on your child's mind?

I'm relieved that I finally told Mom and Dad.

They seemed pretty cool about it. I hope they're not too worried.

I guess I'm lucky. Some of my friends' parents really freaked out when they came out.

JACOB: Yeah, there's a big group up there. We do things together and it's fun, but there's still a lot of homophobia on campus and that's hard.

DAD: That's not surprising. I'm glad you told us, but I worry about how hard your life is going to be with so much homophobia everywhere. It's not going to be easy.

JACOB: I know, Dad, but I can't change who I am.

MOM: I worry about your health.

JACOB: I do too, Mom. And I promise you I'm not going to take any chances. I would never have unsafe sex with anyone.

MOM: That's good. Are you involved with someone?

JACOB: Well, yeah. I met this great guy through the coalition and we've been seeing each other for a while.

MOM: What's he like?

JACOB: He's pretty good looking and really nice. You'd like him. He's from California and he's been "out" since he was a junior in high school. He's a politics major and wants to go to Washington, D.C., after college and work for the National Gay and Lesbian Task Force.

DAD: Do his parents know that he's gay?

JACOB: Yeah, he told them awhile ago. They didn't take it too well, but he's hoping they will accept it eventually. He has a lot of friends at school, but he's sad that he can't talk to his parents. It makes him feel so alone. I was wondering if I could bring him home for spring break?

MOM: Sure you can. We'd like to meet him.

DAD: You know, son, we'll always be your parents, and no matter what, we'll always love you.

JACOB: Thanks, guys.

What's going on.

Jacob's parents were able to focus on his feelings. This represents a model scenario but one that may not reflect the time, care, and concern necessary to absorb the impact this revelation can have on families. It may take years for parents to come to terms with having a gay child; this interaction does not take place once and get settled for good.

It's normal for parents initially to wonder what they did wrong and to question their parenting. Parents often see their children as a second chance at life, and they want their kids to be richer, smarter, happier, and wiser; coming out can mean lost hopes and expectations for parents. Jacob's parents set their feelings aside to let him know that they accepted his sexual orientation and that they would always love him. They have begun a dialogue that is respectful of Jacob and have shared their concerns with compassion, not judgment. Because of this attitude, Jacob can continue to share his life and choices with them openly as he explores his gay identity.

What to do.	What to avoid.
• Try to focus on your child and the importance, to him, of coming out. • Recognize how difficult this is for him. • Ask him if he is involved with someone and be open to meeting his boyfriend, just as you would if he had a new girlfriend. • Let him know what your concerns are in a reasoned and loving way.	• Making this your problem. • Letting him know how disappointed you are. • Blaming yourself or your parenting for his choice. • Keeping this a secret from friends and family.

What you need to know.

There is a great variation in the age at which individuals identify themselves as homosexual. Most gay men realize they are gay in high school or earlier; others may not know this about themselves until they get to college. Coming out to parents is a critical event, one during which parents need to separate how they feel about their child's sexual orientation from how they feel about their child. Acceptance is the most important gift a parent can give a gay, lesbian, or bisexual child.

Many parents feel grief when their child comes out. They often struggle with "a double loss: one, the loss of the child they thought they knew and two, the loss of a basic belief that everyone is born heterosexual and only deviates because of calamity or willful perversity."[12]

Coming Out/Your Daughter

Your daughter is home for fall break and has brought a girlfriend with her. At breakfast on Saturday morning, Mom and Rebecca have the following conversation:

MOM: Hi, honey. How did you sleep?

REBECCA: Fine, Mom. What's for breakfast?

MOM: You can have cereal, eggs, or I could make waffles.

REBECCA: Waffles. I love your waffles!

MOM: What about Lauren? Is she coming down for breakfast?

REBECCA: I doubt it. She's definitely not a morning person. We probably won't see her 'til noon.

MOM: Lauren seems like a nice girl, but I was wondering, does she always dress like that?

REBECCA: What do you mean, "like that"?

MOM: Well, she just looked so man-ish, with those boots and all. I mean, she's not very feminine is she?

REBECCA: Mom, she's a lesbian!

MOM: Honey, you don't have to yell at me. I was just asking.

REBECCA: Well, aren't you going to ask about me? After all, I'm sleeping with her.

MOM: I know she slept in your room last night. I made the beds.

REBECCA: No, we didn't just have a "sleep over," Mom. I mean we're sleeping together; we're in love.

MOM: Why are you shouting at me?

REBECCA: Because I want you to wake up! I'm a lesbian, okay?

MOM: You can't be! You've had lots of boyfriends.

REBECCA: I'm not saying I don't like guys, I'm saying right now I'm in love with Lauren.

What's on Mom's mind?

Rebecca can't be a lesbian. I don't even know what that means, really.

She's always had boyfriends.

This is just a phase. She'll get over it.

Why is she so confrontational with me?

What's on your child's mind?

I can't believe I finally told my mother and she won't listen.

This is important to me and she is treating me like I'm ten years old.

I wish I hadn't said anything.

Mom: Rebecca, I don't understand this. Are you trying to pick a fight?

Rebecca: No, Mom, I'm just trying to tell you I'm a lesbian or I may be bisexual. I'm not sure.

Mom: Honey, I've heard lots of kids go through phases like this. It's okay. I know you'll find a nice young man some day and settle down.

Rebecca: Mom, you are so clueless! Don't you hear what I'm saying?

Mom: Yes, I do and I don't like you raising your voice like that.

What's going on.

When Rebecca tried to tell her mother about her relationship with Lauren, her mother dismissed her announcement and that made Rebecca escalate the issue. They shouted at each other, neither one really listening to the other. Rebecca's mother started the interaction by commenting on Lauren's looks, which made Rebecca feel defensive and blurt out the fact that she is a lesbian. This is probably not how Rebecca envisioned "coming out" to her mother.

### What to do.	### What to avoid.
<ul><li>Listen to your child. Respond to what your child is saying.</li><li>Ask her what she means if you don't understand.</li><li>Recognize that she is going to make her own choices and that it is difficult for her to be open with you.</li></ul>	<ul><li>Brushing off your child's announcement. Scolding her for being confrontational.</li><li>Telling your child that this is just a phase that she'll get over.</li><li>Letting your fears ruin your ability to listen.</li></ul>

What you need to know.

Young women often experience a long period of "coming out." Many don't even identify themselves as lesbian or bisexual until very late in their adolescence or after they are out of college. Parents often believe that their daughters are involved in this one unusual relationship and that they'll "grow out of it" in time. Many young people switch between bisexual and gay/lesbian orientations at different points in their identity development. If a child identifies as bisexual, parents should not assume that this is just a phase or confusion. Bisexuality exists and it's not necessarily a fifty-fifty situation. Interviews with college women revealed a wide range of behavior. Some bisexual women reported that only 20 percent of their attractions were for women and others reported that 80 percent of their attractions were for women.[13]

Whether young people identify as gay, lesbian, or bisexual can depend on their current relationship. For many lesbian and bisexual women, the primary concern is not "labeling" themselves but the importance of the relationship they currently have. More women than men "come out" in the context of a singular relationship. This doesn't necessarily mean that the child is confused about her sexual identity or simply going through a phase. In fact, most gay men and lesbian women have agonized for years about their sexual orientation before coming out to their parents. Parents need to realize the struggle involved when their kids come out; usually it is not a "phase" or an adolescent rebellion. This statement requires that both parents and children exercise patience, while recognizing that it may take time for them to feel comfortable with this reality. Parents need to stand by and support their children as they mature into their identities as homosexual, lesbian, or bisexual men or women.

PFLAG (Parents and Friends of Lesbians and Gays) is an organization devoted to helping parents learn about homosexuality and support each other in coming to terms with being the parent of a gay, lesbian, or bisexual son or daughter. This organization has chapters all over the country, and it may be something you want to explore. See the "Want to Know More?" section at the end of this chapter for additional resources to help parents of gay, lesbian, or bisexual individuals or look at the website <http://www.pflag.com>.

Autonomy

A natural outgrowth of achieving an individual identity is a desire for autonomy or independence from parents and family. This doesn't mean disconnection or detachment. In fact, the healthiest adolescents remain connected to family as they become increasingly self-directed and independent. But one of the disturbing parts of a child's search for autonomy is that it often begins with a rejection of parents in favor of friends.

Parents' Weekend

When you called your daughter to talk about your trip to campus for parents' weekend, she seemed excited at the prospect of seeing you. However, when you arrived at her dorm room at noon, she had left a note on the door saying she had to study for a midterm and would see you at dinner. You were surprised and slightly hurt. When you returned at 6:00 P.M. to meet your daughter, you had an awkward dinner together. You excitedly grilled her about college life, and she responded with one-word answers. The only time she seemed to engage in the conversation was to remind you that she had to get back to the dorm to get ready for a party. The weekend went downhill from there—you hovered and felt unwelcome; your daughter spent a lot of time sleeping, in the library, and with her new friends. The only shared activities were having dinner and going to the mall to buy things for her room.

What's going on.

Parents' weekend is often a disappointing time for parents. Your child may not be comfortable enough yet at college to welcome you into the social mix. The independence your child is beginning to feel is not strong enough to "test" by including parents in this new reality. Your child is taking the first steps toward autonomy and needs to shift dependence on you to dependence on friends as a step toward independence. This shift usually begins in middle or high school, but because you were a part of your child's everyday life, it probably didn't seem so dramatic. Eventually, he or she will see how to maintain a relationship with you while still being independent and self-directed. It will help if you can step back and see the big picture regarding your child's development.

> **What's on your mind?**
>
> Why did I even bother to come for parents' weekend?
> I feel hurt and rejected by my child.
> All she wants from me is money.
> I want to be a part of her life.

> **What's on your child's mind?**
>
> Why did my parents have to come this weekend? I have so much to do.
> What am I supposed to do with them when they're here? They don't fit in.
> I wish I could just be with my friends.

What to do.	What to avoid.
• Prepare yourself before you go to parents' weekend. • Ask your child if he or she really wants you to come—midterm exams or papers may loom ahead. • Make your needs and expectations clear and find out what your child's needs and expectations are before you make travel plans. • Ask your child to arrange a dinner with some of his or her friends' parents—at least the other parents will talk to you. • Plan some activities for yourself. Don't expect your child to be an attentive host/hostess all weekend.	• Feeling rejected and angry. • Arriving with expectations that are hard for your child to fulfill, such as spending lots of time with you. • Expecting your child to be thrilled to see you and be able to entertain you all weekend.

What you need to know.

First, it's helpful to remember your child as a two year old. You can probably recall your child shouting, "No," and running away from you. Seconds later, that same child would clutch your legs and want to be picked up. The two year old needs to push away and separate from parents; at the same time, he or she is completely dependent. Two years olds and adolescents have a lot in common—they both tend to ricochet between the security needs of being a child and the individuality needs of learning to be a separate person from their parents. While it is frustrating and confusing to deal with these extremes, it's comforting to know that this "push-pull" process of trying to separate from parents is absolutely necessary and typical behavior—in a two year old and in an adolescent.

The tumultuous twos were followed by the relatively placid childhood years when your child idolized you, followed by the preadolescent and teen years when your child began to break away from you in favor of peer relationships. All of these stages happened while you were there, playing the traditional role of parent—

monitoring, supporting, directing, caring, and being involved in your child's daily life. Now your child is away from home for most of the year, and truthfully, you don't have much contact or daily influence on your child's behavior. You can't know what is going on, and you may not want to know all the details!

How can you maintain a good relationship while your child is on this roller-coaster quest for identity and autonomy during the college years? How can you still be a positive influence as your child takes on the privileges and responsibilities of fully independent adulthood? We suggest that you review chapter 1 for pointers on laying the groundwork for a new kind of relationship with your child.

Big Trouble

You call your son Peter one night and the following conversation takes place:

PETER: Hello?

MOM: Hi, Pete. How are you?

PETER: All right, I guess. I've been meaning to call you.

MOM: Why, is something wrong?

PETER: Well, I'm sort of in a bit of trouble.

MOM: What kind of trouble?

PETER: A couple of weeks ago at a fraternity party I was in a fight with a real jerk from another house who crashed the party. He started hassling me and I just lost it. I punched him and he was so drunk he fell down and broke his arm. Now I'm in deep trouble with the dean of students.

MOM: Oh, Peter. That's awful. What's going to happen? Is the other boy all right?

PETER: I don't know what's going to happen yet. Yeah, the other guy has a cast, but he'll be all right, I guess.

MOM: Well, what's going on now?

PETER: The dean of students has decided to bring me in front of the Student Judicial Board and let them decide the

What's on your mind?

I can't believe Peter is in so much trouble and we didn't even know it.

These frat parties seem really out of control.

I hope Peter doesn't get kicked out of school. That would be hard on all of us.

I'm worried about him and feel so helpless.

What's on your child's mind?

Boy, I really blew it this time.

I'm glad my mom wasn't totally mad at me. I wonder what Dad will think.

I sure hope I don't get kicked out. What would I do?

This is so unfair. I'm not the only one who gets in fights.

punishment. I'll have to present my case. I have witnesses that the other guy was hassling me, but I don't know what they'll do to me.

MOM: That sounds really serious.

PETER: I know. I could get kicked out of school. I just can't believe this is happening. It's a nightmare.

MOM: Why didn't you call and tell us?

PETER: I just thought I could handle this myself. Now, I'm not so sure. I guess the dean wants to talk to you and Dad. Could you call him?

MOM: Yes, of course. But, Peter, what can we do to help you?

PETER: Nothing really, Mom. I have to argue my case and hope it comes out okay.

MOM: Do you need an attorney?

PETER: No, it's just the School Judicial Board. I don't think they have lawyers.

MOM: Do you have anyone who can advise you on preparing your case?

PETER: I don't know. I can ask the dean.

MOM: I hope you can get some help.

PETER: I'm really sorry to worry you and really sorry I did something so stupid.

MOM: I guess we all make mistakes and have to learn from them the hard way. What have you learned from this so far?

PETER: Not to let your emotions get control of you, especially after you've had a few drinks. And how scary it is to really hurt someone. I mean, what if he had hit his head and died? This mistake has really made me think.

MOM: That's good, Peter. It's important that you learn something from this and that you let the dean and others on campus know what you've learned.

PETER: Do you think I should tell them that? Isn't that kind of like admitting I did something wrong?

MOM: Yes, it is. But, you know, and they know, that you did something wrong. They need to know that you learned something from this incident that will help you grow into a more mature person when faced with these situations in the future. Do you see what I mean?

PETER: Yeah, I guess so.

MOM: It's called being an adult and taking responsibility for your actions, Peter. Sometimes we learn the most from the most painful situations. I'm sorry you have to learn this hard lesson. Remember that we love you and think you are a good person in spite of what you did.

PETER: Thanks, Mom. I'll call you tomorrow after I meet with the dean again. Maybe we can work something out so I can stay in school. I hope so.

MOM: So do I, honey. You know you can call on us if you need help, and I'll wait to hear from you tomorrow. Take care and try not to worry too much.

PETER: Okay. Bye, Mom.

What's going on.

Peter is trying very hard to be independent and handle the consequences of his behavior. He didn't automatically call on his parents to straighten things out for him. In fact, Mom and Dad are not likely to know much about what is going on at school unless a crisis like this erupts. While it's not easy for his parents, Peter is showing healthy signs of achieving autonomy and taking responsibility for his actions.

What to do.	What to avoid.
• Accept the fact that this is your child's dilemma to resolve, not yours. • Be supportive and make suggestions as he handles this problem without trying to "fix it" for him. • Listen to his fears and anxieties and let him know that you sympathize. • Remind him that you are willing to help if you can and that you love him.	• Scolding your son. He knows he screwed up. • Imposing punishment of your own. The college will see to it that he suffers the consequences of his behavior. • Calling the dean and trying to plead your son's case for him. It's appropriate to let the dean know that you are aware of the situation and that, while you support your son, you understand the gravity of the infraction and can appreciate the college's point of view as well.

What you need to know.

Adolescents who have become autonomous can relinquish their dependence on their parents and take responsibility for their actions. Students who have achieved a sense of themselves as separate and responsible people still need parents as trusted advisors. They don't, however, expect or want their parents to bail them out of difficult situations. In this instance, Peter's mom exhibited what we would call an authoritative style of parenting—valuing her son's developing autonomy and independence while still providing a loving and supportive connection.

The development of identity and autonomy is a complex and interactive phenomenon. You have had significant influence on your child's development from the beginning, and your child's unique personality has, no doubt, affected the parenting style you adopted. This is a two-way street and it's important to keep in mind that, particularly when your child is a late adolescent, his or her behavior is not necessarily a direct response to your parenting style. But it is still true that the way you parent, especially during the college years, can continue to have an impact on your child's ability to develop his or her own identity and autonomy.

How Parenting Styles Relate to the Search for Identity and Autonomy

Researchers have developed the following scheme for classifying parenting styles.[14] They have identified two aspects of a parent's behavior toward a child as critical: parental responsiveness and parental demandingness. In the following chart you can see that authoritative parents are high on responsiveness and demandingness.

PARENTING STYLES

| | | Demandingness | |
		High	Low
Responsiveness	High	Authoritative	Indulgent
	Low	Authoritarian	Indifferent

Authoritative parents are warm but firm, setting high expectations that are consistent with the child's developing abilities and needs. They value their children's developing autonomy and self-direction and provide a solid and loving base of support for their exploration. When disciplining their children they explain their rules and decisions. Authoritative parents are more likely to have healthy, supportive, and satisfying relationships with their children.

Authoritarian parents value obedience and believe that children should accept their authority. They tend to discourage independence and do not want their children to question the standards they set. There is little give-and-take in these relationships. However, researchers have found that some authoritarian parents (particularly those in cultures in which authoritarian parenting is the norm) are perceived as supportive and have positive relationships with their children.

Indulgent parents take little interest in shaping their child's behavior. They impose few demands and allow their child a great deal of freedom. They tend to believe that their child will continue to rely on them for help and that any imposition of expectations would be an infringement on their child's freedom to develop.

Indifferent parents spend as little time as possible interacting with their children and know very little about their children's activities, friends, and school performance. Indifferent parents structure their lives around their own needs and interests, rarely engaging their children in discussion or considering their children's opinions when making decisions. In extreme cases, indifferent parents may be considered neglectful parents.

In summary, researchers have found that adolescents raised by authoritative parents are more responsible, confident, socially competent, self-reliant, adaptive, creative, curious, and successful in school. Adolescents raised in authoritarian homes, in contrast, are more dependent, passive, and anxious about social comparison and less socially skilled, self-assured, and intellectually curious. In addition, they tend to have poor communication skills and difficulty initiating activity. Adolescents raised in indulgent households are often more irresponsible and conforming to their peers, less mature, and less able to assume positions of leadership. They often have difficulty abiding by rules and regulations and exercising self-control and, hence, are less socially adept. Adolescents raised by indifferent parents are often impulsive and more likely to be involved in delinquent behavior and in precocious experiments with sex, drugs, and alcohol.[15]

Authoritative parenting, combined with mentoring, provides a healthy balance between restrictiveness and autonomy. This style allows you to have continued influence in your college student's life, while being supportive, warm, and loving as he or she experiences the challenging process of developing identity and autonomy in the world. Of course, most parents do not rigidly adhere to one style of parenting. Some situations (such as living in a dangerous neighborhood) require more restrictive parenting. Moreover, your child's temperament, for example, whether your child is compliant or defiant, will have an affect on your parenting style as well.

It is a major task for college students to forge an individual identity and to achieve autonomy from parents. This process starts in early adolescence and may extend beyond the college years. During the college years, however, students live in a kind of "bubble of safety" in which they can safely explore and experiment with the key question—Who am I? Being out from under parental supervision and control and not having the day-to-day responsibilities of taking care of themselves (i.e., earning a living and paying bills), they are free to "try on" a number of identities to see if they fit. This is not frivolous "acting out," it is a necessary step along the path to adulthood.

Parents who understand and expect this behavior can relax a bit and enjoy watching this process unfold during the college years. While it may be disturbing to witness your child ricochet from one lifestyle, major, or fashion statement to another, it is reassuring to know that, while you may not have much influence on their tastes, friends, and fashions, the vast majority of young adults do not stray far from the basic values that are important to their parents.

It's also useful to know that this process of developing identity can be significantly different for individual students. The amount and extent of experimentation a college student engages in depends largely upon his or her social class, family background, temperament, ethnicity, race, and/or gender. Some students, due primarily to family circumstances, do not have the freedom to engage in this sort of experimentation.

Understanding that your child is working hard at adjusting to college life, developing a unique identity, and working toward being an independent adult will help you to see the big picture in all kinds of situations throughout your son's or daughter's college years.

Want to Know More?

Comer, James P., and Alvin F. Poussaint. *Raising Black Children: Diversity in African American Identity.* New York: Plume, 1992.

Berstein, Robert A. *Straight Parents, Gay Children: Keeping Families Together.* New York: Thunder's Mouth Press, 1995.

Griffin, Carolyn Welch, Marion J. Worth, and Arthur G. Worth, eds. *Beyond Acceptance: Parents of Lesbians & Gays Talk About Their Experiences.* New York: St. Martin's Press, 1986.

1. Erik H. Erikson, *Identity: Youth and Crisis* (New York: W. W. Norton, 1968).

2. Lyn Mikel Brown and Carol Gilligan, *Meeting at the Crossroads: Women's Psychology and Girls' Development* (Cambridge, MA: Harvard University Press, 1992).

3. Duane Buhrmester, "Need Fulfillment, Interpersonal Competence, and the Developmental Contexts of Early Adolescent Friendship," in *The Company They Keep: Friendship in Childhood and Adolescence,* eds. W. Bukowski, A. Newcomb, and W. Hartup (New York: Cambridge University Press, 1996), 158–185.

4. James Marcia, "The Empirical Study of Ego Identity," in *Identity and Development,* eds. H. A. Bosma, T. L. G. Graafsma, H. D. Grotevant, and D. J. De Levita (Newbury Park, CA: Sage, 1994) 67–80.

5. William G. Perry Jr., *Forms of Intellectual and Ethical Development in the College Years* (New York: Holt, Rinehart and Winston, 1970).

6. Erik H. Erikson, "Youth and the Life Cycle" in *Adolescent Behavior and Society: A Book of Readings,* 5th ed., eds. R. E. Muuss and H. D. Porton (New York: McGraw-Hill College, 1998), 252–60. Reprinted from *Children* (March–April 1960): 43–49.

7. Lyn Mikel Brown and Carol Gilligan, *Meeting at the Crossroads: Women's Psychology and Girls' Development* (Cambridge, MA: Harvard University Press, 1992).

8. Mary Field Belenky, Blythe McVicker Clinchy, Nancy Rule Goldberger, and Jill Mattuck Tarule, *Women's Ways of Knowing: The Development of Self, Voice, and Mind* (New York: Basic Books, 1986).

9. Myra and David Sadker, *Failing at Fairness: How Our Schools Cheat Girls* (New York: Touchstone, 1994); Bernice Resnick Sandler, Lisa A. Silverberg, and Roberta M. Hall, *The Chilly Classroom Climate: A Guide to Improve the Education of Women* (Washington, D.C.: The National Association for Women in Education, 1996).

10. William E. Cross Jr., *Shades of Black* (Philadelphia, PA: Temple University Press, 1991).

11. J. S. Phinney and V. Chavira, "Ethnic Identity and Self-Esteem: An Exploratory Longitudinal Study," *Journal of Adolescence* 15 (1992): 271–81.

12. Mary Borek, *Coming Out to Parents: A Two-Way Survival Guide for Lesbians and Gay Men and Their Parents* (New York: The Pilgrim Press, 1983).

13. Lisa Diamond, "Development of Sexual Orientation Among Adolescent and Young Adult Women," *Developmental Psychology* 34, no. 5 (1998): 1085–95.

14. Diana Baumrind, "The Influence of Parenting Style on Adolescent Competence and Substance Use," *Journal of Early Adolescence* 11 (1991): 56–95; E. Maccoby and J. Martin, "Socialization in the Context of the Family: Parent-Child Interaction," in *Handbook of Child Psychology: Socialization, Personality and Social Development,* ed. E. M. Hetherington (New York: Wiley, 1983).

15. Laurence Steinberg, *Adolescence,* 5th ed. (Boston: McGraw-Hill College, 1999).

Chapter 5

Just When You Get Used to the Empty Nest, They're Back!

Coping with Continuing Changes in the Family

We were all looking forward to having Lauren come home for fall break, but the weekend was a nightmare. None of us had anticipated how different she would be. She was rude and ignored us most of the time. We were all hurt and disappointed. The truth is, we could hardly wait for her to get on the bus back to school so that we could return to our normal family life again.

Your Family System

The family system is like a mobile. Just as a mobile must find a new balance when a piece is removed, the family, too, needs to readjust when a child goes off to college and creates an imbalance in the family system.

Let's say you are a family with a mother, father, and two children. When one of your children enters college, several changes take place. You will notice a 50 percent decrease in child-related responsibilities and activities. You may refocus your attention on the remaining child, who essentially becomes an only child overnight. The remaining child may feel at a loss without a brother or sister and may not welcome your undivided attention. You will probably also notice a change in your relationship with your spouse.

The balance in a family system is altered if any member leaves the fold, but the adjustments can be particularly unsettling when a child goes to college because that child will leave and reenter the family group many times. Your child will breeze in and out of the family home during breaks and vacations, and you may feel more like you're running a respite home for a stressed-out student rather than welcoming your child back into the family unit.

Whether you live in a family with a mother, father, and children, or in a single-parent, blended, or in other ways nontraditional family, your family will change dramatically, especially when your first or last child goes off to college. Single parents who are left alone at home for the first time may notice this change the most. This chapter will help you understand your family as a system that can support the growth and development of all of its members.

The Empty Nest

A few weeks after Courtney left for college, her parents had the following conversation:

What's on Martha's mind?

I miss being a mom. Who am I now?

It's strange spending so much time alone with Dan.

Our family will never be the same again. That makes me sad, even though I know it's for the best.

What's on Dan's mind?

I miss the kids too, but Martha seems really heartbroken that they're gone.

I wonder if she still loves me as much as she did before we had the kids?

Why can't she enjoy just being with me?

MARTHA: Boy, it sure seems quiet around here without Courtney and her gang of friends coming in and out all of the time. I can't wait until she comes home for fall break.

DAN: I know. It's funny, but I even miss her arguing about her curfew, running up to her room, and slamming the door.

MARTHA: Yeah, I can't believe I complained about driving to all of her soccer games and having dinner on the table at a certain time to fit her schedule.

DAN: I guess we have a lot more freedom now. We can eat whenever we want and we could even go away for the weekend on the spur of the moment. Maybe we should drive up north this weekend and look at the fall colors. What do you think? I could get us a reservation somewhere. We could sleep late and go for walks in the woods.

MARTHA: I guess we could. Just the two of us, huh?

DAN: Hey, it could be fun. Just the two of us on a romantic weekend alone. Let's do it!

MARTHA: Okay, but we'd better call Courtney and let her know where we'll be in case she needs something.

DAN: Yeah, I'm sure she's going to miss the homecoming activities worrying about where we are! Seriously, hon, I doubt if she cares much about what we're doing, but go ahead and call her if you want to.

MARTHA: Okay, but what will we do for a whole weekend up north?

DAN: We'll just enjoy each other's company. Remember when we used to spend whole weekends just talking and hanging out together, before we had the kids?

MARTHA: Sort of. But what's there to talk about?

DAN: I'm sure we'll think of something. You don't sound too excited about getting away. What's the matter?

MARTHA: I don't know. It's just been so long since we've been alone together. I guess I still feel pretty sad about Courtney leaving home. It didn't seem so dramatic when Matt left for college. That seems like ages ago. Doesn't it feel strange to have our kids gone?

DAN: Yeah, but it could be worse. They could both still be hanging around here! Come on, hon, lighten up. We've been good parents; now we get to be a couple again. This will be fun.

What's going on?

Martha and Dan feel that odd combination of emptiness and freedom now that their last child has gone off to college. They are not sure how to relate to each other without the buffer of children and the involvement that child rearing required for so many years of their married life.

What to do.	What to avoid.
• Talk to your spouse about your feelings. • Give yourself time to come to terms with the changes occurring in your family and in your relationship. These adjustments don't feel comfortable overnight. • Consider getting some marriage counseling if you feel that your relationship needs work and that unexpressed frustrations are surfacing now that the kids are gone.	• Ignoring the major change that the empty nest presents. • Expecting your spouse to be cheerful about this loss. • Criticizing your spouse for not having the same reaction to this change that you do.

What you need to know.

When your last child leaves home for college, it is not unusual to feel confused and conflicted about your relationship with your spouse. You may have put your marriage on hold during the all-consuming task of parenting, and it may now be obvious that your marriage has been neglected. Suddenly, the focus in your relationship with your spouse changes from raising children to the satisfaction, comfort, and enjoyment you feel in each other's company. More than ever, your reasons for being together stem from what you have to offer one another as life partners and less from your roles as parents. If there are problems in your marriage, they will probably surface now.

Even though your child will reappear from time to time during the college years, and your older adult children undoubtedly will have a presence in your life, the old family structure has changed forever. In fact, many couples find this a liberating and rewarding change. They now have the opportunity to rediscover who they are as a couple and as individuals. Letting go of your parenting role doesn't happen overnight, but it can bring long-term satisfaction.

What's on your mind?

What's wrong with Aaron?
I thought he'd be happy with all of the attention.
Maybe he misses Chad more than he wants to admit.

What's on your child's mind?

It seems so strange here without Chad.
Mom and Dad are either breathing down my neck or ignoring me.
I wonder what Chad will be like when he comes home. I bet he's forgotten I exist.

The Lone Sibling

You're a little disturbed by the following conversation you had with your younger son a few weeks after his older brother left for college:

MOM: Aaron, what's the matter with you? You spend all of your time in your room lately.

AARON: It just seems so quiet around here without Chad.

MOM: I thought you couldn't wait 'til he left and you had first dibs on the car!

AARON: Yeah, he was a pain most of the time, but it really feels weird with him gone.

MOM: Well, he'll still come home for vacations.

AARON: But that's a long time from now. You and Dad don't seem to miss him too much. I guess you get to bug me full time now.

MOM: Of course we miss him. What do you mean we're bugging you full time?

AARON: It just seems so weird without Chad here. I can't wait 'til I can go to college too. It's so boring here! Could we call Chad and see what's going on at college?

What's going on.

It's easy for parents to overlook the impact this change can have on younger children. Aaron may not like to admit it, but he's feeling the loss of his big brother. It will take time for the family to readjust to Chad's absence and realign their relationships as a family group. Everything Chad is doing seems exotic and interesting, while Aaron is just the same old Aaron, hanging around the house and having to deal with his parents on his own.

What to do.	What to avoid.
• Talk to Aaron about his feelings about Chad's departure. Ask him how you can help him cope with this transition. • Let him know that it's natural to feel ambivalent about being left home alone. • Ask Aaron if he'd like to talk to Chad on the phone once a week or plan a weekend visit to Chad at school. • Be honest about your feelings of loss, but reinforce how important Aaron is too.	• Reminding Aaron of how anxious he was to get rid of his older brother and have the house to himself. • Ignoring his feelings of loss, even though he doesn't express them directly. • Telling him not to worry, that Chad will be home soon for break.

What you need to know.

It's easy for parents to dwell on their own feelings of loss when a child goes to college and overlook the feelings that their other children may have. Parents need to engage younger siblings in discussions about how they feel when an older child leaves. Even though your children might have had a contentious relationship, that doesn't mean that the younger child will accept this change easily. In many families, the younger child genuinely misses the older child's companionship. The older child may have played the role of mediator between the younger child and the parents and now the younger child must deal with the parents directly without much experience in doing so. Moreover, the older child may have been a caregiver to the younger one, almost a surrogate parent, as well as a pal. These are big changes for a younger sibling.

It's usually not a coincidence if younger children act out when an older child leaves for college. The family is thrown into imbalance, and the younger child may question his or her identity within the family group. Your younger child may believe that you expect him or her to fill the vacuum left by the absent child, and this can make a child feel angry and isolated. The child left behind needs to be reassured that he or she is still a unique and valuable member of the family.

What's on your mind?

I was really looking forward to seeing Audrey.

She acts like this is a bed and breakfast, not her family home.

Why doesn't she want to spend any time with us?

What's on your child's mind?

Boy, it's nice to be home.

It's so great to get some sleep, and eat good food.

It's fun to compare college experiences with my old high school friends.

The Boomerang Effect

Your daughter Audrey is a freshman at college. When she comes home for fall break, the whole family is eager to reconnect with her and listen to her stories of college life. Audrey, however, has a different agenda. She arrives home late Friday night and immediately phones her old high school friends. She dumps her dirty laundry in the basement and announces that she's going out. You don't see her again until she drags herself out of bed at 1:00 P.M. the next day and calls her college roommate. The rest of the break you hardly see her—she's either sleeping, holed up in her room, hanging out with friends, or talking on the phone.

What's going on.

Audrey has been away from home long enough to feel like a free agent in the world. It doesn't occur to her that she has some responsibility to interact with the family. She's on break and enjoying the comforts of home, oblivious to the family's needs. Her family is excited about being together again but has some unrealistic expectations for the weekend.

What to do.	What to avoid.
• Talk to Audrey about what she wants to do during her break.	• Planning family activities before discussing them with Audrey.
• Discuss your expectations with her. If you don't want to stay up worrying about her coming in at 3:00 A.M., let her know that.	• Letting yourself feel rejected because Audrey doesn't spend much time with the family.
• Have a family meeting to discuss important issues: who gets to drive the car and when, planned family meals or get-togethers with relatives, chores you expect your child to resume, and his or her hours.	• Being a doormat—cooking all of her favorite foods and putting your life on hold while you wait for Audrey to interact with the family.
• You will need to re-negotiate her hours and family responsibilities while she's home from school. Remember that she's been able to set her own hours at school. Don't assume that she'll easily revert to the curfew you had for her when she was in high school.	
• Prepare yourself and other family members. Don't expect to welcome home the same child you sent off to college.	

What you need to know.

Family members need to prepare themselves for an adjustment every time a college student comes home and every time he or she leaves again. Most students get used to having complete autonomy at school, and they may have trouble returning to rules and siblings during weekend and vacation visits. Parents who have grown accustomed to the relative peace and quiet may be dismayed by the influx of friends, loud music, and phone calls when their child returns for a visit. And those same parents may find the loneliness and adjustment hard when their child returns to school. Imagine how it would be if any member of the family went away for significant periods of time, only to return for a few days and then leave again.

It's appropriate and necessary to set new guidelines with your college student about his or her behavior during breaks. Don't assume that your child will fall right back into the family routine. Before vacations, talk to your child about your expectations. For example, if you had a curfew during high school, talk about whether it still applies. It's okay to ask your child to make some adjustments when he or she comes home. While your child has no curfew at school, it's different when your child comes home and is part of the family again. It's not helpful to say, "You're living under my roof now; you'll do what I say." You might say, "I understand that you have lots of freedom to set your own schedule at school and that's okay; however, when you're home with the rest of the family, we expect you to respect our schedules too. Can we compromise on your hours?"

It's important that you recognize the shifting family roles and relationships. You may expect the same high school child to return home from college; however, your child will want to be seen as different and independent from the family. This family change requires that you talk about your needs and be clear about your expectations. You have a right to expect that your son or daughter treat you and other family members with respect when he or she returns home for visits from college. You also need to prepare yourself for the inevitable range of feelings you'll have as your son or daughter moves between college and home many times during each year.

Single Parent

Anna is surprised at her daughter Leah's behavior in the following phone call:

MOM: Hi, Leah. How are you doing?

LEAH: Oh, Mom, I'm so glad you called. I've been wondering how your new job is going. What's it like?

MOM: It's good. I think it's going to be a good change for me.

LEAH: That's great.

MOM: There's another change in my life too.

LEAH: Really? What?

MOM: Well, I met this really nice man last week and we've already gone out a couple of times. We had the best time last night. We went out for dinner and a movie.

LEAH: You're dating someone?

MOM: Pretty amazing, huh?

LEAH: So do you like him? Are you going to go out with him again?

MOM: I hope so.

LEAH: Mom, you sound like a teenager. What are you doing?

MOM: I'm just having a good time.

LEAH: Well, I guess that's cool. So are you still coming down for parents' weekend or do you have a hot date?

MOM: Leah, *really*, of course I'm coming, I can't wait to see you!

What's on your mind?

Leah seems almost annoyed at me for going out on a date. What's her problem?

I have a right to have some fun too.

What's on your child's mind?

I can't believe my mom's dating. This is so weird.

I wonder who this guy is.

It's always been just my mom and me. What will happen now?

What's going on.

Anna and Leah have had a close relationship since Anna divorced Leah's father when Leah was three years old. Anna has focused on being a good parent and put her own needs on hold as a single parent while raising Leah. Now that Leah is in college, Anna feels that it's time for her to move on with her life. This is not a comforting thought to Leah, who has relied on her mother being there for her always.

What to do.	What to avoid.
• Recognize that Leah may feel threatened by this new relationship. • Let her know that she will always be very important to you. • Remind yourself that Leah's reaction is probably temporary, but that she may continue to have trouble with this new development in your life.	• Putting your life on hold for your child. • Expecting her to accept this new relationship without some questions and concerns.

What you need to know.

A single parent with an only child can be the tightest family unit. A dramatic change occurs in a single parent/only child family when the child goes off to college and can result in a particularly wrenching separation. If the single parent begins to have a life separate from the child, the child feels abandoned. Or, conversely, when the child leaves home, the parent feels abandoned. In either case, one or both may try hard to keep the same family balance. Moreover, the child may feel guilty that he or she has left the parent to go to college, or the parent may feel guilty if he or she goes out and creates a life for him or herself. The changes in this type of relationship can be difficult to manage.

What's on your family's mind?

We're so proud of Carlos.
When will we see Carlos again?
I wonder how he'll be treated; will there be other kids like him?
Now Mariana will have to get a job and help out more.

First Generation to Go to College

When Carlos left for the university in another state, the whole family went to the bus station to see him off. All the grandparents, aunts and uncles, cousins, brothers, and sisters waved good-bye to the first family member ever to go to college. When Carlos got on the bus, you felt excited, but also worried and sad. Although he received a full scholarship, his departure created a financial hardship for your family. Not only had he provided a steady part of the family income for years through his after-school job, he had also taken care of his younger brothers and sisters while you worked.

What's going on.

Carlos is a pioneer in his family. The first child in his family's history to go to college will deal with many unknowns. His parents don't understand nor are they able to prepare him for the college experience. They may feel intimidated about interacting with the university. While his family knows that education is the key to upward mobility in the culture, they also value the close family ties that exist and wonder if Carlos will return to the family group. Moreover, Carlos's departure creates very real burdens for the rest of the family.

> ### What's on your child's mind?
>
> I'm going to miss all of them so much. They have always been there for me.
> What will it feel like to be all alone at college?
> I feel excited, but also sad.

What to do.	What to avoid.
• Take pride in your child's accomplishments. • Encourage Carlos to express his feelings, even though they may be upsetting to you. • Write to him regularly to keep him up to date on events in the family. • Try to support him in any way you can, because this will be an enormous change and challenge for Carlos.	• Making Carlos feel responsible for your feelings of sadness. • Pressuring Carlos to do well at school to make the family proud of him. • Insisting that he get a job at school and send money home to help out.

What you need to know.

Individuals who are the first in their family to go to college face many difficult obstacles and challenges. A study of three thousand first-generation students found that they needed more support than other students as "they often were less skilled than their peers in reading, math, and critical thinking at the beginning of their college careers." The study also found that first-generation students were "less involved with peers and teachers in high school and consequently were unprepared mentally for the college experience. They required longer to complete their degrees, took fewer courses in the humanities and fine arts, were less likely to perceive instructors as being concerned about students and were more likely to report personal experience with discrimination."[1]

Even though first-generation students may have been stars in their high schools, they will find the adjustment to college-level work challenging. In addition, they often feel great pressure to succeed and excel. First-generation students may carry the hopes and expectations of a large family group, as well as those of a neighborhood, church, and sometimes an entire community. These pressures are intense, especially when a student has academic or social difficulty. Many first-generation college students feel the loss of the extended family's support just when they need it the most, and this can add to the student's feelings of detachment and isolation. At the same time, a student may feel ashamed of his family's lack of education and status and want to keep family members hidden from new friends at school.

Other Family Changes

In addition to changes you can anticipate when a child goes to college, there may also be unexpected changes in the family and in your child during these years. Even though your child is living away from home most of the year, it's important to acknowledge the impact the following situations can have.

A Family Move

You're a bit surprised by your daughter Betsy's reaction when you told her that the family would be transferred to a new city in a few months:

MOM: Hi, Betsy. I've got great news.
BETSY: Really, what?

MOM: I just found out that I'm getting a big promotion at work. I'm going to be head of a whole new division of the company starting next May.

BETSY: Wow, Mom, that's awesome!

MOM: Yeah, I'm really excited. It's going to be lots of work, but this is such a great opportunity for me.

BETSY: So I bet Dad and Billy are really proud of you, huh? Were they surprised?

MOM: Well, I've been working for this for a long time, but I don't think any of us thought it would happen this year.

BETSY: That's cool, Mom. I'm happy for you.

MOM: There's just one drawback.

BETSY: Yeah?

MOM: The new job is in Seattle, and it means we'll have to move.

BETSY: What? Move to Seattle? When?

MOM: Well, I'll probably go out to Seattle in the beginning of May, but Dad and Billy will stay here at least through June so that Billy can finish eighth grade here. Dad also has to find a new job in Seattle, which may take a few months. We hope we'll all be living there by the time school starts for Billy in the fall.

BETSY: But what about me? What's going to happen to me?

MOM: Well, it probably makes sense for you to look for a summer job in Seattle and then you'll be going back to school in the fall.

BETSY: What about our house?

MOM: We've already put it on the market. It may take a few months for it to sell. There's so much to do. My head is spinning.

BETSY: I can't believe you're selling my bedroom without even asking me!

MOM: Betsy, relax, you'll have a bedroom in our new house.

BESTY: But what about my friends at home? I'll never see them again. Why do you have to take a new job now?

MOM: I don't have to. I want to. This is a great opportunity for me. I can't say no to this. It's important to me. I know that all of you will have to move and adjust to a new

What's on your mind?

Why is Betsy so upset? She's hardly home anymore anyway.

She only cares about herself. I didn't realize she was so selfish.

What's on your child's mind?

I can't believe Mom is doing this to me.

They obviously don't care about me!

I don't know anyone in Seattle. It will be terrible there with no friends.

place, but we'll be doing it together. I think you'll love Seattle—it's such a
beautiful city and there are so many things to do there.

BETSY: Maybe I'll just stay here for the summer if I don't have a home anymore.

MOM: Don't be silly, Betsy, you'll always have a home. You're away at school most
of the time anyway, and it won't be long before you have a home of your own.
Dad and Billy are going to have to adjust to a new place too; it's not just
about you. Can't you be happy for me?

BETSY: No!

What's going on.

College students can be pretty self-centered. They want everything at home to stay
the same while they explore their world away from the family. For some students,
this is not a big deal; for others, it's really upsetting.

What to do.	What to avoid.
• Try to give your child as much advance notice of a move as possible.	• Springing the news on her.
• Recognize that this may be a major adjustment, even though your child is away from home for most of the year.	• Expecting her to be happy for you.
	• Criticizing her for being so selfish.
	• Demanding that she spend the summer in the new city.
• Listen to your child and empathize with his or her feelings.	
• Understand that leaving hometown friends and a house they grew up in is a big deal to most college students.	
• Be flexible about your child's summer plans. Offer choices.	

What you need to know.

College students go through so many developmental changes that they will resist
a shift in the family home and hometown with great vigor. Fear usually underlies

the reaction; it's important for parents to be aware of that and help their child adjust to the change. Students who are in the process of transferring their sense of identity from family to friends find it hard to return home for breaks and vacations when they don't have any friends in the new city. They have to leave behind old friends and can be pretty miserable in a new place.

It may be a good time to consider alternatives to having your child come home for every break if you are relocating the family to a new city. He or she may welcome the opportunity to stay with old friends in your hometown, and you won't have to deal with a moping and angry child. You might also suggest that he or she bring a friend from school to your new home for break. This adjustment is a tough one for everyone, but it can be especially hard for a student who has relied on home as a safe haven during a time of great change in his or her life at school.

Divorce

Ned and Jan have known for a long time that their relationship wasn't satisfying and close anymore. They had talked about divorce or a trial separation on many occasions when their children were teenagers but they couldn't face the disruption that such a move would have caused their children; therefore, they put off the decision. Now they are alone. Their last child has gone to college and the deficiencies in their relationship are visible and pervasive. They decide that it's time to move forward with a separation agreement. And now they must tell their children, the youngest of whom is in his first year of college.

What's going on.

Ned and Jan are typical of thousands of couples every year who decide to separate once their last child leaves home. They believe that this change won't be so devastating for their children because they are now away from home and less dependent on them on a daily basis.

What's on your mind?

I just want to get this over with.

We've waited a long time to make this decision.

Now that the kids have their own lives, this shouldn't affect them too much.

What's on your child's mind?

I can't believe my parents are doing this to me. How long have they been lying to me?

What's going to happen to me?

Will I still have a home?

What to do.	What to avoid.
• Realize that this may come as a big shock to your child, even though he may have been aware of your marital difficulties for many years.	• Keeping this change a secret until you have divorced and surprising him with it.
• Choose an appropriate time to tell your child. Don't do it over the phone and don't burden him with this news during a stressful period at college, such as final exam time.	• Putting your child in the middle of any difficult negotiations such as who will pay for college from now on.
• Be honest and frank with your child without blaming one another for this situation.	• Expecting your child to behave rationally and counting on him to accept this decision more readily now that he's away from home.
• Reinforce that you love him and his sister and that you'll always be their parents regardless of changes in your relationship.	
• Make specific arrangements for how you will handle your child's support and share those plans with your college student.	

What you need to know.

Many parents think that, if they hold their relationship together until the last child goes to college, the effect won't be as damaging. In fact, a divorce during the college years can have a devastating effect on college students. As a child searches for identity and autonomy during the college years, the need for a stable family becomes paramount.

While it may seem to parents that their child is grown up, independent, and not in need of their daily attention during the college years, he or she still needs to be able to count on a secure base at home. This decision can rock a child's foundation profoundly and have a dramatic effect on the child's ability to form his or her own intimate attachments and to trust in relationships. Parents planning to separate or divorce while their child is in college need to be especially aware of the consequences and try to understand their child's reaction. The more parents discuss this decision with their child, and listen and empathize with their child's feelings, the better it will be for the whole family over time.

Some parents have a pattern of placing their child in the middle of their relationship; this creates a triangle that can have damaging long-term effects on the child. A triangle occurs in the family system when two people are unable to solve a problem and they draw a third person into the controversy. Parents need to ensure that they don't place their child in this situation. It happens most frequently in families when the parents will not work on their relationship.

If a child often mediates disagreements between the parents, that child may feel that the divorce is his or her fault and may try to fix things between the mother and father. Parents need to make it clear to their child that this change has to do with their relationship, not with the child's behavior.

The most important thing you can do for your child is clearly explain your decisions and accept responsibility for them. Communicate to your child that this is a difficult situation but one that you can manage without his or her help. Treat your spouse with respect, even though you may be angry and hurt. Help your child to believe that you, as parents, are united in your love and caring for him or her. At all costs, avoid the pitfall of asking your child to take sides in the dispute and handle the divorce negotiations without involving your child. Reassure your child that you are still a family that cares and provides for one another. Make sure that what you *do* speaks as loudly as what you say.

Death of a Grandparent

Stephanie, a junior in college, received the following phone call from her mom:

STEPHANIE: Hello?

MOM: Hi, sweetie. How are you?

STEPHANIE: I'm okay, how's Grammy?

MOM: Well, I've got some bad new for you, honey. Grammy died this morning.

STEPHANIE (STARTING TO CRY): Oh, Mom, no. What happened? I thought she was
   getting better.

What's on your mind?

I knew Stephanie would be
    upset, but I figured she
    knew Grammy wouldn't be
    with us much longer.
Stephanie seems so sad and
    angry.
She'll have the whole weekend
    here. Why is she insisting
    on coming home tonight?

What's on your child's mind?

I can't stop crying.
I loved my grammy so much.
    I can't believe she's gone.
She was the only one in the
    family who really under-
    stood me. What am I going
    to do without her?

MOM: She did seem a little better when we saw her on Sunday, but she was still very sick, you know.

STEPHANIE (NOW SOBBING): But I thought she was *better!* I can't believe she's gone and I never got to say good-bye. Why didn't you call me? I could have come home. I can't believe I've lost my grammy. I'll pack my bag right now and get the next bus home.

MOM: Stephanie, I know you're upset. We all are, but there's no need for you to rush home. The funeral isn't until next Saturday and you have work to do at school. There's nothing for you to do here right now, honey.

STEPHANIE: I don't care. I'm coming home right now. I wouldn't be able to concentrate on anything here anyway.

MOM: But, Stephanie, you have classes and exams coming up. I think you should stay at school through the week and come home Friday night. That's plenty of time to be here for the funeral.

STEPHANIE (STILL CRYING): Mom, I just want to come home. I want to see Grammy right now.

MOM: Honey, she's, well, her body's at the funeral home. It won't matter to Grammy when you get here.

STEPHANIE: I just wanted to say good-bye. Now I'll never be able to see her again. I can't imagine home without Grammy.

What's going on.

When students are in college, they rely on everything staying the same at home. The death of an important person in a student's life can be a traumatic experience. Even if Stephanie was at home, she might not have been right there when her grandmother died; but being away at school, she feels left out and angry that she couldn't say good-bye. Stephanie's mother doesn't seem to understand the depth of Stephanie's feelings, urging her to be rational and sensible while Stephanie is understandably very upset.

What to do.	What to avoid.
• Listen to your child's feelings of loss and grief and let her have those feelings. • Ask her what she would like to do. • Respect your child's feelings and encourage her to do what feels right for her. • Ask her if she has a friend she can talk to at school.	• Trying to manage your child's feelings and reactions to this loss. • Insisting that she be mature and get on with her life. • Imposing your expectations on her behavior.

What you need to know.

Students often lose a favorite grandparent while in college, and this loss can be devastating, especially if the relationship was a close one. With life expectancy what it is today, students might well believe that they'll have grandparents in their lives for many years after graduating from college. Most college-aged students have had little experience with death, and the death of a beloved grandparent can be a great shock, even if that grandparent is old and sick.

Grandparents can play a unique role in the lives of children, offering unconditional love and support. It's not unusual for children to be as close to a grandparent as they are to their parents. In fact, many grandparents take an active role in their grandchildren's lives, providing for them emotionally and financially from infancy through the college years and beyond. Parents need to be especially sensitive to what this loss means to their children and make sure that their children have opportunities to express their grief. It's important, too, that their child has a support system at school to help him or her through this difficult time.

Religious Changes

Your son Patrick has become engaged to a young woman at college who is an orthodox Jew. He is taking classes to convert to Judaism and has announced that he and his fiancée will have a Jewish wedding, keep a kosher household, and raise

What's on your mind?

How can Patrick dismiss his
  Christian heritage?
Why can't his fiancée become
  a Christian?
Our family will never be the
  same.

What's on your child's mind?

I really love Joan and respect
  her Jewish faith.
Religion is very important to
  Joan.
I think I can happily adopt Ju-
  daism.

their children in the Jewish faith. You are puzzled about how this could have happened; your family has always been Christian.

What's going on.

As college students begin to form their own values and make lifestyle choices, parents may find departures from the family traditions hard to accept. While this may bother parents and other family members, they need to respect their child's choice. You may worry about the consequences of your son's or daughter's decision, but during this time you need to be open to understanding his or her choices, not taking action to change your child's mind. Having a son or daughter reject deeply held values, such as religion, can be a difficult issue for parents. Parents need to give themselves time to adjust to these changes and allow themselves to feel the loss and sadness that this represents.

What to do.

- Ask your son to help you under-stand his choices.
- Make an effort to learn about Judaism.
- Let your son know that you respect his right to make choices even if they differ from the family's traditions.
- Remind yourself that this is not a rejection of you as much as it is an expression of your child's emerging adult identity.

What to avoid.

- Threatening to disown him if he converts to Judaism.
- Trying to break up the relationship.
- Making disparaging remarks about Jews or Judaism.
- Sharing your worries about how the family will respond.

What you need to know.

Parents need to remember that they don't have to agree with their child's choices in order to respect their child's right to make those choices. Studies of identity development have shown that religious commitments are shaken and questioned during the college years; religious exploration is often the result of the college student's quest for autonomy regarding values and lifestyle choices. It is generally understood that late adolescence is a time when individuals "begin to form a system of personal religious beliefs rather than relying solely on the teachings of their parents."[2] As they seek their own religious beliefs, some young people explore other ideologies and eventually return to their family's religion; others make a commitment to another religion or belief system. In both situations, however, through this process adolescents engage in a fundamental task of developing individual identity and autonomy—that is, making their own personal decisions about religious beliefs.

This may represent a significant change in the way your family celebrates holidays, as well as more fundamental changes, such as eventual child-rearing practices. Indeed, this is one of those decisions that will mean lifelong changes for you and your family. Your challenge is to accept the change (even if you don't agree with it), support your child, and keep your eye on the ultimate goal of establishing a good relationship with your son or daughter and his or her future spouse.

Lifestyle Changes

Your daughter Shelley has become a vegetarian and is living in a vegan co-op at school. She's told you that being a vegan means that she doesn't eat any animal or dairy products. You're wondering how to accommodate her new diet when she's home for summer vacation.

What's on your mind?

Who ever heard of a vegan?
Is this a healthy diet?
Does this mean preparing special meals for her?

What's on your child's mind?

I feel so much healthier now.
I'm never going to eat animals again.
How am I going to survive while I'm home over?

What's going on.

Shelley's interest in being a vegetarian may have begun within her new circle of friends at college or it may have originated in high school. If most of her friends at college are vegetarian, she will be more likely to become a vegetarian. College students, for better or worse, tend to be influenced by their peer group when it comes to lifestyle choices. Whether this is a temporary or lifetime commitment, give them the respect that comes with taking this choice seriously.

What to do.	What to avoid.
• Find out more about what it means to be a vegetarian. • Ask your daughter about this change in her diet. • Expect your daughter to take care of her special dietary needs when she is home and let her know this.	• Jumping to the conclusion that this is some sort of unhealthy fad diet. • Insisting that your daughter eat the same food as the family when she's home on breaks. • Ridiculing or criticizing her weird lifestyle and choices. • Trivializing this choice, assuming that it's just a "phase" she'll outgrow in time.

What you need to know.

Vegetarianism, practiced intelligently, is a healthy food regimen and shouldn't alarm you. In fact, it is generally accepted that eliminating animal products is a responsible and healthy dietary choice. The key with vegetarian diets is to ensure that the individual is getting adequate protein, vitamins, and minerals to promote healthy growth and development.

Food can be a major source of contention between parents and adolescents. If you have maintained an open dialogue with your child about health-enhancing behaviors and choices, it should not come as a surprise when your child makes the decision to become a vegetarian. A child who makes a healthy choice of diet needs encouragement and support. Rather than viewing this choice as a rejection of *your* lifestyle, learn more about alternative diets and congratulate your child for making healthy decisions.

It's not easy to keep up with the explorations and changing habits that characterize late adolescence. While the changes may occur quickly and seem whimsical to you, that doesn't mean they are superficial or transitory to your child. Learn about these lifestyle choices, even if you are not interested in adopting them yourself. It can provide an opportunity for you to begin to interact with your child on a more adult level.

Families That Resist Change

Roles and relationships in some families become fixed over time. If parents are not able to accommodate the changes in their children during the college years, they force their children to make a choice between remaining part of a rigid family system or continuing to grow and develop.

The Inflexible Family

You are upset and surprised when your only daughter Debbie calls to tell you that she's coming home from school:

DEBBIE: Hi, Dad. How's Mom?

DAD: She's pretty good, considering how much she misses her little girl. What's up with you?

DEBBIE: I've got some bad news, Dad. I've been asked to take a leave from college. My grades are so bad that they want me to take a semester off and take courses somewhere else to prove that I can handle the work here.

DAD: Oh, Debbie, what happened?

DEBBIE: I don't really know. I just can't seem to focus on my schoolwork. I think about you guys all the time. I know Mom's been really depressed since I left for college. Do you think she's all right, Dad?

DAD: I think so. It's been hard on her to have you gone. But, Deb, you were such a good student in high school. I'm surprised you're having trouble in college.

DEBBIE: I know, but it's really hard here. I miss you and Mom.

DAD: We miss you, too, honey. So are you coming home?

DEBBIE: Yeah, I guess so. Can you pick me up this weekend? I really don't want to stay here any longer than I have to.

DAD: Okay, I guess you can still get into some courses here at the community college. Do you want me to check it out to see if it's not too late?

DEBBIE: I don't know. Maybe I'll just come home and decide what to do later.

DAD: But, Debbie, what will you do here?

DEBBIE: Well, I thought I could talk to Mr. Miller about getting my old job back for a while.

DAD: Is that what you really want to do?

DEBBIE: I don't *know*, Dad. I'm so confused right now. I just want to come home.

DAD: Well, okay, I'll call you later about picking you up on Saturday. I'll tell your mother. She's not home right now, but I know she'll want to talk to you later. Are you going to be in your room tonight?

DEBBIE: Yeah.

DAD: We'll talk to you later then.

What's going on.

Debbie is an only child and she has always been close to her parents. In fact, her parents have taken so much responsibility for her daily life that she finds being away from home extremely difficult. She's confused about what it means to be on her own at college and has spent most of her time missing home and communicating with her parents nearly every day. She's also been her mother's friend and support for so many years that she feels responsible for her mother's happiness and for keeping the family in balance. We know of children who actually quit or flunk out of college so that they can go home and reclaim their place in the family, trying to preserve those relationships as they've always been.

What to do.	What to avoid.
• Try to understand how unhappy Debbie is about flunking out.	• Taking on responsibility for Debbie's difficulty; making it your problem to solve.
• Ask her what she thinks is going on and empathize with her feelings of homesickness.	• Blaming her for not working hard enough to get passing grades.
• Think about getting some help for Debbie. She may benefit from talking to a counselor who specializes in family systems.	• Expecting her to understand how embarrassing and difficult this is for you.
• Discuss with her what she plans to do while at home.	• Making your child feel responsible for your happiness.
• Let her know what your expectations are if she comes back to live at home.	

What you need to know.

Debbie and her parents are stuck in a family structure that no longer works when she goes to college. Instead of recognizing her departure for college as a normal change in the family, her family was unable to find a new balance when a piece of the mobile was removed. Debbie felt the need to return home to restore that former balance. Her parents might support that return because they, too, were unable to adjust to the new family structure with Debbie gone. This disruption to the family can cause a student to inexplicably drop out or flunk out of college.

Salvador Minuchin, a family therapist and pioneer in the field of family systems theory, describes three ways that families interact with each other: disengaged, clear about boundaries, or enmeshed. When family members are disengaged, they become extremely autonomous and lack feelings of loyalty and belonging. This type of environment makes it difficult for individuals to find support from other family members when they need it. A college student may feel cut off from parents and unable to count on support unless the need is extreme. The family that establishes clear boundaries among it's members has the healthiest interaction of the three. It allows for appropriate dependence when children are young, encourages independence when children begin to mature into adulthood, and values the interdependence that results when children are fully functioning adults.

Debbie's family is an example of an enmeshed family system. In order to belong in a highly enmeshed family, the members must relinquish a measure of independence and autonomy. The family responds to the slightest problem immediately, often with excessive speed and intensity. The family does not have clear boundaries and members take on everyone's problems as their own. Because of this enmeshment, Debbie can't break away from her parents and may even feel an inappropriate responsibility for their happiness and well-being. Hence, she sabotages any situation in which she has to act autonomously and independently from her family—she fails out of school so that she can return home and restore the family balance.

Debbie's parents, perhaps unwittingly and with the best intentions, have done her a great disservice by encouraging her dependence on them. They probably raised her with an authoritarian or indulgent parenting style, as discussed in the last chapter, thus limiting her ability to be independent or secure in herself without constant parental support and reinforcement. Debbie has been asked to serve her parents' needs at the expense of her own development. With help, however, Debbie's family can address the issues of enmeshment and help her move on to find her own identity and establish interdependence with her parents in a healthy, affirming way.

As Minuchin has found:

Families are organisms that evolve and develop over time. Each stage of growth in members of a family requires accommodation and change. Every family member's behavior is influencing and influenced by every other family member. In order to feel secure, people must be part of a predictable interaction. Unfortunately, predictability may congeal into limiting molds, so that patterns become inflexible and family members are limited by the small range of behavior available to them.[3]

In healthy families, changes in roles and relationships will occur during the college years. As your child moves from dependence, to independence, and on to interdependence, the family system will change and flex, much as a mobile responds to the natural movement of wind and air around it. Think of your family as a wonderful work of art in progress.

What to Know More?

Shapiro, Patricia Gottlieb. *My Turn: Women's Search for Self After the Children Leave.* Princeton, NJ: Peterson's Guides, 1997.

1. "First-Generation Collegians Lag Behind," *USA Today,* September 1997, 126, 2628, 8.
2. Laurence Steinberg, *Adolescence,* 5th ed. (Boston: McGraw-Hill College, 1999), 299.
3. Salvador Minuchin and Michael P. Nichols, *Family Healing: Strategies for Hope and Understanding* (New York: Touchstone Books, 1993), 111.

Chapter 6

What to Expect from the College/University

Faculty Advising and Other Services for Students

Doonesbury

BY GARRY TRUDEAU

DOONESBURY © 2000 G. B. Trudeau. Reprinted with permission of UNIVERSAL PRESS SYNDICATE. All rights reserved.

At orientation the college faculty and staff members all encouraged new parents to "let go" and allow our kids to get on with the business of becoming independent. They didn't say much about what we, as parents, could expect in return for the enormous amount of money it's costing us to send our children to college. I guess I'm supposed to take it on faith that they're going to make sure my son has a good college experience.

As you move toward a new relationship with your child, you will also have a different type of relationship to your child's educational institution. The quality of that relationship may depend on the size of the institution; in fact, the services and support that your child can expect to receive will certainly depend on the size of the school. This chapter will help you to understand the differences among institutions and to balance your need for involvement and information with your child's need to learn to manage his or her own life during college.

The Academic Experience

Faculty members expect students to be able to manage a demanding academic workload and to take the initiative in formulating and carrying through on a course of study during their college career. Adjusting to the academic expectations of college is a challenge for most students and, at times, it may be confusing for you as well. These scenarios will help you understand how the learning environment is structured in college.

Faculty Advising

Your son is in his first semester at a large state university. He calls to complain that he can never find his faculty advisor and that his course list for next semester has to be signed tomorrow.

What's going on.

Students often wait until the last minute to have their course list signed by an advisor. At large institutions where faculty members have a large list of advisees, this may be a problem. While students complain that their advisor is "never there," sometimes the student hasn't made a reasonable effort to see the advisor in order to meet course enrollment deadlines. In fact, faculty often complain that they hold office hours and no one schedules an appointment.

What's on your mind?

Why isn't his advisor there when he needs her?

Does this advisor care about my son's education?

What's on your child's mind?

My advisor is never in.

I should have signed up for her office hours, but I didn't get around to it.

What am I going to do now?

What to do.	What to avoid.
• Recognize that this is not your problem to solve.	• Taking on the problem for your son.
• Listen to your son's frustration and offer some ideas: for example, he could ask the department office staff or registrar to assist him in getting his course list approved in time. Most universities have back-up systems in case a faculty advisor is not available when deadlines are looming.	• Calling the university and demanding that his advisor do her job.
• Ask him to think of ways that he can avoid this situation in the future.	
• Remind him that he can request a change of advisor if the relationship isn't working for him.	

What you need to know.

The relationship between advisor and advisee at a university or college is best described as a professional consultation in which the student and the academic advisor accept joint responsibility for the success of the relationship. This is new territory for most students—dealing with a professional consultation that is fundamentally different from the high school student-teacher relationship. Most students have never experienced this sort of relationship without parental involvement and guidance.

Particularly at large universities, students need to be assertive about meeting with their advisor; scheduling time with an inaccessible advisor can intimidate some students. Parents can reassure their children that advising is part of a faculty member's job and a service that they are entitled to when they need it. At the same time, parents need to recognize that their children bear responsibility for this relationship as well. College students need to take the initiative in scheduling appointments, preparing for advising meetings, and changing advisors if the relationship is not working.

Students have a right, however, to expect their academic advisor to be knowledgeable about the curriculum, be able to refer students elsewhere when necessary, help them select courses and formulate an academic plan of study, and encourage them to think about their undergraduate education in the context of long-range goals.

My (Helen) older son, who attended a large research university, received minimal help from his academic advisors and felt intimidated by his interactions with one advisor, who was a Pulitzer Prize–winning novelist. My younger son, who attended a small private college, was invited to have dinner at his advisor's home during the first week he was on campus and, hence, felt much more comfortable about calling on his advisor for guidance during his first semester in college.

In reality, academic advising can vary a great deal, depending on the commitment of both faculty member and student to making the relationship a productive one. A student at a large university may have to be more assertive to receive advice and guidance from a faculty advisor. At a small college, this relationship will be easier to establish and more personal. In either case, however, a college student is entitled to adequate advice and counsel from a faculty advisor. It's generally the student's responsibility to make that relationship work or to seek alternative advice if it doesn't. Your role is to encourage your son or daughter to get the advice that he or she needs to successfully complete an undergraduate degree.

Professors vs. Teaching Assistants

Your daughter is in her second semester at the university and she still hasn't had any contact with a "real" professor. One of her classes is actually taught by a graduate student who is a teaching assistant. Your daughter is having trouble in chemistry class, and her teaching assistant can't speak English well enough to explain concepts to the class.

What's going on.

Particularly at large research universities, teaching assistants play a significant role in teaching first- and second-year undergraduate classes. While some graduate student teaching

> ### What's on your mind?
>
> I'm paying an enormous tuition bill, and my child isn't even being taught by a professor.
> No one told us that this would happen.
> What can I do about this?

> ### What's on your child's mind?
>
> I can't understand half of what the TA is talking about in my chemistry lab.
> Who should I go to for help?
> The classes are so big here. I feel like just a number.

assistants make excellent teachers, this is not always the case. In many undergraduate classes, a professor will provide the weekly lectures and rely on graduate assistants to teach discussion or lab sections and assist in grading papers and examinations. Your concern should be the quality of the teaching, whether the job is performed by a professor or graduate teaching assistant.

What to do.	What to avoid.
• Suggest that she make an appointment with her professor to explain the situation. • If she doesn't receive any help from the professor, recommend that she talk to an academic advisor in the department, or the director of undergraduate studies in her department or college, about this problem. • Ask her if she can seek additional help through a tutoring or learning skills center on campus. • Remember that this is your child's dilemma, not yours. Your role is to listen to her frustrations and offer advice about how she might find some help.	• Assuming that her TA really can't speak English adequately. Although this may be true, it may be that the concepts are just difficult to learn and your daughter would need extra help regardless of the teacher's language ability. • Calling the department and demanding that an English-speaking faculty member teach your daughter's class.

What you need to know.

In a recent independent report, the Carnegie Foundation for the Advancement of Teaching found that large research universities often neglect undergraduates, "herding them into dull classes taught by inexperienced faculty and then giving little academic guidance or support."[1] They further discovered that "undergraduate students are often taught by badly trained or untrained teaching assistants, not the famous professors touted in catalogs or recruiting materials and that few student have access to what distinguishes the research universities from liberal arts colleges: the access to diverse, interdisciplinary opportunities for experience-based education."

The quality of undergraduate education generates serious debate on many campuses; the focus of this debate has been directed primarily at universities that emphasize faculty research above teaching. Although research universities comprise only 3 percent of the nation's campuses, each year they graduate about one-third of all college seniors; hence, it is not surprising that the quality of undergraduate education is a serious concern for many parents.

In order to have contact with faculty in large research universities, students need to take the initiative and be assertive. They can make appointments with faculty during their office hours, enroll in small seminars, or do a research project independent study with a faculty member. But students must seek out these opportunities and be persistent. Usually faculty members take an interest in the students who excel in their courses.

Academic Difficulty

Your daughter Laura called home last night and you're disturbed by her predicament:

LAURA: Hi, Mom.

MOM: Hi, Laura. How are you doing?

LAURA: Not so well. I think I'm going to flunk my anthropology course.

MOM: What's happening?

LAURA: I just can't seem to figure out what my professor wants. I failed the midterm and I got a D on my paper. I got it back today and I don't know what to do. I thought it was okay. I really worked hard on it.

MOM: Have you talked to your professor?

LAURA: No. I wouldn't know what to say.

MOM: Well, what are you going to do about this?

LAURA: I told you, I don't know what to do!

MOM: But, Laura, you can't fail the course. Do you want me to call your professor?

LAURA: No!

What's on your mind?

What's happening with Laura? Is there something that I can do to help?

I don't understand why she won't talk to her professor.

What's on your child's mind?

I can't believe I'm going to flunk anthropology.

I just can't figure out what my professor wants.

I've never failed anything before. What's wrong with me?

MOM: But you obviously need extra help. Why can't you ask for it?

LAURA: I just can't, Mom. You don't understand.

MOM: I *do* understand. You're supposed to be learning and passing your courses. What about your other courses? Are you doing okay in them?

LAURA: Yeah, I'm doing okay, but I'm definitely not going to make the Dean's List here.

What's going on.

While it may be unreasonable to expect that your daughter will achieve high grades her first year in college, it also alarms you and your daughter that she may flunk a course. Many students find the competition and quantity of work required in college courses a surprise. It takes time to adjust to increased academic demands, and students often feel overwhelmed by the challenge.

What to do.	What to avoid.
<ul><li>Listen to your daughter's feelings about her failing grades.</li><li>Empathize with her anxiety about the workload at college.</li><li>Reassure her that you know she is capable of handling college-level work.</li><li>Continue to encourage her to talk to the professor of the course she is failing.</li><li>Suggest that she seek help through a writing workshop, learning skills center, or by engaging a tutor.</li></ul>	<ul><li>Taking on her dilemma as your own.</li><li>Overreacting. Calling her professor to find out what's going on.</li><li>Threatening to take her out of school if she can't get good grades.</li></ul>

What you need to know.

It's not unusual for a student to receive his or her first failing grade in college. Even the brightest high school student will find the adjustment to college life and academics a challenge. This doesn't mean that your child won't be able to do the work and get a degree. It may mean that he or she will have to learn new study skills and habits to cope with the rigors of college-level work. There are services on campus that can help students who are overwhelmed by their workload. Most colleges and universities have learning skills centers, writing workshops, and tutors available to help students through academic difficulties. It is important, however, that the student take the initiative to get help. A good first step is to encourage your child to seek information and advice from the professor of any course in which he or she is struggling. Your role as a mentor is to advise and counsel on what the child can do to improve his or her situation; it is not your role to take over and decide what your child should do.

If your child continues to perform poorly in college, he or she will probably be placed on academic probation and you may be notified of this decision by the college. In this case you may need to be more actively involved; not in solving your child's problem for him or her, but in making sure that your child gets the assistance he or she needs to achieve passing grades. Your role may be to contact a faculty advisor (with you child's knowledge and consent) to find out what services are available and help devise a plan to take advantage of the academic support services on campus. Your skills as a mentor will be useful in helping your child receive the help he or she needs, especially if your child is shy, overwhelmed, or temporarily incapable of seeing the forest for the trees.

Grade Reporting and Transcripts

You have had a frustrating call to the registrar at your child's college. Your daughter is out of the country on a semester abroad program and has asked you to fill out the forms for her financial aid and scholarship package for the following academic year, as the deadlines will pass before she returns. You called to get a copy of her transcript and were told that you could not have it without your daughter's written authorization.

> ### What's on your mind?
>
> Why can't I have her transcript? I pay her tuition. What am I going to do now? By the time I get a note from my daughter, the deadlines will have passed.

What's going on.

Most colleges and universities will not release grade information over the phone to a so-called third party. Students who are over eighteen years old have the legal right to privacy regarding their academic and financial records while in college. Most parents are unaware of this regulation and are angry when they can't have ready access to their child's records.

What to do.	What to avoid.
• Explain clearly to the registrar's office that you need the transcript in order to complete scholarship and/or financial aid forms for your daughter, who is out of the country. Most registrar's offices will be happy to mail the official transcript directly to the scholarship or financial granting agency.	• Simply asking for your daughter's transcript without giving the reason for the request.
• Have your daughter file a release form with the registrar so that you don't have to deal with this again.	• Threatening to withhold tuition payment until you can get the information that you need.
• If you want to see a grade report every semester, make that clear to your child and ask her to share it with you.	

What you need to know.

As your child adjusts to the academic challenges of college, you too will adjust to a new set of procedures for reporting grades. When your child was in primary and secondary school, you were probably used to seeing report cards.

The Family Education Rights Privacy Act (FERPA) was passed in 1974. It guarantees an emancipated student (one who is financially independent) the right to privacy of his or her educational and financial records. A third party (parents or others) cannot have access to that student's grade reports, transcripts, or financial records without the student's written permission. Under this act (also referred to as the Buckley Amendment), institutions are authorized to protect the privacy rights of all students who are eighteen years of age and older, whether or not they are emancipated. However, most institutions will honor the disclosure of grades and financial records to parents who can provide documentation that they contribute more than 50 percent of that student's financial support.

Some institutions simply assume that parents or guardians are providing more than 50 percent of the student's support and automatically send grades to parents. As a practical matter, however, most colleges and universities are not willing to spend the additional money to mail two grade reports—one to students and one to parents—so they may send only one grade report to students at their home addresses.

As technology continues to play a larger role in organizing and reporting information, more students will have instant access to all of their academic and financial records. In the not-too-distant future, it will be possible for you to log on to your child's records, but most colleges will allow parents access only with their child's permission. At least one college currently has a system whereby students can choose what information they want made available to parents who log on to the college's record-keeping system.

Parents whose children attend a college with a policy of not sending grades to parents, need to ask their children about their grades and financial situation. Some parents are angry when they don't automatically receive grade reports from the institution. They need to keep in mind, however, that this privacy protection can work to their child's benefit. For example, if the institution provides information on a student to any third party, a stranger can have access to their child's course schedule, grades, financial data, and maybe even an unlisted address. Several tragedies have resulted from the disclosure of this kind of information. For example, an estranged boyfriend might have access to a former girlfriend's class schedule and confront her after class.

Parents who are engaged in a struggle about grades need to have a frank discussion with their child. This controversy usually is symptomatic of a deeper communication problem. Your child may have any number of reasons for being reluctant to share grades with you, but if you provide most or all of your child's support in college, you do have a right to know how he or she is doing in school.

Life Outside of the Classroom

Most college graduates would agree with the person who said, "I learned a great deal in college, but only about 10 percent of that learning took place in the classroom." Colleges are living-learning laboratories in which students receive an education both inside and outside of the formal classroom setting. Some of the most valuable and lasting learning experiences occur as students learn to live with others and discover who they are as responsible adults in the college community.

Social Adjustment

What's on the professor's mind?

Why is this father calling me?
I don't know how to deal with students' psychological problems.
I'm a teacher, not a counselor.

What's on your mind?

I'm really getting worried about Tim. He seems so unhappy.
Can't someone at the college help him?
I don't think he's in serious trouble, but I don't really know.
I don't want Tim to know that I called and how worried I am.

You are worried about Tim's social adjustment to college and decide to call the department office. They connect you with the faculty member who is director of undergraduate studies:

PROFESSOR: Hello?

DAD: Oh, hello, Professor James. My name is Mike Farrell and I'm calling about my son Tim, who is a second-year transfer student in your department. I'm concerned about him.

PROFESSOR: Is he having difficulty in his classes?

DAD: No, classes seem to be going fine, but he seems so lonely and isolated. He hasn't really met any new friends, and I guess he's spending all of his time studying alone in his room. He calls home almost every day and complains about being bored.

PROFESSOR: So he isn't finding the course work challenging?

DAD: No, I think the courses are going fine, but he doesn't seem to have any social life. He spends too much time alone. I'm concerned that he's becoming depressed.

PROFESSOR: Ah, I see. Are you worried that he might be depressed enough to harm himself in some way?

DAD: I don't think so. I just think he needs to meet some other kids and have some fun once in a while.

PROFESSOR: Well, you see, I'm a professor here, and I don't have much to do with student life outside of the classroom. I think we have a counselor on staff in the college who might be able to help if Tim would go and talk to her. Would you like me to transfer you to Ms. Taylor in our counseling center?

DAD: Well, maybe Ms. Taylor could call Tim and ask him to come in. I could give you his phone number to give to Ms. Taylor. I don't want him to know I called about him. Maybe she could just say that she was interested in seeing how the transfer students were doing.

PROFESSOR: Why don't I transfer you to Ms. Taylor and you can ask her about that?

DAD: Well, okay.

What's going on.

Students who have a difficult social adjustment to college often complain to their parents and the parents feel at a loss to know how to help them. This is especially true of transfer students who come into a new situation where it seems that everyone else has already found a group of friends. Social life is an important component of the learning environment at college, and parents should be concerned if their child feels isolated and lonely most of the time.

What to do.	What to avoid.
• Take Tim's unhappiness seriously. Let him know that you empathize with his feelings of isolation. • Reassure him that you have seen him make friends in the past and that you know he can do it again. • Ask Tim if he needs some help finding out about what services are available on campus to help transfer students adjust. • Suggest that he talk to someone in the college counseling office. • Tell Tim that you'd like to be in touch with him more often just to see how he's doing.	• Jumping to the conclusion that Tim's chosen the wrong school and will never be happy there. • Calling the college yourself to get some help before talking to Tim about it. • Making an appointment for Tim with the counseling center and insisting that he go talk with someone.

What you need to know.

It's difficult, if not impossible, for a parent to assess from afar how unhappy their child is at school. A student may call on parents when he or she needs to make a "stress dump," and this can be upsetting to the parent. The student may feel much better, having just unloaded his or her anxieties onto a parent, but the parent now feels rotten.

In these situations, it's important for the parent to be able to talk openly with the child. Don't be afraid to ask your child if he or she feels too depressed to cope at all. If this is the case, you need to act to get your child some help. We discuss these kinds of crisis situations in chapter 9. This usually isn't the case, however. Tim's situation is a fairly common one. It's tough to be a transfer student in a new place. He may not have realized how difficult it would be to make new friends, so he begins to spend too much time alone instead of taking steps to meet new people. He could be shy in new situations, or he could be overwhelmed with all of the adjustments he has to make.

It would have been helpful for Tim's father to know that faculty members are typically not useful in situations like this. Tim's father may not have known where to turn for help and assumed that the college or department office would be able to assist him. While this may be true in a small college, where faculty members tend to have more interaction with students and take an active interest in student life outside of the classroom, this is usually not true in a large college or university. But all institutions have a Dean of Students' Office that can help parents in these situations. The Dean of Students' Office is a good place to begin if you want to find out about services for your child. Someone in that office will be able to help or make a referral.

In this case, maybe Tim will gradually begin to make friends and handle this situation for himself. He may not be seriously depressed and in need of counseling; he may simply need to share his frustrations with his father and get it off his chest. It's crucial that the parent listen and empathize with the child rather than overreact and come up with a quick fix for the situation. It's especially damaging to the parent-child relationship if the parent goes behind the child's back and forces a solution. This urge to do something to make you feel better will backfire and certainly break the trust you have established with your child. In fact, most college counselors will not agree to engage in subterfuge in getting a student to come in for counseling. They may, however, be willing to counsel you on the worries *you* have about your child's situation. Difficult as it is, your role is to listen, sympathize, encourage, and support your child in finding a solution to what is essentially his or her problem.

Psychological Services

Your daughter Samantha has suffered from a mild, but persistent, form of depression since she was sixteen years old. She's now at college, and during an argument when she was home over fall break, she blurted out that she was seeing a shrink at school. You asked her to tell you about it, and she yelled, "It's none of your business," and stormed off to her room. You're worried that she's getting worse and decide to call the counseling office and find out what's going on with her. You're angry and frustrated to find that no one will talk to you about your daughter's therapy.

What's going on.

It's natural for a parent to want to know what's going on when a child is depressed and seeking psychological counseling. The parent may have been involved in a family counseling situation with that child when she was in high school and now the mother feels left out and worried. However, Samantha is now taking personal responsibility for her mental and physical health and doesn't feel she has to share anything with her parents if she doesn't want to.

What's on your mind?

I've always been involved in Samantha's therapy before.

Why won't they tell me anything?

I have a right to know. I'm her mother.

What's on your child's mind?

My mom is so nosy. Believe me, she doesn't want to know what I'm talking to my counselor about!

This is my problem, not hers.

When is she going to start treating me like an adult?

What to do.	What to avoid.
• Let Samantha know that you are proud of her for seeking help. • Ask her if she wants to share what is going on with you. • Respect her right to privacy if she doesn't want to talk about it. • Be grateful that you have a child who is mature enough to take care of herself.	• Insisting that she tell you what's going on. • Threatening that you're going to find out even if she won't talk to you. • Telling her you're going to withhold financial or emotional support if she doesn't talk to you. • Reminding her that she's still your daughter and you have a right to know.

What you need to know.

If your child is eighteen years of age or older, he or she is entitled to the right of patient confidentiality when seeking medical or psychological treatment. This means that you will not have access to your child's medical or psychological records and that doctors and psychologists will not talk to you about your child's condition without the child's permission. This may trouble a parent who spoke to doctors or therapists in the past about his or her child's treatment.

Most health care professionals working at colleges will encourage a student to talk with his or her parents, particularly if they feel it will help the student. They are mandated by law, however, to keep their interactions and prescribed treatments for any patient confidential. This assurance of confidentiality is often crucial to a student's willingness to seek and receive treatment, and it will not be broken unless the health care provider feels that the student is in an extremely dangerous situation. Even then the provider will first attempt to get the student to deal directly with his or her parents before breaking the confidentiality rule.

It's difficult to respect your child's status as a legal adult when you know, as a parent, your child is not yet truly independent and not always capable of making mature and responsible decisions. Now, more than ever, you need to be patient, honor you child's right to privacy, and trust that he or she will be able to take care of him or herself. Your child may need to exercise extreme autonomy from you for a while, and you need to work on respecting that.

Residence Hall Staff

You've been trying to call your son for over a week and he's never in his room. He hasn't responded to the messages you left on his answering machine. The last time you talked to him, he was feeling pretty sad about the breakup of his relationship with his girlfriend. You're beginning to worry and wonder who you could call. You don't know any of his friends' last names or phone numbers.

What's going on.

It's easy for parents to forget that social life and relationships are important to college students. The breakup of a close relationship can leave a student feeling lonely and isolated from the social scene. Many students want to withdraw from everything. The last thing on Craig's mind is to worry about how his parents feel. His own pain is the only thing that's real for him.

What's on your mind?

I wonder if Craig is all right. The last time we spoke he sounded really unhappy. I wonder if anyone would notice if he just disappeared.

What's on your child's mind?

I'm really bummed out over Lisa.
Will I ever have another girlfriend who I like as much?
I'm so lonely without her.

What to do.

- Try to respect your son's need to withdraw and lick his wounds for a while.
- Call your son's residence hall director and ask if anyone has seen your son lately and if they noticed anything different in his behavior.
- Ask the residence hall director to check on Craig and ask him to call home.

What to avoid.

- Jumping to the conclusion that your son is in serious trouble. He's probably just trying to cope and doesn't need to have any further demands placed on him.
- Blaming him for not calling when you finally reach him.
- Deciding immediately that you have to get to campus and find out what's going on.

What you need to know.

Residence hall staff are a wonderful resource for parents who are worried and need to check in with someone. Resident directors are usually professionals hired by the college to manage the problems, large and small, that confront students living in residence halls. Some schools have directors and resident advisors, as well, who are usually graduate students or third- or fourth-year undergraduates. They live in the residence hall and are trained to deal with situations that arise when large groups of students share living quarters. They know all of the students in their hall and may even see them on a daily basis; they are usually aware of changes in behavior and are there to intervene, if necessary.

Residence hall staff members mediate roommate disputes, check on students in trouble, and notice if a student is withdrawn or appears depressed. At least one staff member is on call at all hours of the day and night, available to help a student deal with the problems and difficulties he or she faces, either personally or academically. Moreover, staff members tend to be people who students can relate to because they are not that much older and have recently gone through the college experience themselves. They are the most likely of all college staff to notice if your child seems to be in trouble, and they can be a great resource for parents who are concerned about, but removed from, their child's daily life. Ordinarily, however, you should not call on residence hall staff members without your child's knowledge and permission unless you are convinced that your child is in serious danger.

What's on your mind?

How could she be so stupid?
Where did she get a fake ID?
Now she'll have a "record" and
    she may even be expelled.
What can I do to help her?

What's on your child's mind?

Why did I have to get caught?
I should have let someone else
    buy the beer.
What's going to happen to me?

Legal Trouble

Your daughter Gabriella, a sophomore in college, was caught with a fake ID buying beer for her friends at a local convenience store. She's been arrested and has to appear in local court and deal with sanctions from the college as well. You're upset and angry with her, but you want to help.

What's going on.

Fake IDs are common on most college campuses, and many students each year get caught buying liquor or beer using fake IDs. Because the legal drinking age in almost every state is twenty-one, it is illegal for students to be in possession of or purchase alcohol during most of their college years. If this is her first offense, Gabriella will probably not be treated too harshly by the local authorities, but she will have to appear in court and will also be punished in some way by the college.

What to do.	What to avoid.
• Ask Gabriella if she's thought about what she's going to do. • Listen to her fears and let her know that, while you are unhappy with her behavior, you still love and support her in coping with her predicament. • If you are willing, help her find legal counsel if she wants it. • Let her know that you expect her to behave more responsibly in the future and that you do not condone her breaking the law for any reason.	• Letting your anger and embarrassment take over. • Telling her that you'll get her an attorney and deal with the authorities at school. • Agreeing with her that everyone has a fake ID and that you think it's unfair that she happened to get caught when everyone breaks the law about alcohol at college.

What you need to know.

While it's true that most college students break the law by drinking alcohol sometime during their college years, having a falsified driver's license or other form of identification is a serious offense and should not be taken lightly. The law is especially harsh if an individual is caught purchasing alcohol with a fake ID.

The consequences and punishments for this behavior can vary widely, but the college has no other choice than to respond to students who break the law. Underage drinking is a major issue on most campuses and a great deal of energy and resources are spent trying to control students' drinking. In large part those efforts fail, and drinking remains a major social activity carried out with varying degrees of secrecy and ingenuity on the part of students. Falsifying a legal document, such as a driver's license, however, escalates the offense and the local police department may well be involved when this occurs.

Parents may need to act when there is an arrest and their child needs support and help in getting legal counsel. No parent wants to deal with this situation, but it is, unfortunately, quite common on college campuses today. Parents do, however, have the right to insist that their child refrain from breaking the law and make it clear that they expect their child to obey the laws and the rules of the college and accept the consequences if he or she doesn't.

Additional Programs and Services on Campus

Even parents who have attended college themselves often find the structure and organization of higher education a bit confusing. And not all colleges and universities are organized in exactly the same way. We hope this listing of offices, programs, and services will help you make sense of the college's unique way of doing business and ensure that you receive the assistance you need when you have questions and concerns.

Dean's Office

The Dean's Office is the central location for all academic matters of the college or university. If your child is at a large university within which there are several colleges or schools, each of those units will have a Dean's Office dealing with the administrative issues relevant to the academic business of the college. The Dean's Office usually coordinates academic advising and oversees the hiring and promotion of teaching and research faculty members. You may want to contact this office if you are concerned about your child's academic-advising situation or if you have questions about course requirements or other academic issues.

Dean of Students' Office

The Dean of Students' Office oversees the wide range of student life issues on campus. They may be in charge of new student orientation, parents' weekend, student activities, fraternities and sororities, student government, and may run special programs, such as assertiveness training and self-defense workshops, among others. They may also coordinate public service and volunteer activities for student involvement on campus and/or in the local community. The Dean of Students' Office is the appropriate place for parents to get information and referrals on all aspects of student life. For example, parents might call this office for information on rules and policies governing the Greek system.

Bursar's Office

A strange name for a rather ordinary function—keeping track of student accounts and sending bills for tuition and room-and-board payments. Although ordinary, the processes are not necessarily simple or easy to understand. One parent complained that even though he was a certified public accountant, he couldn't understand the bursar's bill.

Depending on how the office is organized at your child's college, all kinds of charges may appear on this bill: some include tuition, room and board, campus store purchases, parking fees, dry cleaning and laundry, computer lab charges, and even pizza ordered from campus dining services. Many colleges have a student ID card that doubles as a charge card at many locations around campus. Make it clear to your son or daughter what charges you are willing to support. It may take persistence to get answers to your questions, but you should feel free to contact the Bursar's Office if you have questions about your child's bill.

Financial Aid

You may be quite familiar with the Financial Aid Office even before your child begins college. What you need to know is that your child's financial aid is calculated on a yearly (and sometimes on a term-by-term) basis. If there are changes in family circumstances, such as a parent losing a job, the Financial Aid Office should be willing to readjust your child's aid package to reflect your change in financial status. Financial aid offices have counselors to assist you and your child in unraveling the sometimes arcane financial award systems. Encourage your child to make an appointment with a financial aid counselor if there are questions or problems regarding the financial aid package.

Campus Security and Police

Even the smallest campuses employ security guards and often have a resident police presence. On most colleges and universities, the campus police officers have all of the jurisdictional rights of a regular community police force and are charged with enhancing safety and security on campus. They are authorized to enforce local, state, and federal laws.

Most college police personnel are individuals who have shown a particular interest in and sensitivity to working in a college environment. They are usually considered a part of the student services team and work around the clock to ensure that the campus environment is a safe one. They must comply with all of the federal and state-mandated reporting and advisory requirements.

You and your child are entitled to the information on campus crime that colleges and universities are required by law to compile and make available to the campus community. Many campus police and security operations offer free escort services and all of them provide emergency help twenty-four hours a day.

Student Employment Office

If your child is eligible for federal work-study funds, he or she can be employed on campus as a part of the financial aid package. Most colleges do not assign students a job; students are responsible for seeking out available opportunities and deciding where they want to work. Studies have found that students who work on campus find this a very positive experience if the work hours are kept to a manageable number each week. Having to work for ten to twelve hours each week can actually help a student structure his or her time and learn useful time-management skills.

Campus jobs can provide a valuable connection to the campus community and many students develop close relationships with their supervisors, thus benefiting from additional mentoring and adult support. Some students who do not qualify for the federal work-study program also take jobs on campus and reap the benefits of this connection.

Learning Skills Centers and Writing Workshops

It's not unusual for even the brightest high school student to find the adjustment to college-level work a challenge. Most colleges and universities recognize that they need to provide additional support to students who need to develop more effective study skills and who may need help in writing college papers. Many offer supplemental instruction in introductory-level science, mathematics, and economics courses, as well as tutoring and workshops in critical reading and thinking. Urge your child to take advantage of these helpful services, which are usually provided free of charge.

Career Services

All colleges and universities have a Career Services or Career Development Office that provides a range of services to help students make the transition from college to a first job or to graduate or professional school. Most offer advising and programming tailored to the curricular and career goals of students. They can help your child identify his or her career goals, develop job search skills, and apply to graduate and professional school. Many offer extensive recruiting programs for students interested in summer jobs, internships, and/or permanent jobs after graduation. They also offer a credentials service that records, stores, and transmits confidential letters of recommendation for students. More information about career services on campus is offered in chapter 8.

Campus Crisis Services

In addition to health and psychological services, many campuses operate telephone crisis lines that are available around the clock to students who are dealing with difficult issues. Most college towns also have a crisis hotline service available to students as well as to community members.

Equal Opportunity Office

All students have the right to study in a safe environment that is respectful of their race, ethnicity, gender, sexual orientation, age, veterans status, or learning or physical disability. The Equal Opportunity Office on most campuses is equipped to counsel, advise, and assist students who have experienced bias, prejudice, sexual harassment, or any other form of discrimination in their course of study or in their extracurricular life on campus.

Computer Support Services

Due to the widespread use of computers and computer technologies on campuses today, most colleges and universities have computer support staff who are available to assist students with learning new programs and applications and troubleshooting problems. In addition, many schools have special areas on campus with computer equipment available for student use.

Campus Religious Organizations

Whether it's through the college or the local community, students will have access to religious services and counseling. Most schools employ chaplains and religious advisors and offer a wide range of programs for students. Many also have nondenominational chapels that offer a variety of services.

Minority Students' Programs

If your child is a member of a racial or ethnic minority group, he or she can get support from the college's minority students' program. These programs exist on most college campuses today and provide an important connection for students.

International Students' Office

If your child is an international student, he or she may want to take advantage of the services provided on campus through the International Students' Office. Professional staff can offer assistance and advice on cultural adjustment and on academic, personal, and immigration issues.

Study Abroad Programs

Your child may want to consider spending a semester or a year in a study abroad program. Many parents are pleasantly surprised to find that study abroad is no longer confined to children of the wealthy. In fact, the cost of a semester abroad can be less expensive than studying back home, although studying abroad is not a guaranteed bargain. If your child is interested in this type of program, he or she needs to start investigating programs early because planning such an experience can take a year or more.

Many colleges offer their own study abroad programs, but there are also programs available to all college students through hundreds of American colleges every year. Your child can find out about abroad programs through the college's career center or through the Study Abroad Office on campus. At the end of the next chapter, you will find resources on foreign study programs.

Off-Campus Housing Office

Many colleges and universities do not guarantee student housing after the first or second year of study. And many students prefer to live off-campus in apartments. If your child's college has an Off-Campus Housing Office, they can provide assistance in locating suitable housing and counseling students on the complexities of signing leases and dealing with local rental agents.

Athletics

Whether your child is involved in organized sports or wants to participate in an informal game of softball or soccer, most colleges offer opportunities for your child to engage in physical activity. Intramural or informal sporting events can provide a healthy way for your child to meet other students, get some exercise, and reduce stress. If your son or daughter is involved in an organized sport, you will no doubt have had contact with coaches and will be aware of services and support available to college athletes.

Student Activities

A major part of your child's experience in college will undoubtedly be his or her involvement in student activities and social events. Most schools have a wide variety of student activities that can help your child find friends with similar interests and make the adjustment to college smoother. Typically, the Dean of Students' Office has listings of student activities on campus.

Parents' Programs

Most colleges and universities have a Parents' Program Office. Although the office's main function may be fund-raising, the staff members are attuned to parents' needs and issues and may be able to offer valuable assistance and referral if you have concerns about your son's or daughter's educational experience.

How You Can Get Involved

There are many ways for you to be involved with your child's college or university. Beyond your main job of supporting your child through his or her college years, most colleges offer ways for you to be affiliated through various programs, in addition to being the parent of an undergraduate.

Parents' Programs

In addition to soliciting your financial support, parents' programs offer additional ways for you to participate. You might want to offer to be a parents' program contact in your area, offering advice and support to new parents, and perhaps organizing a "send off" party for new students and parents. Most colleges and universities have a parents' council that facilitates communication between parents and the college and spearheads fund-raising drives for scholarship aid and other worthy causes.

Alumni Clubs

Find out if there is an alumni organization in your town or city. These groups offer a unique way for you to be involved with the college from afar. Programs and activities vary, but often include presentations by faculty members, student "send off" events, luncheons with local community leaders, information on theater trips, and sporting events. Alumni clubs often organize special public service projects and participate in fund-raising events. Many alumni clubs offer special membership for parents. Check with the college's Alumni Office to find out about activities in your area.

Educational and Campus Vacations

Many colleges offer special travel packages, both domestic and international. These often include special seminars and study tours with leading members of the faculty. Some universities offer summer study vacations on campus with activities for the whole family. This can be a wonderful way to get to know your child's campus, learn something, and have the benefit of someone organizing interesting activities for all members of the family.

Athletic Events

You can attend a game or meet in your area. Check with the Athletic Office on campus for schedules.

Career Services

Consider participating by offering an internship or summer job at your place of employment for a college undergraduate. You may even convince your company to begin a recruiting program with the college, or you can contact the Career Services Office if you have a summer internship or permanent job opening. You might also offer to travel to campus to participate in a program or career fair sponsored by the career office or agree to be a mentor or advisor to a student who is interested in a career in your field.

Want to Know More?

Harris, Marcia B., and Sharon L. Jones. *The Parent's Crash Course in Career Planning.* Lincolnwood, Illinois: NTC Publishing Group, 1996.

1. "Reinventing Undergraduate Education: A Blueprint for America's Research Universities," A report on the nation's 125 research universities by the Carnegie Foundation for the Advancement of Teaching, April 1998.

Chapter 7

One Thousand Dollars a Week for a College Education

Dealing with Money Issues and Understanding the Value of a College Education

I know college is a good investment in my son's future, but by the time he and his sister graduate, we'll have a big second mortgage on our house and no savings left. The next few years are really going to be hard on us financially. I sure hope it's worth it!

A few years ago, *Newsweek* asked the parents of young children to list their greatest fears about raising their sons and daughters. More parents cited worry over college costs than worries about daycare or healthcare. The only fear deemed more serious to these parents was kidnapping or violent crime—and it surpassed college costs by only 2 percentage points.[1]

Although only the most elite colleges carry a $1,000-a-week price tag, sticker shock is common when most parents are paying for college. When your generation went to college, it was probably possible to cover a large part of your college costs (at least at a state or public college) through summer job earnings. Now even state schools can cost upward of ten thousand dollars a year. Six out of ten parents surveyed by Daniel Yankelovich, chairman of a well-known polling firm, believe that "higher education overall is too expensive" and that "liberal arts education is a luxury most people cannot afford."[2]

Why is college so much more expensive today? Many factors contribute to the continuing rise in the price of a college education. Those most often cited in studies are increased costs for financial aid, library materials, computer systems and technology, salaries for an aging and tenured faculty, the pressing need to complete maintenance on buildings and laboratories that was deferred during the high-inflation period of the 1970s, and the decrease in government support for research.

Although 50 percent of all students receive some type of financial aid to help defray college costs, the burden on families is still significant. And even though some schools have made a serious effort to maintain stable tuition levels or even decrease tuition, the overall cost of going to college will continue to increase.

Many articles each year in the popular press exhort parents to save early for college, prepay tuition, cash in savings bonds, investigate the new tax breaks, take advantage of scholarship opportunities, encourage children to became legally independent, or invest in tax-free education IRAs. We will not try to unravel the complexities of financial aid and scholarship policies; many good resources are available to help you understand and take advantage of the best method of financing your child's education. Some of them are listed at the end of this chapter.

Our goal is to help you explore two questions:
- How can I communicate with my child about money issues during the college years?
- How can I be sure that my child's education is worth the money I'm investing and the sacrifices I'm making?

Money Issues Beyond Tuition

In chapter 2, we encouraged you to have a frank discussion with your child about how you will pay for the major college costs—tuition, room and board, books, and trips back and forth to school. During the college years, you will undoubtedly be faced with other money issues as well. It's a good idea to talk about "extras" and make it clear to your child what you are willing to pay for in addition to the basic costs.

For example, your child may want to do an internship in another city during the summer or attend summer school, thereby decreasing the amount that he or she can contribute to the next year's cost of school. Are you willing and/or able to consider this "extra"? Perhaps you can support one summer internship, but not two or three. The following scenarios will help you plan for some of the activities and situations that call for additional resources during the college years.

What's on your mind?

Why can't he live in the dorm?
What will this apartment cost?
How will he manage cooking,
   keeping an apartment, and
   studying?

Renting an Apartment

Your son Tom, who has been living in a residence hall and subscribing to the meal plan, calls you in January to tell you that he and his friends have found a great apartment for next year. He wants to sign a lease right away.

What's going on.

Many college students choose to live in apartments after the first couple of years on campus. This can actually be a cost-saving alternative if your son chooses the apartment with care and cooks for himself. Renting an apartment during college can be a learning experience that prepares your child to take on such responsibilities after graduation.

What's on your child's mind?

I really want to get out of the
   dorms next year. All of my
   friends are getting out.
It would be so cool to live in
   an apartment.

What to do.

- Remind your child that these are decisions that require thought and time to discuss.
- Ask Tom to get all of the details surrounding signing a lease and give you a proposal, comparing the costs of living in the dorm and renting an apartment.
- Go through the terms and conditions of the lease agreement with him.
- Ask him to show the lease to the off-campus housing staff or have a lawyer look at it.

What to avoid.

- Immediately saying no before you have explored the possibilities.
- Responding to Tom's insistence that the lease has to be signed immediately. This is rarely the case, except in major cities.

What you need to know.

If your child wants to sign a lease for an apartment, it's important that you get all of the pertinent information regarding that lease before making a decision. Rental agents can be aggressive in trying to get students to sign lease agreements, especially if there is ample rental housing available near campus. It's to their advantage to sign up renters early and beat the competition.

Many apartment owners who rent to college students require what is called a "one for all" lease. This means that each student is responsible for the entire cost of the apartment in the event that one or more of the renters doesn't carry through with the agreement. This could be a problem if one of the renters drops out of school or gets ill and can't return to college for the next year. Ask your child to come up with a fall-back plan if this occurs. Many apartment leases have hidden costs, such as utilities and parking charges. Ask your child to gather all the facts and present them to you.

Spring Break on a Credit Card

Your daughter Anna announces that she wants to go on vacation with her friends over spring break in March. They plan to drive to Mexico and spend a week on the beach. She says she can charge almost everything on her new credit cards.

What's on your mind?

Why can't she just come home?
I've heard these spring break trips are drunken brawls.
I'm concerned about how she'll pay off the credit cards.

What's going on.

Every spring, thousands of college students make the legendary trip to the beach. Some go to ski resorts and others take even more exotic trips abroad during spring break. Students plan eagerly for these trips and feel the pressure to go along with friends. Travel companies offer seemingly great deals for these vacations, inundating campuses with special offers and promotional deals throughout the year.

What's on your child's mind?

Everyone is going on a trip.
It will be so great to go to the beach and relax for a week.
I deserve a break.
I can get an extra job this summer to pay for this.

What to do.	What to avoid.
• Make it clear if you are unwilling to provide the money for a spring break vacation.	• Refusing to let your child consider such a plan.
• Ask your child how he or she plans to pay for this trip.	• Regaling him or her with stories of drunken brawls.
• Ask your child how many credit cards he or she has and what the balances are.	
• Discuss your concerns about your child's safety. Ask your child to provide you with details on where he or she will stay, with whom, and how he or she will travel back and forth.	

What you need to know.

Students can get whipped up into a frenzy about going on spring break trips with their friends. Sometimes these vacations are wonderful, relaxing breaks from studying, and sometimes they are disasters with ten students sharing a motel room, cars breaking down en route, and unregulated drinking and partying around the clock. Make sure that your child has thought this trip through and has a fall-back plan if things get out of control.

While it's a good idea for your child to have a credit card during college for emergencies, students can get into serious financial trouble by having several credit cards and charging goods and services that they can't afford. Students can easily obtain credit cards, even though they do not have a stable or substantial income. Although most credit card companies will offer only a five hundred dollar credit limit, students can have several cards adding up to thousands of dollars in available credit. These are usually cards with the highest interest rates and annual fees so that students can charge far beyond their ability to pay and incur large debts with high interest rates and late fees. It doesn't take long for a student to seriously damage his or her credit record, especially if the parents are unable or unwilling to bail their child out.

It's up to you to teach your child about credit cards and money management, helping him or her to be aware of "teaser" offers and inflated interest rates. Moreover, your child needs to understand the importance of establishing a responsible credit history and learning to set boundaries. Help your child investigate credit card offers. A few companies offer a no-late-fee card with relatively low interest rates. A couple of companies even offer a no-interest card if the student does not exceed the borrowing limit. *Never* cosign a credit card application with your child unless you are willing to pay off the balance. Credit card companies are not required to reveal what purchases are made on the card, but you will be liable to pay off all charges that your child is unable to handle.

Fraternities, Sororities, and Social Clubs

Your son Colin told you during holiday break that he wanted to go through rush and join a fraternity when he returns for his second semester at school. You've heard that fraternities are expensive and you wonder what the additional costs will be.

What's on your mind?
Why does he have to join a fraternity? He seems to party enough already. What is this going to cost?

What's going on.

Fraternities, sororities, and other social clubs can be a good way for your child to feel part of campus social life and to form a close group of friends during his college years. The costs of joining such organizations can vary dramatically from negligible to significant.

What's on your child's mind?
I want to join a fraternity. All my friends are going to rush next semester.

What to do.	What to avoid.
• Have Colin give you all of the details about joining the fraternity, including social dues and fees. • If he plans to live in a fraternity house, ask him to find out what room and board will cost. • Ask him to figure out how he will cover the costs if they are greater than living in the dorm or in an apartment.	• Assuming that fraternities are expensive and that you'll have to come up with more money for him to join. • Telling him that he can't join before you know the facts and have discussed them with him.

What you need to know.

Social life varies from campus to campus. At some colleges, fraternities and sororities provide a major part of the social life, while at others these social organizations play a relatively small role in the overall social life on campus. Just as these organizations vary from campus to campus, the costs of joining can be vastly different as well. It's important to get the information you need to help your child make this decision based on real costs. If your son decides to live in a fraternity house, it may actually cost less than living in a college dormitory or in an apartment. The social dues and fees are usually the costliest parts of joining a fraternity or sorority. Fraternities, however, tend to throw more parties and, therefore, their social dues are usually higher than those of a sorority. If your child was a high-maintenance person socially in high school, this trend will probably continue when he or she goes to college.

What's on your mind?

Why can't she just come home and work as a waitress?
How do we know she'll be able to save the money she needs for next year?

Working Away from Home for the Summer

Your daughter Cindy is finishing up her sophomore year and wants to go to Maine to work in a restaurant for the summer. She has friends who did this last summer, and they earned a substantial amount of money. She plans to go to Maine this summer with two of her sorority sisters who worked there last summer.

What's going on.

Many college students learn a great deal from living on their own for a summer. If they are willing to work hard, they can also earn as much or more money than they might living at home and working.

What to do.	What to avoid.
• Ask Cindy to do some research on what other students have earned. • Let her know if you expect her to contribute the same amount to her college costs next year. • Ask her to do an estimate of her living costs away from home and discuss them with you before she makes a decision.	• Insisting that she come home and work at the local restaurant again. • Deciding she shouldn't do this before you find out what's involved.

What you need to know.

Waitressing is one of the few high-paying jobs that students can do during the summer to earn money for their college expenses. The key is finding the right position and often that information is passed word of mouth from student to student. If your daughter can find a good waitressing job, it's likely that she can earn enough money to pay for her living costs and save ample money to pay for her expenses the next year at school.

It's important, however, that she makes realistic plans for this experience and has written assurance that a full-time job is awaiting her. She should ask her potential employer about what she can reasonably expect to earn and talk to other students who have worked there, if possible. Then she needs to arrange affordable living quarters, in order to meet her saving goals for the summer. She needs to be aware of the temptation to spend too much of her earnings on social activities while she is away for the summer.

The Unpaid Summer Internship

Your daughter Abigail calls home excited about applying for a summer internship:

What's on your mind?

I can't believe these businesses hire students for the summer and don't pay them anything.

I wonder if it's true that there aren't any paying internships in advertising.

This summer experience could cost a couple of thousand dollars.

What's on your child's mind?

I really want to apply for this internship.

It would be so cool to live in Chicago and work in an ad agency for the summer.

I hope my parents will let me do it. It shouldn't cost that much if we can get a cheap sublet.

ABIGAIL: Hi, Dad. I have some great news. I just found out about an awesome internship at an ad agency in Chicago, and I was wondering if it's okay with you and Mom if I apply for it. It sounds so cool. It's one of the best agencies in the whole country.

DAD: That sounds interesting, Abby, but where would you live for the summer?

ABIGAIL: One of my friends is going to work in Chicago too. We thought we could get a place together. I heard that you can sometimes sublet an apartment from another student for the summer.

DAD: Sounds like it might be an expensive summer. How much does the internship pay?

ABIGAIL: Well, that's the bad news, Dad. It's unpaid.

DAD: What? You're going to work for someone all summer and not get paid anything?

ABIGAIL: Dad, there aren't any paid internships in advertising. At least there aren't any that I know of. Lots of students want to intern at this agency because it's such good experience, and I've heard that it's impossible to get a job in advertising after graduation if you don't have any experience. I think it's really worth it, don't you?

DAD: Well, it seems like it's going to cost a lot of money. I mean, you'd have to pay rent, buy your food, probably get some professional clothes, and just getting to Chicago and back is going to cost money. And you won't be earning any money to help with the expenses. What are you going to do for spending money next year at school if you don't earn any money this summer?

ABIGAIL: I don't know. Maybe I could get a higher paying job on campus next year. I just want to apply for this internship so much.

What's going on.

Internships and career-related summer jobs can give students the opportunity to test their interest in a particular field, but students need to research the financial feasibility of these options. If Abigail has a serious interest in advertising as a career, it may be wise for her to try for this internship. If, however, you feel that she's only interested in spending the summer in Chicago, you may want to encourage her to try an advertising internship closer to home for the summer and suggest that she plan for an internship away from home another summer.

What to do.	What to avoid.
• Ask Abigail to provide you with more information about this opportunity and a budget for what it will cost, including the loss of her regular summer job earnings. • Help her brainstorm ideas for getting work experience at home. • Discuss what you are willing to support in the way of an unpaid internship experience.	• Dismissing the idea of an internship without getting all of the details. • Telling her there is no way she can spend a summer without getting paid.

What you need to know.

It can be especially difficult for liberal arts or fine arts students to find summer jobs or internships that relate to their career interests. It's ironic that engineering or business majors, for example, are sought for the well-paying internships while liberal arts students, who also need "real world" work experience, often are unable to find paying internships.

But there are ways that your child can manage an unpaid internship. It's possible to get an inexpensive sublet in Chicago, room with friends, or stay in another university's residence hall. Your child could find a second job and earn some money while doing the unpaid internship. Or your child could arrange an internship in a similar organization at home, save the cost of living away for the summer, and work an extra job to earn money for the next school year.

If your child qualifies for federal work-study funds, it may be possible for him or her to be paid through the summer as well. Many employers who are unable to offer paid summer jobs will consider taking on a work-study student because they will only have to pay a small portion of that student's summer salary. Have your child check with the Financial Aid Office early in the year to see if such an arrangement is possible.

This internship, while unpaid, may be the best choice because it offers a chance to explore a career field and acquire some job experience. Most employers now expect students to have career-related experience on their résumés when they seek an entry-level job after graduation. And in some fields, paid internships are simply not available. You need to discuss the options with your child and remember that an internship experience may be a worthwhile investment in your child's future career prospects.

Students who attend college in a major metropolitan area can often find worthwhile internships during the school year, sometimes requiring only a few hours a week. It may be possible to have an internship and remain on campus in a regular academic program. Students can also gain valuable job-related experiences through volunteer work on campus or in the community during the school year. If your child attends college in a rural area or small town, however, these options may not be available.

What's on your mind?

This sounds pretty exotic.
How much will it cost?
Will her credits transfer?
Will she be safe?

Study Abroad

Your daughter Nicole is in her sophomore year of college. She wants to spend next year in France with her college's junior year abroad program. She's just chosen French as her major and feels that a year in France, being exposed to native speakers, will improve her language skills.

What's going on.

Overseas study by American students is on the rise. Each year more than one hundred thousand students receive credit for studying in a foreign country. Many colleges and universities have their own study abroad programs or help students take advantage of the hundreds of programs offered by other institutions. In fact, study abroad is seen as such a positive experience that some colleges offer attractive financial incentives for their students to spend time in another country during their college years.

What's on your child's mind?

It would be so amazing to spend a year in Paris. I could travel all over Europe. I can try out my French and I'll meet so many interesting people.

What to do.

- Ask your child to provide you with detailed information on the program she's considering.
- Talk to her about the advantages and disadvantages of living and studying abroad.
- Find out how the costs abroad compare with the cost of remaining on campus for the year.
- Read all of the literature about the study abroad program.

What to avoid.

- Resisting the idea without knowing all of the facts.
- Assuming that this is going to cost much more than studying in the States for the year.

What you need to know.

Studying abroad can cost the same as—or even less than—studying in the States. Make a concerted effort to gather all of the information available and discuss the possibilities with your daughter. Be a wise consumer of these offers and make sure that credits will transfer, adequate housing is available, relative safety is assured, and the costs are manageable for your budget.

Some schools offer short-term study/travel abroad, but, again, investigate the offers and ensure that they are appropriate for your child. Many students experiment with an abbreviated travel program abroad to decide if they really want to study abroad for a whole semester or year. At the end of this chapter, we have listed some of the many excellent reference books available on study abroad programs.

A Car on Campus—Luxury or Necessity?

Your son Max insists that he needs a car on campus next year:

MAX: Dad, I really need a car next year at school.
DAD: Why?
MAX: I'm going to be student teaching next semester and the school where I'll be teaching is a long way from campus.
DAD: How far?
MAX: A few miles at least.
DAD: Can't you ride your bike? Or get a placement nearer to campus?
MAX: No, this is the only school where my professor could place me. And I have to dress up and look professional. I can't be riding my bike to school through the rain and stuff. How would that look?
DAD: We just can't afford to get you a car right now, Max, and your mother and I need our cars to get to work. Isn't there any public transportation? I thought there was a bus system there.
MAX: There is, but they don't come often and I'd waste a lot of time waiting around for one to come. I have to study too, you know.
DAD: How many weeks do you have to student teach?
MAX: I think about ten.
DAD: Well, maybe your brother would lend you his car to take to school for those ten weeks. You know he's worked

---

What's on your mind?

I don't think Max really needs a car on campus.

We can't afford to buy him a car.

We can probably work out something if it's only for ten weeks.

What's on your child's mind?

I don't see why I can't have a car.

It would be so much easier if I had a car on campus.

All of my friends have cars.

hard at his after-school job to get his car, but he might be willing to let you borrow it, if it's only for part of the semester. It's kind of an old jalopy, but it should be able to get you back and forth.

MAX: What's Brad going to do?

DAD: He could take the school bus for a while, I guess. Why don't you ask him? Maybe he'll make a deal with you if you get it tuned up and serviced for him.

What's going on.

While it's true that many students have cars on campuses today, usually it is not a necessity but a luxury and a convenience. Rarely do students need a car on campus to fulfill course requirements, but there are extraordinary situations, such as Brad's, when a car may be needed for a period of time. Students may find life easier if they have a car, especially if they live off-campus and there are no grocery stores nearby. Many students, however, want cars for social or recreational reasons; few really need a car while in college.

What to do.	What to avoid.
• Find out if your child really needs a car and why he or she needs it. • Ask your child to come up with alternatives if a car isn't possible. • Explore the advantages and disadvantages of having a car on campus. For example, most colleges charge a lot for parking, in part to discourage students from bringing cars to school. • Remind your child of the responsibilities that accompany having a car and the additional costs involved.	• Saying no before you find out the specifics. You child *may* actually need a car for a legitimate reason. • Being pressured into buying your child a car before you know the situation.

What you need to know.

A college student rarely needs to have a car on campus in order to fulfill his or her academic requirements. There may be exceptions, however, and you may need to make a car available to your child for a specific purpose and for a limited time.

If you are in favor of your child having a car on campus, make sure that he or she knows what this responsibility involves. Cars need servicing and care; your child needs to know how to handle car emergencies. Students don't automatically know that cars need periodic oil checks and fluid replacements, for example. Be prepared for parking and other expenses if your child has a car on campus.

Change in Family Income

What's on your mind?
What if I can't find a job? I can't see how I'm going to support Tom in school. This layoff couldn't have come at a worse time. I should have saved more money.

You have just been informed that your job will be eliminated in six months due to your company's downsizing program. Your son is in his junior year of college and you feel awful after telling him the bad news.

What's going on.

What's on your child's mind?
What if I can't finish school? How are we going to survive?

Many families face this problem every year as companies downsize and lay off workers. In addition to worrying about basic financial survival, parents have to consider interrupting their child's education. This is a very difficult situation for parents, as their first reaction may be to shield their child from upsetting news.

<table>
What to do.	What to avoid.
• Tell your child as soon as you know that you will be losing your job. • Try to stay calm and confident about coping with this crisis. • Let your child know what you are doing to find other employment. • Get in touch with your child's financial aid counselor and explain the situation.	• Immediately announcing that your child will have to quit college. • Blaming yourself for not being able to support your family. • Accepting the fact that you'll be unemployed.
</table>

What you need to know.

While you may feel anxious about giving your child unpleasant news, it is almost always preferable to keep your child informed about what's going on at home. You need to address your own anxieties about the situation first and then prepare to explain the circumstances to your child. It's easy for parents to overreact and even to go to extreme measures to shield their children from worry. In our experience, however, students who feel included in family decisions and events, even when they are not living at home for most of the year, are able to adjust to changes more successfully. These situations offer opportunities to mentor your child, treating him or her as an adult. You must take the lead in devising solutions and alternatives, but your child should be kept informed.

Circumstances change for many families when they have children in college. Because colleges realize that no one has a completely secure job, they are prepared to renegotiate financial aid packages when a family's ability to contribute to their child's education changes dramatically. They may ask students to take on additional loans, work at campus jobs, or even take a semester or a year off to earn money to help pay for college. Whether parents are paying the full cost themselves or helping their child put together a financial aid package that includes grants, loans, and summer earnings, the cost of college can burden most families—especially when a family's major wage earner loses a job.

The Value of a College Education

Living a Life *and* Earning a Living

What's on your mind?

Will he be able to support himself?

If he accepted a job in the computer science field, his future would be secure.

What's on your child's mind?

I'm really excited about being able to work in the theater. Now I can see how useful my computer skills will be.

Your son James went off to college with the intention of becoming a computer science major. You were pleased that he had chosen a major that would provide him with a good job upon graduation, even though his first love had always been the theater. In his sophomore year of college, he found an internship with a local theater company updating their reservations system on the computer. He also helped design the computerized lighting for a couple of productions. He sees now that he can combine his computer science knowledge with his love of the theater and is thinking of looking for a job with a theater company when he graduates. You're not so sure about theater as a career path.

What's going on.

Students who have the benefit of work experience in college often modify their educational goals as they begin to see how they can apply their skills in the workplace. This does appear to be the best of both worlds. James will continue his computer science education and add theater courses so that he'll be able to work in a field that interests him.

What to do.

- Encourage your child to explore internships or summer jobs in the theater to obtain more experience.
- Remember that computer science is a good background regardless of whether the theater job works out.
- Let go of your expectations—it's James' life and he has a right to follow his heart as well as his head.

What to avoid.

- Trying to convince James that a job with a computer company would be much more stable and lucrative.
- Discounting his interest in working in the theater as a passing fancy.
- Expressing your disappointment in his choices for his future.

What you need to know.

While it is true that computer science, engineering, economics, and math majors can expect to earn among the highest starting salaries of college graduates, these fields also contain low earners. No specific college major is a guarantee of financial success, according to a study by the U.S. Department of Labor.[3] The key determiner of success in any field is the individual's motivation to succeed. You'll find more about academic majors and career expectations in the next chapter.

Majoring in Underemployment

You're upset by the following conversation with your daughter Paige, who is currently a business major at the state university:

PAIGE: Mom, I've been thinking about changing my major.
MOM: Really? To what?
PAIGE: To fine arts.
MOM: Fine arts? You're kidding, right?
PAIGE: No, Mom, I'm not. I took this great sculpture course as an elective and I really loved it.
MOM: But I thought you wanted to work in a small business.
PAIGE: Well, I like business, but I love art. I've even been doing some painting again, and I'm so happy when I can be creative.
MOM: I know you love art, honey, but you could paint and be a business major too.
PAIGE: Not really. I checked with the Fine Arts Department and if I want to pursue fine arts, I'll have to change my major and really concentrate on studio courses. You know, painting, sculpture, and drawing. I can even study printmaking and photography if I switch to a fine arts major.
MOM: I just don't understand why you insist on a fine arts career. You can always enjoy painting in your free time.

What's on your mind?

I'm worried that Paige will never be able to support herself.

I'm spending a lot of money for her education, and I want her to have a chance at a good job.

Why can't she see that art is an avocation, not a vocation?

What's on your child's mind?

I love art. I want to be an art major.

I can't see myself as a business person.

PAIGE: But I love art and you always told me that I should do what I love.

MOM: But, Paige, there aren't any jobs for fine arts majors. What will you do when you graduate?

PAIGE: Well, I could work in graphic arts. You know, in advertising or something like that. Or I could work in a gallery or maybe a museum.

MOM: Do you know what people in those jobs earn, if they're lucky enough to get a job in the first place? I can't imagine you could support yourself. Artists live in hovels and have to waitress to pay the rent!

PAIGE: So what would I do with a business major? Work in some boring company analyzing spread sheets! I just want to be an artist. I don't care if I have to struggle for a while.

What's going on.

It's natural for parents to show concern when their child switches from a "secure" major to one that doesn't seem to promise much in the way of career potential. Parents necessarily want to see a payback for the money they have invested in their child's education. They also want to know that their child has a chance at being self-supporting after college.

What to do.	What to avoid.
• Try to be supportive of Paige's love for art.	• Insisting that your daughter remain a business major.
• Encourage her to explore the career possibilities available to fine arts majors.	• Denigrating fine arts as a major.
	• Threatening to cut off support if she changes majors.
• Remember that students who have a passion for their major tend to excel in college and find satisfying work eventually.	

What you need to know.

Regardless of what your child's major is in college, his or her earning potential is far greater than if he or she had just graduated from high school. A college graduate's income, according to the U.S. Department of Commerce,[4] will be double that of his or her peers who only have a high school diploma. While it may take a student longer to find a career niche, your investment in his or her college education, over time, will yield anywhere from an 8 to 22 percent return, depending on his or her earnings. It's hard to imagine a better return on an investment.

The New York Times recently reported that "throughout the economy, the earnings boost from a college degree has risen nearly twice as fast as tuition. In 1980, for example, the typical 25- to 34-year-old male graduate earned 19 percent more than his high-school counterpart; by 1995, the gap had widened to 52 percent. That's an increase of 173 percent at a time when inflation-adjusted tuitions were rising roughly 100 percent."[5]

Parents who have sacrificed to put their child through college must balance their expectations with their child's initial earning potential. Fine arts and liberal arts graduates often go through a floundering period after college and take longer to become comfortably self-supporting. Parents need to keep in mind that the return on their investment in college costs may take several years to materialize if their child chooses a career path that doesn't bring immediate financial rewards. Most students five or ten years out of college are working in careers that do not directly relate to their major. In fact, few work in the career field that they thought interested them in college. Chapter 8 will explore career expectations and academic choices in greater depth.

When faced with high tuition bills, it's easy to forget that there are enormous intrinsic rewards in the pursuit of higher education. The experiences your child has in college—the opportunity to study a field of interest in depth, the chance to interact with students from diverse backgrounds, and the challenge of making decisions and taking responsibility for those decisions—will contribute enormously to his or her ability to live a satisfying life as well as to earn a living.

Want to Know More?

Detweiler, Gerri. *The Ultimate Credit Handbook: How to Double Your Credit, Cut Your Debt and Have a Lifetime of Great Credit.* New York: Plume, 1997.

Hoffa, William. *Study Abroad: A Parent's Guide: For Parents of College and University Students Contemplating a Study Abroad Experience.* Washington, D.C.: NAFSA: Association of International Educators, 1998.

Web sites:

Institute of International Education (www.iiebooks.org)

Peterson's Guides (www.petersons.com)

Financial Aid (www.finaid.org/nasfaa or www.ed.gov)

---

1. "Anxiety over Tuition: A Controversy in Context: A Special Report," *The Chronicle of Higher Education* (30 May 1997): A11–A19.
2. Richard H. Hersh, "Intentions and Perceptions: A National Survey of Public Attitudes Toward Liberal Arts Education," *Change* (March–April 1997): 29, 2, 16–23.
3. "Earnings of College Graduates, 1993," *Monthly Labor Review* (December 1995): 118, 12, 3–18.
4. Statistical Abstract of the United States, 1997, 117th ed. The National Data Book, U.S. Department of Commerce, Economics and Statistics Administration, Bureau of the Census, October 1977.
5. Matthew Miller, "$140,000—and a Bargain," *The New York Times Magazine,* 13 June 1999, 48–49.

Chapter 8

So, YOU Always Wanted to Be a Doctor

Career Expectations, Academic Choices, and the Value of Practical Experience

Doonesbury

BY GARRY TRUDEAU

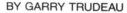

Marisa always wanted to be a doctor and we were thrilled. Some people have a family doctor, but we have a family of doctors! You can imagine how disappointed and confused we were when she told us that she had decided to drop premed and major in French. We never should have agreed to let her study for a semester in Paris. She fell in love—with a language! We're dumbfounded and worried about her future.

Your Expectations and Your Child's Choices

You are spending thousands of dollars for your child's education and his or her future seems uncertain. The job market changes so rapidly, it's hard to follow. None of us can predict the future, and very few careers can offer permanent security.

Even medical doctors, tenured teachers, and computer scientists fall prey to the changes in national and world economic and employment circumstances.

In our culture, careers indicate social status and social class mobility. Many people define themselves by their job, and it's hard not to see your child's career choice as a reflection on you as a parent. You have high expectations that a college education will guarantee your child a personally rewarding and secure future. In a work environment that constantly changes, you may wonder how your child's education will translate into a good job upon graduation and how you can help as your child makes career decisions.

You can do three things:
1. Encourage your child to get practical experience to prepare him or her for a first job.
2. Use your mentoring skills and put your child in touch with other mentors as he or she explores career interests.
3. Be open to learning about career areas and how they relate to college background so that you understand the myths and realities about the world of work.

You don't have to become an expert on every possible job and career field. You don't need to find out if computer software engineers have higher salaries than chemical engineers, or what the five hottest career fields are predicted to be in two years. Even if you had all this information and could choose the ideal career for your child, your child has his or her own ideas. Your child may not be interested in the career fields that you would choose. Your role is to offer support and guidance as your child tries to make sense of the many options.

How Majors Relate to Careers

As students explore the academic offerings of college, they may change majors and career aspirations several times. These scenarios will help you understand the sometimes confusing relationship between college majors and career potential.

Changing from Engineering to Liberal Arts

Your daughter Amanda is a sophomore and it's time for her to declare a major course of study. She went to college wanting to be an engineer and you're proud that she's chosen such a viable career field. You're surprised and troubled by the following conversation you had with her:

Amanda: Hello?

Dad: Hi, Amanda, it's Dad.

Amanda: Oh, hi, Dad, what's up?

Dad: Well, I was just reading *The Wall Street Journal* and came across this article about how well engineers are doing in the business world and it made me think of you. So I thought I'd call and see how you are doing.

Amanda: I'm fine, but to tell you the truth I'm having second thoughts about engineering.

Dad: Second thoughts? But you're a sophomore; you can't change your major now.

Amanda: Well, I'm not sure I can't. You know how much I like psychology courses—and I've had three of them. I met with my psychology professor yesterday and he said I would still have time to finish the major and graduate on time.

Dad: What could you possibly do with psychology? I can't picture you as a therapist.

Amanda: Dad, there are lots of things you can do with psychology besides being a therapist.

Dad: Oh yeah, name one.

Amanda: My professor said lots of his former students have been successful in business jobs. Psychology involves working with data—it's a lot like science, Dad. But the data in psychology is more interesting to me than the data in engineering.

Dad: You can't be serious. Women in engineering are in demand now, honey. I read an article about it in *The New York Times.* Women can move up the corporate ladder really fast. Are you wimping out on me? I know dealing with all that math is tough, but it will be worth it in the end.

What's on your mind?

What is Amanda thinking?
This psychology professor has her brainwashed.
Who cares if psychology is fascinating? You can't support a family by being fascinated—you need practical skills.

What's on your child's mind?

Dad just doesn't understand that you can get a good job without majoring in a professional field.
I just love psychology. It's intriguing.
I'm not wimping out, am I? Psychology is full of hard math and science.

AMANDA: Dad, psychology has lots of math too. It has nothing to do with the math. Besides, my psychology professor says that all the experience you get in quantitative analysis in psychology prepares you for business. They do a lot of number crunching in business. And I think psychology is fascinating—all those things about what motivates people and whether intelligence is inherited or depends on your environment. You would love it, Dad. And I think it would prepare me to be a manager in business. I would understand people and what makes them tick.

DAD: Amanda, if you're going to abandon engineering then why don't you just major in business? At least you'll be able to get a job when you graduate.

AMANDA: The business courses are so boring, Dad. Remember, I took one last semester. I don't think you need to sit through such boring courses to be prepared to go into business. At least that's what my psychology professor says. It's better to major in what fascinates you, and as long as you have good basic skills in critical thinking, analytical reasoning, writing, and quantitative analysis, you'll be fine.

DAD: Your psychology professor sounds like he doesn't know anything about the real world.

AMANDA: But, Dad, I also went to the career center and they said that recruiters look for students who have been in leadership positions in student organizations. They told me that being president of my sorority is giving me experience that I couldn't get just by taking courses. I know I'll be able to get a good job when I graduate.

DAD: Just last week I read in *Newsweek* that the average starting salary of chemical engineers is $45,000 and liberal arts majors were starting at $26,000. That's almost a $20,000 difference. You know, college costs a lot of money; I hope you think long and hard before throwing away $20,000 a year in salary.

What's going on.

Amanda's dad tries to keep up with trends in the job market and accurately noted that engineers have higher average starting salaries than psychology majors. It's also true that businesses value engineers and scientists for their quantitative skills, and women engineers are particularly in demand. Her dad is taking the short-term view: What major will make Amanda the most marketable immediately after graduation? While it's true that the rigor of psychology departments will vary from campus to campus, many departments are staffed by research scientists and provide a solid scientific and quantitative background. Amanda may have identified a department with some of the best faculty and courses on campus.

## What to do.	## What to avoid.
• Encourage your daughter to research what psychology alumni are doing five to ten years out of college, as well as immediately after graduation. Many schools have networks of alumni who are available to talk to students about their careers.	• Making assumptions about an academic field without investigating it. The career center or Psychology Department should be able to tell you what psychology majors at your child's school do after graduation.
• Suggest that she take electives or think about minoring in business.	• Having your daughter believe that she is a failure if she abandons engineering.
• Recommend that she talk to some women faculty and alumni in engineering. If she likes the field, but simply needs a mentor and helpful advisor, she may be able to find one this way.	• Threatening that you will not pay for her education unless she majors in something practical like engineering.
• Be prepared to accept your child's choice of major.	
• Encourage your daughter to gain practical work experience during summer and school vacations.	

What you need to know.

A recent national survey showed that most parents (75 percent) and college-age kids (85 percent) believe that the goal of a college education is to learn practical skills that will help in finding a good job right out of college. This is not an unreasonable goal. The problem occurs in how parents and students define practical skills. They may believe that practical skills are only developed in professional programs that lead to specific jobs in business, computer technology, or engineering. But only 37 percent of business leaders surveyed agreed with this belief. "CEOs say they value the long-term outcomes of a college education—those that prepare one not only for a first job, but for a long and variable career . . . to them practicality means the ability of higher education to produce people of strong character with generalized intellectual and social skills and a capacity for lifelong learning."[1]

What are these generalized skills? They include problem-solving, critical thinking, and "learning to learn," especially the ability to grasp new information quickly and apply it to problems. Employers also value a proficiency in writing and speaking clearly and persuasively in order to help others understand complex ideas and the capacity to work collaboratively with others from diverse backgrounds. Corporate managers believe that these skills are usually best developed through a liberal arts education. Leadership skills gained through extracurricular activities are also highly regarded by potential employers.

What is a liberal arts education? It is the traditional study of the humanities (for example, English and philosophy), the social sciences (psychology and political science), and the natural and physical sciences (biology, chemistry, and physics). These are the precise subject areas that many parents and students identify as impractical in today's job market. But studies of successful professionals in a variety of fields have shown that a liberal arts education allows for more long-term flexibility, while narrower preprofessional study can eliminate future options. Given the explosion in technology in recent years, all graduates should have computer skills. And in an increasingly global economy, foreign language skills are in demand as well.

Flexibility and the desire and capacity to learn can be the keys to success in the long run. In our experience, it usually takes more effort for a liberal arts major to land the first job, but studies of liberal arts graduates, over time, reveal that they move up the organizational ladder faster than graduates who have pursued narrow, preprofessional majors in college.

We want to emphasize that we do not believe that every college student should be a liberal arts major, especially if that child's skills and interests make her better suited for a particular preprofessional major. We believe that everyone is better off if they find a field that is a good match for their interests and abilities. We have focused here on students who change from preprofessional programs to the liberal arts because we have never met a parent who was concerned that his or her child was changing majors from English to computer science!

The Importance of Practical Experience

Your daughter Tina announced over Thanksgiving dinner that she's not sure she wants to attend law school when she graduates, and that she's thinking of changing her major from political science to philosophy.

What's going on.

While not everyone changes majors in college, a significant number of students do. In fact, some students change majors several times and often choose a major based on the quality of the faculty in that department. It can be unsettling for parents when their child shifts to a course of study that seems lacking in career potential or abandons a goal of pursuing a lucrative and prestigious graduate degree. It's natural to worry about your child's future prospects; after all, you have the benefit of a lifetime's experience and knowledge about work and making a living. However, you can support your child's academic exploration during college and help him or her to be more "career ready" when he or she graduates.

> ### What's on your mind?
>
> Is she crazy? Philosophy?
> She's always wanted to be a lawyer, what happened?
> What in the world is she going to do with this degree?

> ### What's on your child's mind?
>
> I love my philosophy courses.
> The faculty in the Philosophy Department are some of the best teachers here.
> Why are my parents so surprised? Everyone I know at school is changing majors.

What to do.	What to avoid.
• Listen to Tina's interests and ask her questions that will help you understand her fascination with the study of philosophy.	• Refusing to accept Tina's change of major. If you insist on controlling her choice of major, she could be less motivated and do poorly.
• Ask her to visit the career center on campus and find out what careers students with philosophy majors have pursued after graduation.	• Believing that she'll never find a good job.
• Talk to her about the career areas that she's interested in.	• Threatening to withdraw support if she changes majors.
• Encourage her to apply for an internship or summer job in one of those areas.	
• Suggest that she network with alumni who studied philosophy and find out what they have done with their degrees.	

What you need to know.

Tina's interest in philosophy will give her marvelous thinking, analytical, and writing skills that will serve her well no matter what career she eventually chooses. These skills are in great demand in a variety of career fields today and will be as important in years to come. It's critical, though, that liberal arts majors have some practical work experience during college in order to be competitive for jobs upon graduation.

Although your child can gain this experience from a summer job or internship, don't overlook field studies that can be done during the academic year. Many colleges have Washington, D.C., semesters in which students participate in seminars and internships for academic credit. These opportunities for practical experience may be called internships, field study, or co-op placements. Graduates tell us that these experiences were the single most useful tool in helping them define their career goals and become more marketable upon graduation. Some colleges offer programs of study and experiential education in another city; others offer study abroad programs that will help your child become fluent in a foreign language and learn to adapt to another culture.

These experiences can help students focus their career goals and be more attractive to employers who seek a demonstrated interest in their career field and an understanding of the world of work, as well as the general writing, speaking, and analytical skills developed through liberal arts study.

Philosophy provides a solid background for law school and other areas of study if Tina decides to go to graduate school later. More important, however, is Tina's enthusiasm about majoring in philosophy—students who love what they study perform significantly better in college than students who are pressured into majoring in a subject they don't enjoy. You may be concerned if your child chooses a major based on the teaching skills of certain professors, but your child will receive a better education from better teachers.

Studies have found that the vast majority of people today change careers an average of six to eight times during their working lives and that most people do not ultimately work in a field directly related to their college major. In fact, a recent U.S. Department of Labor study found that workers hold an average of nine jobs before turning 32. The critical issue is that students major in something that engages them and helps them become an adult who is prepared to continue learning and growing.

Evolving Career Goals

Even students who begin college with clearly defined academic interests and goals often change their focus and decide to pursue a different path. This can be a disconcerting process for students and parents alike. Your mentoring skills will be valuable as you help your child cope with changing goals and aspirations during the college years.

Choosing Teaching Instead of Premed

Your son Bill has always wanted to be a doctor but now, in his second year at the university, he's having second thoughts about medicine:

What's on your mind?

Bill's always wanted to be a doctor.

Where did he get this idea to be a schoolteacher?

How could he not get into medical school?

What's on your child's mind?

I never thought about the fact that I might not get into medical school.

I'm not sure if I want to be a doctor or a teacher.

I just know that I want to help people, and I could do that either way.

These college chemistry courses are just too hard; I don't think I can ever get As in them.

Mom: Hello?

Bill: Hi, Mom it's me, Bill.

Mom: Oh, hi, how are you?

Bill: I'm pretty good. I called because I've been thinking a lot about whether it makes sense for me to stay in this premed program.

Mom: What? You aren't thinking of dropping out of school are you?

Bill: No, I'm not talking about leaving school. I'm just thinking about changing my career goal. You know how I've been having trouble with these premed courses, especially the chemistry.

Mom: Yeah, but you told me you had talked to an advisor in the Minority Students Office, who said that it wasn't unusual for kids to struggle with chemistry. I thought you were getting extra help in the Learning Center with your chemistry. You're still doing that aren't you?

Bill: Yes, I am, and it's helping. My grade has improved. But Bs or Cs are still not good enough to be accepted into medical school. Besides, I started thinking about why I really wanted to be a doctor. It's always been important to me to be able to help people, and I want to be able to come back to Brooklyn and help people in our neighborhood. But I'm really not that interested in being a research scientist.

Mom: Wait a minute. Who said anything about being a research scientist? You've always said you wanted to be a doctor—since you were a little boy. You told me, you told Grandma—you told everyone at church—that you wanted to be a doctor. You don't want to be a doctor anymore?

BILL: It's not so much that I don't want to be a doctor. I'm just not sure. Anyway, my advisor told me that I should have a back-up plan in case I don't get into medical school.

MOM: What's this about not getting into medical school? You were the smartest kid in your high school, weren't you? Who says you might not get into medical school?

BILL: Mom, that was high school. It's different in college. I'm just not sure that I can get high enough grades in chemistry and physics. I could stay a biology major and go into teaching. My advisor says there's a need for good science teachers, especially in neighborhoods like ours. Half the people teaching don't even have degrees in science. I could come back and be like Mr. Williams, my tenth-grade biology teacher. He really inspired me to go on in science.

MOM: What? You're thinking of being a schoolteacher? After all this hard work and sacrifice, you want to be a teacher instead of a doctor?

What's going on.

Bill is working hard, but he can't seem to get better than Cs and Bs in his chemistry courses. It's not unusual for students to struggle with science courses in college. College courses often move at a much faster pace than high school courses, and students are expected to learn and digest large amounts of information. In high school teachers often guided students step-by-step, while in college they expect them to figure out more on their own. This can overwhelm even the best students. At the same time, it's hard to understand why your child isn't the top student he was in high school. If you have little or no experience with college, it's even more difficult to understand why hard work may not result in As.

In small colleges, students can receive individual help and guidance from faculty in science courses, but at large universities, introductory science courses often serve to weed out all but the hardiest and best prepared students. It can be extremely hard to get As. At these large universities support services and learning centers can help students, but some will need this extra support in order to get Bs and Cs. Students who have not been challenged in high school will have to learn new study skills; they will no longer be able to manage on raw ability.

What to do.	What to avoid.
• Try to listen to Bill and find out what he is thinking and feeling.	• Insisting that he has to be a doctor to meet your expectations and not disappoint so many people who are proud of him in your family, church, and community.
• Focus on your son's needs rather than your own desire to have him be a doctor.	
• Express understanding about how hard college chemistry must be and give him credit for getting extra help and working hard.	• Letting him know that you are disturbed that he may become a schoolteacher.
• Encourage him to think carefully about whether he wants to pursue teaching or if he simply feels discouraged about getting into medical school.	• Acting as if medical school is his only option, and he will have failed if he doesn't follow through with his plans.

What you need to know.

Getting accepted into medical school can be a confusing and daunting process. You may have difficulty determining if your child is giving up his dream of medical school because he's losing confidence in his ability to get in, or if he has seriously thought about the alternatives and decided that he is better suited for a career as a teacher. You may wonder how you can help your child as he struggles with this difficult decision.

The most effective role you can play is one of helping your son explore the alternatives and urging him to gather the information he needs to make an informed decision. Bill can obtain a realistic assessment of his chances of getting into medical school by talking to the premed advisor and finding out what kind of grades and scores he needs. Encourage him to explain his goals to the premed advisor and map out a realistic plan, including a fall-back plan in case he does not get accepted into medical school.

We know of many students who fall short of the stringent requirements to get into medical school right out of college but who eventually do get accepted and go on to successful careers as doctors. If it's clear that your son wants to be a doctor, you need to encourage him to take whatever steps he can to strengthen his case for admission. He may need to take a preparation course for the MCAT exam, or take time off between college and medical school to gain some relevant experience to enhance his application. He could work as a research assistant in a medical school laboratory, join the Peace Corps as a healthcare volunteer, or take additional science courses to prove that he can excel in them. Today, increasing numbers of students who want to go to medical school take time after college to do what they can to improve their chances of acceptance to these extremely competitive schools. The average age of entering students at some medical schools today is twenty-five.

If, however, your son persists in wanting to teach, you can encourage him to acquire some experience in a classroom to help him decide if this is the career path for him. Many college students volunteer in local schools for a few hours a week or work in a summer program. He could apply for the Teach for America program, try teaching in a private school, or take the courses necessary to get certified to teach in a public school after graduation. While it's true that few teachers have high salaries, it can be a financially stable and personally rewarding profession. If he decides after a couple of years that he really does want to be a doctor, having worked as a teacher will not hurt his medical school chances; in fact, it will provide support for his interest in helping people.

You can play an important role in helping Bill explore his options, but you need to be prepared to accept his decisions along the way. It can be hard to give up your dreams for your child's career, but you can provide the most help by raising questions, offering guidance, and ultimately supporting the decisions he makes for himself. As difficult as it may be, you need to remember that this is *his* life and these are *his* decisions to make.

In our roles as career counselors, we have had students ask us if they can have their parents call us to talk about why it's a reasonable decision for the student to change plans from medical school to some other field. It may help you to call a staff member at the college to gain a better understanding of your child's situation and options. Don't call the college to take care of your child's business for him or her, but do call if you want to get some of your own questions answered.

You Want Your Child to Be a Doctor or Lawyer

When your daughter Clare is home over spring break, she says that rather than use her neurobiology background to go to medical school, she thinks she wants to apply to clinical psychology programs. She's taken enough psychology courses, she adds, to have a double major in psychology and biology.

What's going on.

You don't know much about professional jobs in America, but you know that medicine and law are respected and financially rewarding professions. Meanwhile, your daughter, who has done quite well academically and could certainly get into medical school, has discovered the field of clinical psychology, which better fits her interests.

What to do.

- Encourage your daughter to learn as much as she can about medicine and clinical psychology.
- Have her spend a day or two with her cousin, who's a doctor, and find out what he does on the job.
- Suggest that she contact people in clinical psychology who can help her explore the field.

What to avoid.

- Ruling out all fields except medicine and law.
- Giving your daughter an ultimatum: She goes to medical school or you won't pay for her education.
- Putting your daughter in the position of having to choose between your love and support and a career that interests her.

What you need to know.

Clinical psychology is a prestigious field that allows students to pursue many career options. They can become private therapists, university professors, scientific researchers, or work in hospitals, clinics, and mental health agencies, or in a variety of private business concerns. It can be quite difficult to get into graduate programs in clinical psychology because each program takes a very small number of applicants; it is often harder than getting accepted to medical school.

If you force your daughter to choose between the only two professional fields that you know anything about, chances are she won't be happy. Given the choice of a daughter who is a successful clinical psychologist or an unsuccessful doctor—or even worse, one who can't face her parents or other relatives if she isn't a successful doctor—we hope you would support her decision to become a psychologist. You may have difficulty accepting your child's change in career choice, especially if you have sacrificed a great deal and had one specific dream for your child, but you must remember that this is your child's decision, not yours, to make.

The Value of Internships

Internships and career-related job experiences make classroom learning more meaningful and eventually help your child make the transition from college to the world of work. Students who have the opportunity to test their skills in a real-world setting have a distinct advantage when they graduate and begin their first job search.

Internships Can Help Focus Career Goals

Your son Jeremy, a sociology major, always thought that he would be a social worker someday. He took a course in urban issues and found out about a summer internship working at a nonprofit community housing agency. Because they couldn't pay him much, the agency agreed to work with his school so that he would receive academic credit for his summer's work.

At the end of the summer, he had an entirely different view of his career prospects and began thinking about a career in nonprofit administration. The agency director expressed interest in interviewing him for a permanent position when he graduates.

> ### What's on your mind?
> This summer internship really changed Jeremy's perspective.
> He seems so confident about his future now.
> I guess a sociology major is good for a number of different jobs.

What's on your child's mind?

I thought that sociology majors usually became social workers or teachers.

I found out that I can do many different things with my academic background.

I really enjoyed working at Neighborhood Housing Services. I can see the impact that this organization has on people's lives.

What's going on.

Many students find an internship or summer job a great opportunity to learn about a little-known career area. Jeremy had the opportunity to meet with many different kinds of professionals, from architects and planners to real estate brokers and lawyers, as well as community activists. He worked on a report to the mayor, and his sponsor recognized that he had strong writing skills. He did some preliminary analysis using a spread sheet, interviewed clients, and gave part of a major presentation to the city's board of zoning appeals. He discovered how useful his writing, research, and presentation skills were in a professional setting. Through this experience, Jeremy was able to refine his career goals, expose himself to a whole new field, and add valuable practical experience to his résumé.

What to do.

- Reinforce how useful his academic work will be in a workplace.
- Congratulate him on doing so well that he may be offered a permanent position.
- Encourage him to explore other nonprofit jobs by visiting his Career Center and contacting alumni who work in this field.

What to avoid.

- Asking him why he's not interested in social work anymore.
- Dampening his enthusiasm for working in a nonprofit job.
- Assuming that his sociology degree is now "wasted."

What you need to know.

Students with internships or summer jobs in small organizations often have an excellent experience and use a variety of skills. Many small agencies are sparsely staffed and need students who can take on major responsibilities and make a significant contribution to their organizations.

The difference between a summer job and an internship can confuse parents. Usually an internship implies that the organization will structure the work experience to ensure that learning takes place, especially if they cooperate with the college to offer course credit. Internships for course credit need the support of a professor who will supervise and evaluate the student's experience on the job. Some schools have rather formal relationships with internship sponsors and others handle these requests on a student-by-student basis.

While some summer jobs and internships offer significant learning experiences for student employees, others simply expect students to handle routine work and make little effort to see that the job or internship offers the student valuable training or instruction in the field. Students often have to take the initiative by presenting their internship sponsor with written learning goals and requesting weekly meetings to assess their progress.

Some employers insist that students receive academic credit for their internships or summer jobs for liability reasons. A student who receives credit for work is considered primarily a student and not eligible for the organization's worker's compensation insurance if he or she should be injured on the job. If an employer pays a student, the organization has to accept liability for that student, just as they do with their other employees.

In some cases, your child will have to be assertive in convincing his or her department to agree to sponsor an internship for college credit. Your child will also have to invest a certain amount of time in planning, applying, and making sure all parties agree to this arrangement. Some colleges refuse to give course credit for internships, and the students may be forced to do the internship as an unpaid volunteer. Even if this is the case, an internship can be enormously valuable in acquiring practical skills and making contacts for future employment. Internships are usually well worth the time and energy required and can make a significant difference in how employable a student is upon graduation. Most employers today expect a certain degree of work experience on a graduating student's résumé and, in some fields, that requires a commitment of extra time, energy, and resources during the college years.

Employers often hire student workers in order to assess their performance on the job so that they can recruit these students for permanent positions later. This summer experience can provide a major advantage for a liberal arts student who may otherwise have found his or her job search at graduation a confusing and frustrating experience.

Job Security

What parent hasn't worried about whether their child will be self-supporting after college? Parents who have lived through years of job market ups and downs may be particularly concerned about their child's prospects for future job security.

The Aspiring Actress—Parent to Parent

The other night you had the following phone conversation with your sister:

> **What's on Stacy's mind?**
>
> Are we nuts to let Natasha go to New York?
> What if this whole experience is terrible for her?
> Why couldn't she be interested in something more stable?
> Marjorie and everyone else must think we're too indulgent with Natasha.

STACY: Hi, Marjorie, how are you doing?

MARJORIE: Great. Jed just got his acceptance letter from MIT. We're all so excited. We're going out to dinner tomorrow night to celebrate. Now if we can just afford to pay for it!

STACY: That's great! You must be so proud of him.

MARJORIE: We sure are. He worked really hard for this and he's definitely ready for college. How's Natasha doing?

STACY: Well, she's almost done. We're going down for graduation in late May. As to what happens next, we're kind of clueless, to tell you the truth.

MARJORIE: What do you mean? Does she have any job prospects?

STACY: Are you kidding? She's a theater major, remember?

MARJORIE: Yeah, well, I guess that's kind of hard, huh?

STACY: Hard? It almost seems impossible! She's had lots of roles in college, but who knows if she'll ever get a paying acting job.

MARJORIE: What's she going to do?

STACY: Well, she wants to go directly to New York and give it a try. To tell you the truth, I'm really scared. It's not only living in New York City, but what if she doesn't find anything? She's so eager and committed to being an actress. I worry about her being disappointed. It's such a hard field to break into.

MARJORIE: I can imagine. I'm so glad my kids wanted to be business and engineering majors. At least I don't have to worry about them getting jobs after college.

STACY: Yeah, they probably won't be working in a restaurant waiting for that big break. It's just that Natasha has always dreamed of being an actress since she was a little girl and she's worked so hard at learning her craft. I guess Bill and I are going to have to help support her until she gets on her feet, and New York is so expensive. We've told her that we'll help her for a year and talk about what the prospects are then. Sometimes I wish she had been more like me, content to be a teacher or something more predictable. Maybe they switched her in the nursery at the hospital! She's so different. Everyone else in the family has such practical careers. You know, Mac's in computers and Taylor is in sales. They both had great jobs right out of college.

MARJORIE: Well, you know, you could just tell her that she has to be more realistic and get a regular job. I mean, acting is such a shot in the dark.

STACY: I know, but I can't bear to tell her that she can't follow her dreams.

MARJORIE: I know, it's hard. It sounds like you've accepted the fact that she's going to need a lot of support. But what if she hasn't made it in a year?

STACY: I don't know. We'll just have to see what happens. At least she'll know she gave it a chance. To tell you the truth, right now I'm more worried about her being safe in New York. Sometimes she's so naive and trusting.

MARJORIE: I don't blame you. I don't know if I'd be so understanding if one of my kids wanted to go to New York and become an actress.

> ### What's on Marjorie's mind?
>
> Stacy and Bill really have their hands full with Natasha, and it looks like they will for a while.
>
> I'm sure glad my kids didn't want to study something so impractical.
>
> I don't understand why they can't just say no to Natasha. They've put her through college. That should be enough. She needs a little dose of reality, I think.

What's going on.

It can be difficult for parents when their child decides to follow a career path that seems impractical or foreign to them. Naturally, you worry about your child's prospects when a career field such as theater or acting is the only thing he or she is interested in pursuing. But you can also take pride in your child's ambition to tackle a difficult career field. Allowing your son or daughter to follow his or her dreams may be a great leap of faith for you, but it is also a great gift to your child. It won't be easy for you or for your child, but you can support him or her in this effort while setting clear guidelines for what you are willing and able to do to help your child succeed.

It may take several years for your child to become self-supporting, and a career in the theater may never offer the kind of security that you would hope for, but it's important to remember that no career choice is absolutely secure forever. You need to set aside your fears and recognize that your child may never aspire to the kind of job security that you value, that he or she may be comfortable living a life of constant change and considerable sacrifice to follow a dream.

What to do.	What to avoid.
• Make it clear to Natasha what you can feasibly do and how long you can support her efforts to become an actress.	• Standing in the way of her trying to make a career for herself in acting.
• Ask her to think about fall-back plans if she isn't able to support herself as an actress.	• Reminding her constantly of how difficult the choice will be.
• Encourage her, while pointing out how difficult this may be at times.	• Refusing to support her efforts even if you are able to do so.
• Let her know that you are proud of her determination to undertake a tough career path.	• Letting her know that this is a fantasy that you hope she'll outgrow soon.
• Educate yourself on the realities of a career in acting; for example, find out about the role of an agent in an aspiring actress' life and read about the theater as a career.	

What you need to know.

While a career in the theater is a long shot for most people, many actually do make a living acting and find their work satisfying and rewarding. Even though it may seem that everyone you know has children who aspire to more practical careers, your child is determined to be an actor or actress. Who's to say that he or she will be less successful and happy than your friends' children, who become computer programmers and may lose their jobs or become disillusioned in their forties?

While it's hard to accept a child's unusual career choice, it's helpful to remember that a degree in theater (if it includes a liberal arts component) can prepare him or her for many careers. Natasha has been educated for more than simply a job as an actress, but her passion to work in the theater is worthy of your support. You will have helped her to follow her dreams and that gift will have a long-lasting impact on her life.

You must, however, be clear with her about how far you will support your child in trying for a career in acting. You can be realistic about the uncertainties of this field without refusing to help or dampening your child's spirit and youthful enthusiasm.

What *Is* Job Security Today—Parent to Parent

A conversation you had today with a colleague at work left you wondering if your son's college major will result in a good job offer when he graduates:

PETE: Hey, Joe, how's it going?

JOE: Pretty good, Pete. I had a talk with my son Jay last night. He's trying to decide if he should get a graduate degree right away.

PETE: What's he majoring in?

JOE: Well, he's in engineering, but some of his advisors have told him that his starting salary will be at least ten thousand dollars more with a master's degree.

PETE: Hey, let me tell you about my nephew. He started college as a chemical engineering major and by the time he graduated four years later, the market for chemical engineers had dried up. He's working in sales for an Internet company. He's not using his chemistry background at all. Who knows what kids should study today? Everything changes so quickly.

JOE: Yeah, I know what you mean. I thought an undergraduate degree in engineering would be golden for Jay. He just finished that co-op job with Intel, and he thinks

> ### What's on Joe's mind?
>
> I read about the future of jobs in the papers and magazines, but it's still pretty confusing.
>
> How can I know what's best for Jay?
>
> Things are changing so fast. It's hard to feel this insecure at my age.

What's on your child's mind?

That additional ten thousand dollars a year in starting salary sounds pretty good.

I'm really sick of school, but maybe I should just go ahead and do the grad school thing now.

It may be hard to come back to school once I'm out and earning money.

they're going to offer him a permanent job. But now his professors are telling him he should pursue a graduate degree. Will the tuition payments ever end?

PETE: Not in our lifetime! Boy, it's tough to know what to do, isn't it? Look at you and me? Working in a company that's constantly threatening to downsize. I've been with this outfit since I graduated from college twenty-five years ago. You've been here almost as long. What kind of job security did that get us? We may be out of a job any day now, and we thought we'd signed on until retirement.

JOE: I know. It's really hard to know what is secure anymore. Jay doesn't really want to go to graduate school, but maybe he should while I still have a job myself and can help him out. Maybe he'll be able to support me then!

What's going on.

It gets harder and harder to predict which career fields will be seeking new hires, even in the foreseeable future. Many of us graduated from college in a relatively stable employment market and find it hard to counsel our children about their future career prospects. The work world that we've experienced differs drastically from the one our kids will enter when they graduate from college.

What to do.	What to avoid.
• Listen to your son's concerns about going directly on to graduate school. • Ask if he's excited about further study or simply doing it to get it over with. • Suggest that he get the names of alumni in the field from his college or Career Office and ask those professionals for advice.	• Telling him he'd better get the graduate degree now or you probably won't be able to help him. • Focusing on the higher starting salary and trying to influence him based on that alone.

What you need to know.

While it's true that a master's degree in engineering may bring a significantly higher starting salary for your son, if he takes a job with a large enough company after his bachelor's degree, the company may pay for him to get the graduate degree. Your son may be swayed by the larger salary, but he doesn't seem very enthusiastic about continuing on to graduate school right away. This is a tough decision and one that doesn't necessarily bring with it any guarantee of future success or job security. If you have experienced corporate downsizing and job insecurity, it's hard to know what to believe and how to advise your child.

If your son sounds hesitant about going directly to graduate school, listen to him carefully. He may be "burned out" by having been in school continuously for so many years, and he may need a change. Moreover, he may discover, after a couple of years in a job, that he's really interested in an entirely different field of engineering and may want to go to graduate school in that area.

Chapter 11 explores how you can assist your child in making informed decisions about life after college and whether graduate school or full-time employment is the best choice after graduation.

Want to Know More?

Harris, Marcia B., and Sharon L. Jones. *The Parent's Crash Course in Career Planning.* Lincolnwood (Chicago), IL: VGM Career Horizons, a division of NTC Publishing Group, 1996.

Phifer, Paul. *College Majors and Careers.* Garrett Park, MD: Garrett Park Press, 1993.

Figler, Howard. *Liberal Education and Careers Today.* Garrett Park, MD: Garrett Park Press, 1989.

———. *The Internship Bible.* New York, NY: Random House, 1995.

---

1 Richard H. Hersh, "Intentions and Perceptions: A National Survey of Public Attitudes Toward Liberal Arts Education," *Change* (March–April 1997): 2, 2, 7.

Chapter 9

When to Worry, When to Act

*Dealing with Problems and Crises
and Knowing the Difference*

Doonesbury

BY GARRY TRUDEAU

> *When Hannah called from college last night, she was crying and unable to tell me what was the matter. She sounded so miserable and unhappy. I didn't know what to do, and she was so vague about what was bothering her. I'm scared that she's really in trouble and can't tell me what it is. I wonder if I should get in the car and go see for myself. It's so hard to tell what's going on over the phone.*

How Can You Know What's Going On?

There is nothing more frightening than the feeling that your child is in trouble, especially when that child is away from home and you're not sure what's going on. As we've said before, college students tend to unload their worries on parents and then they feel better and go on about their lives. How can you tell from afar when there *is* a serious problem?

Whether your child is going through a normal developmental struggle, dealing with a serious problem, or in the midst of a dangerous crisis, you need to know how to identify, distinguish among, and respond to these situations. It is important to recognize when you are being used as a sounding board for normal confusion and unhappiness and when problems are serious and need outside intervention. You also need to know the resources available on most campuses to assist with problems and crises. This chapter will help you evaluate your child's situation and offer strategies for dealing with typical problems or crises.

Normal Developmental Struggles

Most students go through personal struggles during the college years. These struggles, while troubling to you and your child, rarely call for more than understanding and a sympathetic ear. Relationship issues and managing routine stress can consume a great deal of your child's energy and cause you to worry. It's important to recognize, however, that struggles like these are a natural part of your child's development. The following situations illustrate how you can use your mentoring skills to guide and support your child during difficult times.

Breaking Up

Your daughter Vicki has called you every night for the past two weeks. She sounds so listless and unhappy since she broke up with her boyfriend of three years. You suspect that she's spending most of her time alone in her room, skipping classes and meals. Now you're beginning to lose sleep worrying about her.

What's going on.

The breakup of a long-term relationship is a big deal for most college students. It's not unusual for Vicki to call home for support and comfort. Vicki probably needs to unload her feelings and be reassured that you love her. These situations are

> **What's on your mind?**
>
> I'm really worried about Vicki. She sounds so unhappy. What can I do to help her?

> **What's on your child's mind?**
>
> I'm so depressed. I miss David so much. I don't feel like doing anything.

usually hard on parents because they feel helpless. How can you tell from afar if this problem will resolve itself over time or if your daughter is seriously depressed? It is appropriate to be concerned about a child who calls home every night from college, but she may simply need reassurance and care from you for a relatively short time until she can get past this period of sadness. It's difficult for you, too, because you can't see her, give her a hug, and reassure yourself that she's basically okay.

What to do.	What to avoid.
• Listen, listen, and then listen some more. • Let Vicki express her feelings of sadness. • Reinforce how much you care about her. • Tell her how sorry you are that she feels so sad.	• Minimizing her sadness now by telling her she'll get over David in time. • Telling her that you expect her to deal with this and tend to her studies. • Taking it on as your problem too. • Trying to "fix it" for her, offering *your* solutions.

What you need to know.

It is a major task of late adolescence to form and commit to intimate relationships. Friends and relationships are critical to college students; in fact, when most people are asked what meant the most to them in college, they mention friends immediately. When these relationships end, your child may be temporarily devastated. Your job is to listen and attend to the feelings of loss and sadness that your child expresses. Hopefully, your child will also have close friends at school with whom he or she can share feelings. While painful and difficult to experience, most relationship breakups in college are not of a crisis nature. That doesn't mean they are not significant events and important to your child; it simply means that you probably don't have to worry about serious consequences and that your role is to support your child and listen. If your child persists in sleeping most of the time and not attending classes for more than a week or so, you may want to suggest that he or she get some counseling.

Stress

Every time you speak with your daughter Teri she's in a near panic about something going on at school. Your conversations never last long because she's always in a rush to get somewhere or complete something on time. She always exclaims that she's so stressed out.

What's going on.

Many bright and capable students who seemed to breeze through life in high school find the competitiveness and adjustment challenges of college difficult to negotiate. Perhaps because of their motivation, they take on the pressures and stresses of a highly competitive environment even more than less achievement-oriented young people. Moreover, many students don't realize how much they relied on the comfort and security of home and being around people who cared about them on a daily basis. All of these factors add to the already stressful change of being at college and away from home.

A recent national survey of college freshmen found that women are five times as likely to be anxious and stressed out as men, reporting that they frequently felt "overwhelmed by all I have to do." The survey found that "male students spent considerably more time exercising, partying, watching TV and playing video games . . . meanwhile, young women are taking on more and more responsibilities and feel stressed by all they have to do."[1]

What's on your mind?

Is it normal for her to be in such a frenzied state all the time?

She seems pretty overwhelmed by her responsibilities.

I wonder if this college is too much pressure for her.

What's on your child's mind?

I never have enough time to complete my work.

I can't remember the last time I relaxed and had fun.

If I don't keep up, I'll fail my courses and never get into graduate school.

My friends have started calling me a "stress case." I never have time to go out with them.

What to do.	What to avoid.
• Try to remain calm. Don't absorb Teri's stress and anxiety. • Empathize with how hard college life can be. • Remind her that you love her and that you don't expect her to be perfect. • Ask if she's thought of any ways she could make her life more manageable. Mention things that you do to relieve stress. • Suggest that she may want to look into taking a class in stress management or talk to someone who understands the pressure she's under.	• Feeling rejected because Teri never has time to talk with you. • Telling her she's always making mountains out of molehills. • Reminding her that she's not the only one who has a lot to do. • Assuming that she's this way all of the time.

What you need to know.

Feeling stressed out and tense is a natural response to trying to manage the many demands of college life. There are papers to write, classes to attend, reading and lab assignments to complete, tests to prepare for, roommate conflicts to resolve, friendships to develop and maintain, dating pressures, worries about doing well in school, anxieties about the future, in addition to managing all the daily physical needs—feeding yourself, doing the laundry, getting enough sleep, and getting up and showered in time for class.

A certain amount of stress is unavoidable and usually manageable, but when stress becomes excessive, it can lead to great anxiety and actually make you physically sick. If your child is under too much stress, you may see the following signs:

• He or she is always late and rushes to accomplish daily activities.
• He or she is moody and irritable a lot of the time.
• He or she can't avoid striving for perfection in everything.
• He or she can't sleep well and almost never relaxes for any period of time.

- He or she always seems to have too much to do and can't stop worrying about everything.
- He or she "catastrophizes" everything and is sure that something awful will happen by putting off any of his or her responsibilities.
- He or she often complains of headaches, upset stomach, and/or assorted aches and pains.

Most campuses have counselors and programs to help students deal with excessive stress and anxiety. Of course, it's usually the most stressed out students who don't feel they have the time to get help. As a parent, the best you can do in this situation is to encourage your child to get help and remind him or her that he or she is a valuable and worthwhile human being, even if he or she isn't perfect. You can also model behavior that assists you in stress reduction—taking time to relax and have fun, accepting the fact that you cannot be all things to all people in your life, reinforcing the importance of behaving like a "human being," as well as a "human doing," and trying to avoid all-or-nothing thinking, such as, "If I don't complete this task perfectly, I'll never have another chance."

Serious Problems

It may be hard for you to assess from afar when a situation becomes a serious problem. The following scenarios can help you determine whether a serious problem exists and if you need to get involved:

Depression

Recent phone calls with your daughter Marty have left you concerned. She seems to be going through a tough time at school. Even her voice sounds different. You're worried that she may be seriously depressed.

What's going on.

Marty suffers from a bout of depression and it's difficult to determine its severity. You wonder if she feels this bad all of the time, whether she attends classes and studies, and if you can help her in any way. College students commonly do feel depressed, but as in the general population, their depression has varying levels. The highs and lows of adolescence do not lessen during the college years; in fact, they might be intensified. Great stimulation, excitement, and challenges are often followed by frustrations, fears, and disappointments. And students usually struggle with these highs and lows without the benefit of adequate sleep, regular nutritious meals, and the care and nurturing that sustained them during times of stress at home.

A recent study followed high school senior girls for five years after graduation and found that 47 percent reported one or more episodes of major, clinical depression during that time. These girls were at highest risk for depression when they graduated from high school and started college, moving away from home.[2] Another study found that from early adolescence until very late in adulthood, females were much more likely to suffer from clinical depression than males.[3]

What to do.	What to avoid.
• Listen carefully and nonjudgmentally to your child's feelings. Keep your voice and manner calm even if you feel alarmed.	• Overreacting, thus making *your* feelings an extra burden for your child.
• Be patient if your child has difficulty articulating exactly how he or she feels.	• Judging and evaluating the situation: "No wonder you're depressed, you don't eat well and you never get a decent night's sleep."
• Ask when these feelings began and how intense they are.	• Trivializing your child's feelings: "Everyone has their ups and downs. I'm sure you'll feel better soon."
• Empathize with the feelings expressed; accept them at face value even if you find them exaggerated, embarrassing, or painful.	• Taking on the problem yourself or getting angry if your efforts to help are rejected.
• Ask how these feelings are affecting your child's daily life; for example, "Are you finding it difficult to sleep, eat, go to class, etc.?"	
• Ask how you can help.	
• Stay in close touch with your child until you feel he or she is better. A short phone call each day to check in and let your child know you're thinking of him or her can be a great help to both of you.	
• Remind your child that depression is treatable and that he or she may want to talk to a professional counselor or therapist.	

What you need to know.

Depression can come in many forms, from mild to full-blown clinical depression, which may require immediate intervention, treatment, and even hospitalization. Clinical psychologists Paul Grayson and Philip Meilman, who direct counseling services at New York University and Cornell University respectively, give the following description of depression:

> A *depressive reaction* is a reaction to some negative event, such as failure at school, a romantic breakup, or the death of a parent. A depressive reaction is "normal" in the sense that anyone facing the same circumstances would naturally feel bad. However, depressive reactions certainly don't feel normal. Like any other type of depression, they can be intense and profound, can last many weeks or even longer, and, in severe cases, are disabling. But they are related to a specific cause and ordinarily the depression will abate with time.
>
> Other forms of depression aren't due to negative circumstances alone. The person who experiences them also has an underlying biological and/or psychological vulnerability to depression; the cause lies at least partly within. Of these forms, *dysthymia* refers to a long-lasting but comparatively mild form of depression. Dysthymic persons manage to get by from day to day, they can bring themselves to study and socialize, but they view whatever they turn to through gray-colored glasses. One psychologist compared dysthymia to a "low grade infection." Dysthymics never really feel good.
>
> By contrast, a *major depression* has a relatively sudden onset and lasts several weeks to many months. It is paralyzing. College students who suffer a major depression find themselves unable to function and often must withdraw from school. This is the most severe form of "unipolar" depression, meaning that the extreme moods only go in one direction; depression does not alternate with elevated, or high, moods.[4]

Students are particularly vulnerable to feelings of depression because of the significant developmental tasks and the enormous challenges and uncertainties of late adolescence. Anyone, students included, can go into a tailspin if the stresses in their lives exceed their coping abilities at the time. Most students experience some sadness during the college years, but usually the mood passes within a few days. Sadness, however, is a temporary state and a normal human reaction; it's important to be able to differentiate sadness from depression.

You may have difficulty determining if your child is merely temporarily sad or depressed and in need of help. In general, if you feel that your child is depressed, it's a good idea to suggest that he or she talk to a counselor or another trusted adult. Certainly no harm can come from a visit to the college counseling center, and it may help your child to be evaluated by a trained professional. While it is good that your child is confiding in you, it is also important that he or she see someone who can assess whether therapy and/or treatment on an ongoing basis is needed.

Grayson and Meilman have identified some common indicators that can help you decide if your child suffers from serious depression. If you observe one or two of these indicators, you should keep your eye on the situation. If several of these indicators are present for more than a couple of weeks, your child probably needs help.

- Prolonged sad or depressed mood; crying spells, irritability; or an inability to feel anything at all.
- Loss of interest and pleasure in activities and other people.
- Significant weight loss or weight gain, or marked increase or decrease in appetite.
- Low self-esteem; feelings of worthlessness, guilt, and self-blame.
- Poor concentration; inability to read, write, or study for a test.
- Difficulty making decisions.
- Feelings of hopelessness; a belief that the future won't be any better than the present.
- Fatigue and loss of energy or agitation and restlessness.
- Problems with sleep; inability to fall or stay asleep, waking up early and being unable to get back to sleep, or sleeping too much.
- Worries about health and physical symptoms such as digestive disorders and nonspecific aches and pains.
- Recurrent thoughts of death or suicide.[5]

Assessing whether your child needs help is not an easy task, especially from afar, but if you observe several of these indicators over time, you will want to pay close attention. Don't be afraid to ask if your child ever thinks of hurting him or herself or others, and don't be frightened if there is an intense emotional response. Keep talking. Talking about a problem or crisis does not make it worse; it is the first step toward finding a solution.

Manic Depression

What's on your mind?

Rob seems either superhappy or down in the dumps.

He looks awful, like he's lost weight and has never seen the outdoors.

Is this normal adjustment to college or is he in trouble?

What's on your child's mind?

I am really freaked out about the pressure at school.

All I want to do is sleep, and my parents keep bugging me to talk about school.

I just want to forget everything and veg out or hang with my friends.

Your son Rob is home on break after his first semester at college. His appearance and general attitude alarm you. When he isn't sleeping, he seems wound up and irritable. One minute he raves to his friends about how great college is; the next minute he refuses to talk about it and retreats to his room.

What's going on.

Rob's behavior may indicate that he suffers from manic-depressive illness, although some of the symptoms may simply be the result of exhaustion or normal developmental struggles. Manic-depressive disorder (also called bipolar disorder) is characterized by "episodes of being uncontrollably high (mania) alternating with episodes of depression. Both the up and down extremes are grave problems, although in the manic phase the person has no insight into the dangers. During manic episodes judgment is impaired and inhibitions melt away."[6] In the manic state, an individual feels superhuman, able to function on no sleep and tackle any situation; he or she might also go on a spending spree or "act out" sexually. In the depressive state, he or she feels profound despair and may contemplate suicide.

Review the list of symptoms of depression given earlier to begin to assess whether Rob needs help. For example, do his behaviors prevent him from living his life in a reasonably healthy and orderly way? Are his moods either excitedly high or dreadfully low with little in-between or sense of calm?

What to do.	What to avoid.
• Find out the symptoms of this illness and observe Rob to determine if he manifests any of these symptoms.	• Ignoring or criticizing Rob's behavior.
• Ask Rob if he is experiencing any of these symptoms.	• Keeping it a secret if your family has a history of mental illness.
• Reassure him that this disorder is treatable but that he needs help.	• Assuming this is only a first-year-in-college adjustment issue.
• Suggest that he see a counselor at school and follow up on whether he has done so.	
• Keep talking about these behaviors in a nonjudgmental way: "Rob, I notice that you're sleeping a great deal and not eating well. That worries me. Can I help in any way?"	
• Remember that it's important for your child to take the initiative in getting help, but you can intervene and insist that he get treatment if you feel he is in danger.	

What you need to know.

College students are at an age when serious mental illnesses such as depression, manic depression, and schizophrenia are most likely to begin. It can be hard to distinguish if your child is becoming seriously ill or merely reacting to the kinds of stressful habits and lifestyles that are so typical of college students—routine lack of proper sleep, poor eating habits, sleep deprivation brought on by last-minute cramming for exams, and overindulging in drugs or alcohol. Parents need to be on the lookout for these behaviors and this can be especially difficult when they don't have much direct contact with their college child. Even if your child suffers from something serious, such as manic-depressive illness, these conditions are highly treatable. Students who receive professional help can learn about the habits that put them at risk and avoid spending their college years in the grip of mental illness.

College medical or counseling centers usually are not equipped to handle serious mental illness; and even if your child goes to the counseling center, he or she might not see an expert who can diagnose the condition accurately. Most colleges have therapists or social workers who deal with temporary problems, but few have staff with the time or qualifications to diagnose and provide long-term treatment and care for serious conditions. Most students with serious mental health problems are encouraged to take a medical leave of absence (this is a strictly confidential medical record and will not affect your child's future prospects negatively) for as long as it takes to get appropriate treatment.

Margaret Chisolm, former consulting psychiatrist at the Johns Hopkins University School of Medicine, explains: "Fortunately, most mental illnesses are highly treatable. People who have had these problems don't inevitably end up functioning with only marginal success. Nor do they necessarily return to the campus to be merely average students. People who have recovered from mental illness can become vibrant and capable leaders within colleges and universities and in society. However, for disturbed students to recover, their illnesses first must be recognized and treated appropriately."[7]

What's on your mind?

What in the world is going on?

I'm really angry that the college allows creeps like this to teach young people.

Is Virginia taking on more than she can handle?

I worry about the consequences for her whether she wins or loses.

Sexual Harassment

Your daughter Virginia called last night to tell you that she has decided to file sexual harassment charges against her biology professor. She had already met with an advisor in the college's Equal Opportunity Office and was calling to ask if you would support her in taking the professor to court.

What's going on.

Sexual harassment and the handling of such incidents is a hotly debated topic on most college campuses today. Attitudes and behaviors that may have been tolerated when your generation was in college are no longer acceptable. Moreover, most colleges have taken a firm stand with regard to treatment of faculty, staff, or students who are found guilty of sexual harassment. Title VII of the Civil Rights Act of 1964, as amended, has identified sexual harassment as an act of discrimination on the basis of sex. In accordance with Title VII and Title IX of the Civil Rights Act, most universities have adopted the following definition of sexual harassment:

> Unwelcome sexual advances, requests for sexual favors, and other verbal or physical conduct of a sexual nature constitute sexual harassment when (1) submission to such conduct is made either explicitly or implicitly a term or condition of an individual's employment or academic status, (2) submission to, or rejection of, such conduct by an individual is used as the basis for an employment decision or academic decision affecting that person, or (3) such conduct has the purpose or effect of substantially interfering with an individual's work or academic performance or creating an intimidating, hostile, or offensive working or learning environment.

> **What's on your child's mind?**
>
> I'm so glad I talked to that person in the Equal Opportunity Office.
>
> I want to do something so that other students aren't subjected to this horrible experience.
>
> I hope Professor Nelson gets fired for what he's done.

Most colleges have a policy manual and procedures in place governing such infractions and will support any individual member of the academic community who wishes to file sexual harassment charges through the campus review and judicial system.

It's still difficult and humiliating for most students to file charges against a faculty member, and parents may need to get involved if such a charge is taken to the public legal system. Your child is entitled to a safe living and learning environment in which he or she is treated with dignity and respect by faculty, staff, and students. Unfortunately, this is not always the case; conduct that constitutes sexual or gender harassment occurs on many campuses, but it does not have to be tolerated.

What to do.	What to avoid.
• Listen to your child's anger with respect and empathy. • Keep reminding your child that he or she is entitled to respectful treatment. • Help your child assess what type of action is appropriate. • Congratulate your child for being courageous enough to address this issue. • Recognize that he or she will probably waver and question him or herself during this process no matter how strong he or she is in the beginning. • Be prepared for the fact that this may be a long and painful process and that it may require extensive emotional and financial support.	• Asking your child to drop the charges and just stay away from that nasty person. • Suggesting that he or she may have done something to elicit this conduct. • Telling your child he or she will only intensify the pain by taking this public. • Calling the college and yelling at any staff member who will listen. • Threatening to take your child out of school and sue the college yourself.

What you need to know.

Nearly every college and university in the country is dealing with the issue of sexual harassment and has established a policy to respond to complaints by students. If your child brings a charge against a faculty member within the college system, a confidential review board will hear this complaint, determine whether there is cause, and recommend sanctions or penalties if the complaint is upheld.

This poses a difficult situation for a student as the complaint will be the student's word against the professor's. Although these review processes are designed to be fair and impartial, the power imbalance between a faculty member and a student is a real concern in trying to effectively adjudicate these situations within the college system. Very few faculty members are dismissed for alleged sexual harassment, especially if they have tenure. On some campuses, however, the process can work in favor of the student because a college can sanction and punish members of their community without the more stringent rule of law requiring the standard of "beyond a reasonable doubt" in applying penalties for wrong doing.

If the student decides to take the matter to a public court of law, the process could be quite different. Lawsuits of this type tend to be drawn out, expensive, and extremely painful for both student and faculty member. College officials may try to discourage your child from taking a complaint to a public court of law, given that they have to look out for their own interests and would rather not have this matter made public. If your child persists in wanting to go to court, he or she may have to contend with both the college and the faculty member. Having to rely on limited family resources, your child may be compelled to settle the suit without getting the satisfaction he or she sought and having been humiliated and exposed to public scrutiny as well. Taking public legal action to redress sexual harassment is a step that requires resources and commitment.

Parents should talk to their children about the consequences of sexual harassment and sexual assault before they leave for college or early in their college career. If you have a daughter, make sure she knows that she has a support system if she is ever the victim of sexual harassment and that you expect her to take advantage of that support if she needs it. Ensure that she knows she does not have to tolerate any form of harassment based on her gender, including overt acts: a fellow student using an offensive term to refer to females; a faculty member making sexist remarks in class; sexual propositions, innuendoes, or negative stereotypes and attitudes based on gender. Make sure that she knows she is not to blame when these events occur and that she is entitled to a safe environment in which to live and learn. If she is the victim of one of these acts, she will need your love and support to recover and carry on. She will need a calm and rational adult presence, not a hysterical, revenge-seeking parent who takes on the anger and humiliation that belong to her.

Parents also need to remember that recovery from these incidents, depending on the severity of the harassment, may take a long time. Be patient and keep reminding your child you love him or her and that he or she deserves great care and respect.

Eating Disorders

What's on your mind?

Why is she throwing up?
She doesn't seem sick.
Should I approach her about
the vomiting?

What's on your
child's mind?

I am so fat; I hate my body.
All of my friends are thinner
and better looking.
If I could only lose another
five pounds.

You noticed over Thanksgiving break that your daughter Jamie has been acting strangely. She ate some of the family holiday dinner but later that night you heard her vomiting in the bathroom.

What's going on.

Disordered eating is all too common among college students today. While serious eating disorders affect a relatively small percentage of the college population, disordered eating—severe dieting, unusual eating patterns, preoccupation with eating choices, troublesome though not frequent bingeing, anxiety about weight gain, and shame or guilt about one's body—is estimated to affect nearly 50 percent of the college population and can include men, particularly athletes. Serious eating disorders—anorexia nervosa, bulimia, binge eating, and combinations of these—are found in perhaps 5 percent of college students and nine out of ten of these are women. These conditions, particularly anorexia, can have serious consequences and even result in death if not treated appropriately.

Most schools today have staff on hand who are experienced in dealing with eating disorders. In some cases, students who exhibit symptoms of eating disorders are referred to a school psychologist or social worker by a friend or roommate who has become aware of and alarmed by the student's physical condition or behavior. The staff member would then call in the student for a counseling appointment and evaluation. At large colleges or universities, however, this level of attention to individual students may not be present, and you may need to take steps to ensure that your child receives the help she needs. Some small colleges may not have the appropriate staff to deal with these problems, but the Dean of Students' Office staff should be able to make a referral for your child.

What to do.	What to avoid.
• Confront Jamie if she exhibits erratic and/or unusual eating patterns. • Describe the behavior that concerns you in nonjudgmental terms: "Since you've been home, I've noticed that you eat very little at meals and yet I've heard you vomiting later in the day. I'm concerned about your eating habits. Are you eating a lot between meals? What's going on?" • Find out all you can about eating disorders. • Suggest that your child seek counseling and treatment at school. • Reassure Jamie that you love her and have confidence in her ability to make wise choices. • Keep talking about this issue with her. • If the behavior continues and/or escalates, make sure that Jamie seeks professional help immediately.	• Ignoring the behavior and assuming that it is just a phase. • Letting your fears get in the way of finding Jamie help. • Nagging your child about eating properly. • Threatening her or judging her behavior.

What you need to know.

There is a tremendous amount of written material that can help you understand the nature and complexity of eating disorders. Anorexia is self-starvation and can be extremely dangerous, resulting in death in as many as 10 percent of the cases. Bulimia is a disorder in which the individual alternates between binge eating and purging, usually through self-induced vomiting. This purging can also take the form of excessive use of laxatives, diuretics, or diet pills. Compulsive eating, without purging, is known simply as binge-eating disorder.

Two factors conspire to make dealing with eating disorders difficult for parents of college students. First, the child is away from home and cannot be observed on a daily basis, and second, eating disorders are usually accompanied by extremely secretive behavior. It's possible for a child to have a fairly serious eating disorder for a long time and keep it hidden from parents and friends. Moreover, individuals who suffer from eating disorders are usually embarrassed and ashamed of their actions and will often vehemently deny this behavior. Because of these feelings of shame and guilt, it is crucial that the child be reassured that any treatment or discussion of this disorder will be strictly confidential. Parents need to be vigilant about respecting their child's right to privacy on these issues.

Eating disorders are often tied up with feelings of shame, guilt, and lack of control over oneself. Families need to prepare for participating in counseling and/or treatment. Students whose parents are actively involved in dealing with the treatment of eating disorders have a better chance of overcoming this condition. Treatment can be painful for parents and children alike, as eating disorders are often symptoms of family dysfunctions that are difficult to address. For example, a child who witnesses her parents fighting constantly may see food as the only area of her life over which she has control. Hence, the eating disorder becomes a symptom of an unaddressed and unresolved family problem.

Bulimia is harder to detect than anorexia because many bulimics maintain a normal body weight even though they regularly binge and purge. The common symptom is uncontrollable eating—a hunger that stems from psychological rather than biological cravings. Bulimics are often excellent students, highly popular, talented, and extremely clever at hiding their eating disorder. In fact, a drive for perfection and achievement is at the heart of many eating disorders; therefore, it is a significant problem on college campuses filled with intelligent, achieving young people. Students who find themselves in a competitive environment may feel they have lost control over the academic part of their lives and may turn to eating as an area they can master and control.

In fact, on some campuses there is an alarming behavior that experts call "fad bulimia." In dorms and sororities, women get together and gorge themselves and then vomit or abuse laxatives, diuretics, and enemas or engage in excessive exercise to shed the pounds.

Your role as a parent is to help your child acknowledge and accept that she has a problem. Denial is the biggest hurdle in overcoming eating disorders. Compassion, reassurance, love, and support, along with a firm insistence on seeking help, is the surest route to helping your child conquer an eating disorder.

Illness

Your daughter Karen has been sick for a week or more with severe stomach cramps. She has been to the college health center for an examination but the symptoms continue. She's gone back to the health center a couple of times, but the staff there insist that she's just suffering from the intestinal flu bug that's going around campus. She's been told to rest and drink liquids, but she's still in a lot of pain.

What's going on.

It's possible that Karen suffers from an intense case of the flu, but it's also possible that she has something else. It's hard for students, especially when they are sick, to be assertive about receiving adequate health care. Friends and roommates may or may not help a student who is too sick to get out of bed to get food and medicine. This is especially true for an illness that is not minor, but is not a crisis either.

What's on your mind?

Is Karen in danger?
What if something serious is wrong with her?
Should I go see what's happening?

What's on your child's mind?

My stomach really hurts.
I don't see how this could just be the flu.
The health center staff made me feel like a whiner, but I'm really in pain.

What to do.	What to avoid.
• Trust your instincts. You know your child.	• Ignoring your child's complaints and insisting that she handle this herself.
• If you feel Karen is in danger, take action to get her some help.	• Calling the health center and complaining about your daughter's care.
• If you can't get to campus, get in touch with the residence hall advisor or director and have them check on her.	• Telling your daughter she has to go back to the health center until they get to the bottom of this problem.
• Ask the RA to help get your daughter to a physician or emergency room where she can get a second opinion.	

What you need to know.

Health centers at colleges are often overburdened and understaffed. Some have excellent resources and services, and some may not even have a physician on hand to diagnose and treat serious illnesses. Students' complaints can go unheard in a busy health center.

It's difficult and frustrating to have to figure this out from a distance, but if your child isn't improving and you are worried that he or she is in danger, you may have to become directly involved, at least to make sure that your child has the best professional help available.

What's on your mind?

- I can barely deal with this news myself. How am I going to tell Tim?
- Should I just wait until he's home for the summer?
- I'm worried about how Tim will take this news and how it will affect his studies.

Loss and Grief

Your husband has just been diagnosed with terminal cancer. You wonder if you should tell your son Tim, who is a junior in college and halfway through the spring semester.

What's going on.

The death or serious illness of a parent is a major issue for a college student. A college student, above all, needs to know that there is a secure base at home, and news of this kind can create tremendous stress and anxiety. The death of a parent is difficult at any age, but may be most unsettling just as a late adolescent is away from home and preparing for fully independent adulthood.

What to do.	What to avoid.
• Tell your child as soon as you can. It's better to do it in person.	• Keeping this news a secret in hopes of protecting your child.
• Be as clear as possible about the prognosis.	• Insisting that he or she go on with life even though a parent is very ill.
• Ask your child what you can do to help him or her through this crisis.	
• Offer to allow him or her to drop out of school for a while if your child expresses the need to spend time with his or her parent.	
• Honor his or her feelings even though they may be hard to accept.	
• Give your child time and space to adjust to this news.	
• Suggest that your child might want to seek counseling on campus.	

What you need to know.

The death of a parent is a significant life event no matter what the age of the child. When this happens during the college years, your child will need an extraordinary amount of care and compassion. Be prepared for a variety of reactions from your child. Experiencing and accepting feelings of grief, such as sadness, helplessness, loneliness, guilt, or anger, can help your child recover from this loss. He or she may be in denial or shock at first. After the shock has passed, your child may be depressed, panicked, remorseful, angry, and/or experience a variety of physical ailments for up to eighteen months. He or she may need to talk about the parent, tell stories and reminisce, or recall events over and over.

This can be extremely difficult when you too are experiencing feelings of grief, anger, and sadness. Be patient and gentle with yourself and your child. Expect this process of grieving to take a long time, and give yourself and your child as much time as it takes to come to terms with this tragedy. This may be even more difficult with an accidental or sudden death.

Other Problem Areas

During the college years, many issues can arise. Your mentoring skills, coupled with your ability to assess situations and determine whether you need to be involved, will help you weather these temporary situations and problems. If you suspect your child is involved with cult activity, is gambling or irresponsible with money, is behaving in any way that you feel might endanger his or her life, the first step is always to listen to your child and ask questions nonjudgmentally and with love, even if he or she is defensive. This technique alone will go a long way toward opening up communication about difficult topics.

Dealing with Crises

Although extremely rare, some situations becomes crises and require an immediate response. Sometimes you are the person to intervene, and other times you will need to rely on professional help for your child. In either case, you may be the first to recognize how serious the problem is. We hope the following scenarios will help you respond.

Suicide

When your daughter Nancy was home for spring break, she appeared extremely depressed. She complained about how hard it was to do well in school and that she didn't feel she had any real friends at college. She seemed so listless and discouraged. When you asked about her plans for summer break, she replied, "Who cares? I may not even be around by then."

> ### What's on your mind?
> I'm really worried about Nancy.
> I wonder if she's depressed enough to be suicidal.
> What should I do?

What's going on.

College students are among the highest risk group for suicide. The college years are a time in which individuals strive to create an individual identity, adjust to life away from home and

> ### What's on your child's mind?
> Life is just too hard.
> I feel like giving up.

family, form intimate relationships, and plan for the future. These are not always easy and pleasant tasks. In fact, researchers have found that young people in college seem to be more at risk than their peers who are not in college.

The suicide rate among adolescents has increased dramatically in the past forty years. Each year more than a half a million young people attempt suicide. Although completed suicide rates are higher for men, attempted suicide is far more common among adolescent girls than boys. About 60 percent of teens report that they know another teenager who has attempted suicide.

There are several risk factors that have been identified through study of adolescent behavior. Those young people who are at greatest risk are those who suffer from psychiatric problems, especially depression or substance abuse; have a family history of suicide; experience family disruption, significant family conflict, or parental rejection; are under extreme stress, especially in the areas of achievement and sexuality. If a child has one of these risk factors, he or she is more likely to attempt suicide than his or her peers; and if more than one risk factor is present, he or she is dramatically more likely to try to kill him or herself. Moreover, adolescents who have attempted suicide once are at risk for another attempt.[8]

What to do.	What to avoid.
• Take any expression of hopelessness or desire to "go away" seriously.	• Ignoring the behaviors and symptoms.
• Don't be afraid to ask your child if he or she has thought about hurting him or herself. Asking about suicidal feelings never encourages a person to take that step—it may open the door for saving that person's life.	• Underreacting when your child's life may be in grave danger.
	• Becoming hysterical and needy yourself.
• Ask your child what makes him or her feel so hopeless, and allow your child to speak even if what you hear is painful and frightening.	
• Act quickly to get professional help. Better to overreact than underreact in these situations.	
• If your child can't find professional help on campus, arrange for a medical leave of absence.	
• Think about getting some help for yourself. This is a traumatic experience for you as well, and you will need a safe place to talk about your fears and anxieties.	

What you need to know.

If your child suffers from serious mental illness or behaves suicidally, act decisively to get that child some help. Even if your child seems "recovered" after a bout of serious depression or suicidal behavior, you need to remain vigilant. Once people have decided to take their life, they often feel a period of calm before actually committing suicide. It is easy to misinterpret this period of calm as recovery, especially when you so desperately want that to be the case.

While all expressions of wanting to die should be taken very seriously, there are varying levels of risk. An individual who has a plan and a method of committing suicide is a high risk, and an individual who has attempted suicide in the past is an extremely high risk. If your family has a history of mental disorders or suicidal behavior, you should pay especially close attention to your child's mental health. One of the strongest protective influences against adolescent suicide is a cohesive, supportive family that provides a sense of stability. Even one family member who reacts responsibly with love, support, and intervention, if necessary, can make the difference between a student struggling through a rough period and a tragic death.

Rape

Your daughter Tina had been acting unusually withdrawn and uncommunicative since she arrived home for spring break. You finally asked her if anything was wrong, and she broke down and told you that she had been raped by a guy she had been dating at school.

What's going on.

Date rape, unfortunately, is a common problem on nearly every college campus today. One study found that one in four college women have been victims of rape or sexual assault. About 10 percent of sexual assault victims are men. Sexual intercourse forced by an acquaintance or date is rape. In some ways, it is more traumatic than by a stranger because it can seriously damage the victim's trust in others and in her own judgment.

It is a positive sign that Tina has shared this trauma with her mother. Too often, victims of date rape blame themselves and do not get the help they need to deal with the aftermath of this assault. Victims can feel ashamed, dirty, embarrassed, and responsible for the assault, especially if alcohol or drug abuse was involved.

What's on your mind?

I am so angry I could kill this guy.

What can I do to help Tina?

Will she ever get over this terrible violation?

What's on your child's mind?

Maybe I should have told Brian earlier that I didn't want to have sex yet. I must have led him on.

This has turned into a real nightmare.

I feel so ashamed and embarrassed.

I'm glad I told my mom, but now she's really upset too.

Every college has to deal with this growing problem and most have health services and counseling staff to assist victims of sexual assault and rape. Moreover, nearly all colleges have a policy about acceptable and unacceptable behavior in intimate relationships and a judicial or review process to address these infractions in a formal way. A rape victim can also avail herself of the public legal system and press charges that will be heard in a courtroom.

What to do.	What to avoid.
• Listen with empathy to your daughter's pain. • Reassure her that you love her and that she is lovable. • Let her know how important it is that she is able to talk about this horrible experience. Suggest that she see a counselor. • Remind her, often, that this is not her fault and that her feelings, no matter what they are, are appropriate and acceptable. • Ask her how you can help. Offer to go with her if she wants to seek medical attention and/or counseling. • Be patient if she seems to be indecisive and confused. • Support her if she decides to press charges or take any other action. • Respect her right to absolute confidentiality. Don't tell anyone about this event without her permission.	• Becoming hysterical and threatening to take action against the boy yourself. • Questioning your daughter about how this could have happened. • Blaming her for getting drunk and being out of control. • Asking questions that imply that the rape was your child's fault: "Why did you go to his room?" "Why didn't you scream and run away?" • Telling her that she must press charges and make sure this guy pays for what he did.

What you need to know.

If your daughter is the victim of sexual assault, the recovery may take a long time. She may have flashbacks, nightmares, low self-esteem, and bouts of depression and fearfulness for many years after such an experience.

Counseling is extremely important for victims of sexual assault or rape, and parents of victims often avail themselves of counseling as well. If you learn about the rape directly after it's occurred, ask your child if she would consider contacting a local rape crisis organization for information, advocacy, and support. In addition to offering vital emotional support, they will reinforce the importance of immediate medical attention and assist her in reporting the crime to authorities in case she wants to press charges later. Notifying the police does not obligate your child to press charges later.

You may need to support her if she decides to press charges, either formally or informally, within the college system. But you also need to respect your child's right and responsibility to make those decisions herself.

Recovery from a sexual assault can take time. Show your support and love for your daughter, reminding her constantly that it is natural and normal to feel confusion, rage, guilt, shame, insecurity, and depression. You may need to remind her often that she is lovable, precious, and entitled to be treated with dignity and respect, and that she is not responsible in any way for what happened to her.

If you have a son in college, there are a number of issues he needs to keep in mind. College men can be victims of sexual misconduct as well, although it is uncommon. Most often, however, college men need to be aware of their behavior when they express sexual interest in another student. Negotiating a sexual relationship can be confusing, clumsy, and embarrassing, but young men need to be reminded that they are responsible as well to make sure that consent is present before any sexual behavior takes place. Men are rarely the victim of sexual assault by a woman, but many college men regret having sex with a woman they have just met or with a woman who has been drinking too much. Cultural pressure makes it difficult for men to turn down sexual opportunity. Remind your son that it is okay to remain a virgin until he is ready to have sex or to abstain from sex if the situation is not appropriate for him. You can reassure him that making sound choices and acting with respect and constraint is the mature thing to do.

Parents of college men need to be especially clear on their expectations regarding consensual sex. Modeling respectful behavior is a parent's best teaching tool, but it is also necessary to talk about unacceptable and illegal behavior and the consequences of using pressure or force in sexual relationships. He needs to be reminded that under no circumstances should he ignore a no when he hears it, and that it is never his "right" to engage in sex with an unwilling partner, no matter what the circumstances. Being drunk and, therefore, unaware of whether the woman has given consent does not absolve him of responsibility. Neither is he absolved if the woman is too drunk to give consent.

If your son is accused of sexual misconduct, make sure that he gets all the support he can. This is a terrifying process for most young men, and you should encourage him to seek counseling so that he doesn't have to experience this alone.

Alcohol Abuse

What's on your mind?

I wonder if Darrel is an alcoholic?
What can I do to support him even though I am appalled by his behavior?
Where can he get help?

What's on your child's mind?

I am so bummed out that I got caught driving drunk.
I'm not the only one who drinks a lot here. Everyone does.
I can't be an alcoholic, can I?

Your son Darrel has been charged with driving while intoxicated and has to appear in court to answer these charges. You've felt for some time that his drinking has grown out of control.

What's going on.

Underage drinking and alcohol abuse is an enormous problem on most college campuses. If you've read a newspaper or magazine lately, you probably have seen articles on binge drinking and how colleges are trying to limit/prevent alcohol abuse. Despite alcohol awareness and other programs to alert students to the dangers of alcohol abuse, studies indicate that nearly half of all college students engage in binge drinking.[9] Colleges are faced with two unattractive alternatives: One, to clamp down on underage drinking on campus, thereby forcing students to drive to remote drinking locations; or two, to turn the other way and ignore illegal and dangerous drinking behavior on campus.

What to do.	What to avoid.
• Confront your son about his drinking behavior. Let him know that you take this seriously and that you are concerned.	• Blaming, threatening, and punishing him.
• Allow him to experience the consequences of his behavior.	• Ignoring his destructive drinking behavior.
• Ask him if he needs help.	• Assuming this is just a phase that all college students go through.
• Suggest that he find a counselor and/or attend an Alcoholics Anonymous meeting.	
• Let him know that you love him and will support him in getting the help he needs.	
• Model responsible drinking behavior. If you abuse alcohol or condone it's abuse, it's likely that your child will too.	

What you need to know.

Underage drinking has been a major concern for college administrators for some time. Raising the legal drinking age in the mid-1980s left colleges with a serious dilemma. College students who have not reached the age of twenty-one are legally not allowed to purchase or possess alcoholic beverages, but most students break that law. The problem has become so severe that schools have asked Congress to add an amendment to the Higher Education Act allowing them to inform parents anytime a student under twenty-one violates drug or alcohol laws. This amendment was passed in the fall of 1998 and is a departure from the post 1960s recognition that college students who have attained the age of eighteen should be treated as legally independent adults. At a time when extensive efforts to curb alcohol use and abuse on campuses have largely failed, colleges are now turning to their last resort—parents—to help them reverse the often tragic results of underage drinking.

Colleges are now debating whether to use this right to inform parents. Some have instituted a "zero tolerance" rule that results in a student's suspension or expulsion after three alcohol offenses. Some notify parents after a serious violation (such as fighting or requiring medical attention due to excessive drinking) or after two minor violations (such as possession of alcohol). The parental notification plans for most colleges are aimed at high-risk behavior, the kind that may result in accidental death or serious injury to self or others.

While recent national studies of drinking behavior on college campuses have come up with conflicting reports on the increase in alcohol consumption, most agree that binge drinking (defined by researchers as consuming five drinks in a row within a short period of time for men and four drinks for women or taking fourteen to twenty-one drinks in a twelve- to twenty-four-hour period)[10] continues to be a serious problem. The Harvard School of Public Health college alcohol study concluded that there has been a slight decrease (from 44 percent to 43 percent) in binge drinking among college students, but the study also found that the college students who are binge drinking are doing it more frequently. They also found that four of five residents of fraternity houses binge and more than half are frequent binge drinkers. It is not surprising that much of the recent media attention and most of the alcohol-related deaths involved fraternity parties. They also stress, however, that one in five college students nationally abstains from alcohol and that another two in five drink, but not to excess. The fact remains, however, that on most campuses, alcohol is the drug of choice.

Drug Abuse

What's on your mind?

Is my son a drug addict?
What can I do to help him?
What is crank anyway?

Your son Nick called you last night at the urging of a nurse in the college's medical center. He explained that he had blacked out at a party on Saturday night and that tests revealed that he had a high level of crank in his system. The staff at the medical center has recommended that he take a leave of absence and go into a rehab program.

What's going on.

While alcohol is the most commonly used drug on campus today, the use of other drugs—marijuana, cocaine, hallucinogens, and amphetamines (like crank, crystal meth, and ecstasy)—is also a problem at many colleges. There can be significant pressure on students to experiment with illegal drugs in order to be a part of the social scene on campus. Most colleges have extensive programs and other outreach efforts to educate students on the dangers of drug use and abuse, but each year students are harmed by drugs and the danger can be even greater if drugs are combined with alcohol.

What's on your child's mind?

I don't understand what everyone's so freaked out about. I've only used crank a few times.

Are they going to make me leave school?

A lot of kids use drugs here.

What to do.	What to avoid.
• Take this incident seriously.	• Assuming that this is just a one-time event and that he's learned his lesson.
• Accept the fact that your son may have a serious drug problem.	
• Make sure that he gets medical treatment and care to address this problem, even if it means he needs to drop out of school for a while.	• Reacting with outrage and anger and refusing to help.
	• Blaming the person who gave him the drug.
• Let him know that drug use and abuse is absolutely unacceptable to you.	• Refusing to address the seriousness of his situation.
• Remind him that you care deeply about him and expect him to take the necessary steps to deal with his problem.	
• Be prepared to do anything required to help him recover.	
• Educate yourself on the effects of this drug.	
• Prepare yourself for the fact that this may take extraordinary amounts of time, effort, and love.	

What you need to know.

Drug use that results in blackouts is evidence of potentially serious drug abuse. It's important that you recognize this problem and do everything you can to get help for your child. This kind of abuse can have long-term negative and even tragic effects on a student's life and future. The health risks are significant, with the possibility of causing both physical and emotional trauma and damage. It's imperative that you make sure that your child gets evaluated by a professional and that steps are taken to get him or her into a recovery program if necessary. It's customary for the family to be engaged in the counseling portion of rehabilitation and this can be an enlightening, if painful experience.

Coming to terms with serious drug abuse in a child can be an excruciating experience for parents. It's normal for parents to want to deny what is going on, partly because of the social stigma of dealing with a child who has a drug abuse problem and partly because the prospect of acknowledging that you have a drug-addicted child is so terrifying. Now is the time, however, to set your fears aside and do everything you can to help your child through this crisis. Failure to do so could result in real tragedy down the road.

What's on your mind?

Is my daughter safe?
What if this is some crazed serial killer?
I want her to come home where we can protect her.

What's on your child's mind?

How could this have happened to one of my friends?
I am really freaked out.
I don't feel safe here anymore.

Violence/Crime

Your daughter Janet called you at 1:00 A.M. last night to tell you that one of her sorority sisters had been found dead in the park near the sorority house. Janet thinks she was killed by her former boyfriend, who had been threatening her and acting very strangely.

What's going on.

Although rare, violent crime does occur on campuses. Just as domestic violence plagues the larger culture, violence on campus can occur between estranged boyfriend and girlfriend, and usually the boyfriend is the perpetrator. This is a terrifying situation for student and parent alike. Families don't expect that violent crime will be a part of their child's college experience; therefore, many students come to college unprepared to adequately protect themselves.

What to do.	What to avoid.
• Listen to your child's fears without sharing your anxiety and alarm with your daughter. • Ask her if she feels safe. • Encourage her to take advantage of any counseling offered by the college as a result of this tragedy. • Urge her to talk about her fears and sadness with you and others.	• Becoming distraught yourself and insisting that she come home until you're sure she's safe. • Focusing on the crime instead of on the death of your daughter's friend.

What you need to know.

Most students and their parents do not expect to have to deal with violence and crime but colleges are no different than the larger culture. Until recently, colleges did not reveal their violent crime statistics; rarely did colleges share these statistics with incoming students. In 1990, however, the federal government passed the Student Right to Know and Campus Security Acts (now known as the Jeanne Clery Disclosure of Campus Security Policy and Campus Crime Statistics Act), that required colleges and universities to publicize their annual crime statistics to students, potential students, and employees.

It is important for parents to talk to their children about what they can do to increase their personal safety on campus and off during the college years. Seemingly obvious measures such as locking doors, avoiding walking alone at night in secluded areas, and moderating drinking behavior can go a long way toward ensuring safety in a variety of situations.

While most college women will not be victimized by violent crime, "one in twenty women can expect to be stalked at some time during her life and the stalker is usually a man she has dated or married. In a survey among college students in West Virginia, 34 percent of the women . . . said they had been stalked."[11] If your daughter has ended a relationship with a man (or woman) you feel is dangerous and unbalanced, it is important that you talk to her about what she can do to avoid a confrontation. Any behavior that is out of line should be taken seriously and responded to with absolute consistency. Your daughter should zealously protect herself by keeping her address, telephone number, and E-mail address private or unlisted. She should also keep a diary recording incidents with names, dates, and times of every contact and save tapes of phone messages or copies of anything sent by the offending party. She should be careful about locking her dorm or apartment doors and securing her car. She should also contact her Campus Security Office or a police officer if she receives threats or has experienced threatening behavior.

Pregnancy

What's on your mind?

Why didn't Kay tell me about this?

Should I tell her that I know?

I'd like to know if she's okay.

What's on your child's mind?

Should I have told Becky about my abortion?

I thought she should know what can happen if she has unprotected sex.

I wish I could tell Mom and Dad, but I'm afraid they would be so upset.

I still think about that abortion. Did I do the right thing?

Your daughter Kay is in her senior year of college. Over holiday break you overheard her telling her younger sister that she had an abortion when she was a sophomore.

What's going on.

Unwanted or unplanned pregnancies are a serious crisis for many young women in college. They often feel guilty and ashamed, and they may wonder for many years if they made the right choice if they have an abortion.

Although there are fewer unplanned pregnancies on campuses than there were in the 1970s and 1980s, it is still a major dilemma for those young women who become pregnant. Many are afraid to tell family and friends and, hence, have to shoulder this emotional burden alone. This can be a tremendous source of guilt and pain, especially for those students whose religious or ethical beliefs make terminating a pregnancy a difficult choice.

What to do.

- Let her know that you overheard her conversation with her sister.
- Make it clear that you respect her right to privacy but that you'd like to offer support and a chance to talk about it if she wants to. Be open to discussing this issue non-judgmentally.
- Recognize and honor her right to have made this decision, even if you do not agree with it.
- Empathize with the difficulty she's been through and offer her unconditional love and support.
- Ask her how she is dealing with this decision now. You may want to suggest counseling if she's continuing to have feelings of grief, guilt, or self-doubt.

What to avoid.

- Confronting her with having had an abortion.
- Moralizing and preaching about having premarital and unprotected sex.
- Asking Becky to tell you what she knows about Kay's abortion.

What you need to know.

While most colleges do not have adequate resources to support a young woman through pregnancy and child rearing, many student health plans cover abortions. Insurance requirements usually make it mandatory for family-planning practitioners and pregnancy counselors to discuss carrying the child to term as well as the option of terminating the pregnancy. This can be a complicated decision, fraught with emotional and financial worries for a college student. Carrying a child to term will often mean having to drop out of school for a semester or a year and it can be difficult to return to college while raising an infant. Choosing an abortion is also a tough decision.

If your child decides to carry through with an unplanned pregnancy during the college years, you may need to provide a lot of support, both emotionally and financially, for a number of years. This can make it difficult for you to respect her decision and honor it, knowing what hardships may be down the road for all of you. Good counseling is absolutely essential when your family is dealing with this issue.

The incidence of HIV infection and concern about contracting the AIDS virus has encouraged many young women and men to be much more careful about protecting themselves. Some also abstain from vaginal intercourse because of these fears, choosing to practice oral sex instead, although oral sex is not risk-free. Many colleges offer free and confidential AIDS testing, as well as infection checkups to detect any one of a number of sexually transmitted diseases (STDs).

Parents need to be proactive about discussing these issues with their college-aged daughters and sons. Even if the conversation is one-sided, make the effort to inform yourself and talk about pregnancy, AIDS, and STDs with your child. Discuss abstinence as an option, but also encourage your child to practice safe sex and discuss any risk factors with a partner before having intercourse. Stress the importance of making careful decisions about when and with whom to have sex.

Above all, let him or her know that you are available to talk about these difficult topics. You may not know if your daughter becomes pregnant, contracts an STD, or becomes infected with HIV, but you can take the initiative to discuss these concerns with her and be clear about your values and the behaviors that you expect her to adopt when and if she becomes sexually active.

How to Obtain Help from the College if There's a Problem or Crisis

You're not alone if you are puzzled about what to do if you feel your child is in danger or needs help with a serious problem. Every parent sending a child off to college has high hopes that their child will have a successful and rewarding college experience; however, most undergraduates encounter some distress and unhappiness during their college years. Usually these are temporary bumps on an otherwise relatively smooth path. While it's important to allow your daughter or son the opportunity to deal with minor problems and adversity and learn from those experiences, it's also important to know how to get assistance when you're concerned with your child's safety and well-being.

While we nearly always suggest that parents allow their children to experience the consequences and learn from their mistakes, there are times when parents need to get involved and call upon the resources of the college. The first involvement, however, should be directly with your child. Ask your child to share specifically what is going on, and be ready to share your opinion and offer guidance without judgment or criticism. Be wary of "taking over" your child's dilemma, but be prepared with resources and information. It's appropriate to share your values, but then let your child make his or her choices free from your admonishments.

If you feel that intervention is justified, respect your intuition. You know your child and you will likely be able to sense if things are not right. Start by listening to your child carefully and in a calm, nonaccusatory way. Point to the signs or signals that you've observed. Let your child do most of the talking, and assure him or her of your full support, but be ready to deal with rejection if your child refuses to discuss what's going on. If your child slams the door in response to your concern, it may be that there is more going on than your child wants to admit.

You may want to enlist the help of someone on campus to assess your child's situation and provide support. Ideally, you would inform your child before contacting someone on campus. In a crisis situation, however, it may be necessary to consult someone on campus without your child's knowledge. If you do this without your child's approval, there is a good chance that your child will eventually find out and may be antagonistic about your intervention. Hopefully, your child will realize sooner or later that you acted out of love and concern, but you may need to risk rejection or hostility in the short term.

If you decide to seek the help of campus administrators or counselors, you need to come across as a calm, thorough, and systematic person who has a reasonable attitude about determining whether a serious problem exists. Before you contact the college, make notes describing specific aspects of your child's behavior that concern you. Try not to exaggerate or jump to conclusions before enlisting help in assessing the situation.

The Dean of Students' Office is usually a good place to start. Ask for a referral to another office if necessary. The college's Dean of Students' Office is usually administratively responsible for dealing with most aspects of student life outside of the formal classroom or academic setting. This may include offices of health services, counseling, campus security services, career counseling, and residence hall life. Larger colleges may have an assistant dean dealing with specific aspects of student life, such as fraternities and sororities, women's affairs, student activities, minority affairs, and other campus programs.

When you contact a staff person, tell them who you are and who your child is. Then simply lay out your concerns in a systematic and specific manner. Emphasize that you are trying to assess if there is a serious problem and that you are seeking advice on how to proceed. Have a paper and pencil ready to take notes. You should, at this point, receive a caring, professional response and be taken seriously. This does not mean, however, that the staff person will be able to give you any specific information about your child's behavior or activities. Chances are, this person will not even know your child, but he or she is bound legally to maintain your child's right to confidentiality. This doesn't mean that he or she cannot help you with your concerns or offer support and suggestions on dealing with those concerns. They can listen to your worries, advise you on ways of dealing with your son or daughter, and, most importantly, help you assess whether there is a serious problem present. They cannot, however, share with you any information that would compromise their ethical and legal relationship with your child.

Many college counseling staff and residence hall advisors will be willing to contact your child and ask him or her to come see them if they are convinced that a serious problem or crisis is looming. If this intervention is unwelcome by your son or daughter, however, it may not do any good or may even exacerbate the problem. At this point, you may have to go back to your child and be assertive in getting help. This should be a last-resort effort, only used if you sense there is grave danger to your child.

In general, it makes sense to rely on the professional advice and support that you will receive from college staff. In most cases, they have the experience and expertise to help *you* through a difficult time, even if they are unable to share specifics about your child's life on campus.

What to Know More?

———. *Helping Your Child to Choose Life: A Parent's Guide to Youth Suicide.* San Mateo, CA: Youth Suicide National Center.

Parrot, Andrea. *Sexual Assault on Campus: The Problem and the Solution.* New York: Macmillan, 1993.

Grayson, Paul A., and Philip W. Meilman. *Beating the College Blues,* Second edition. New York: Checkmark Books, 1999.

National Sexually Transmitted Diseases Hotline and Public Health Service Aids Hotline, 1-800-227-8922.

American Council for Drug Education, 1-800-488-DRUG, 1-800-COCAINE, web address: http://www.acde.org.

National Council on Alcoholism and Drug Dependence, 1-800-NCA-CALL, web address: http://www.ncadd.org.

American Anorexia/Bulimia Association, 133 Cedar Lane, Teaneck, NJ 07666, 201-836-1800.

---

1. . . . "Female Students Feel the Stress," *Ithaca Journal* (25 January 1999).

2. Karen S. Peterson, "Depression Hits Teens Away from Home," *Ithaca Journal* (26 June 1999).

3. B. Compas et al., "Gender Differences in Depressive Symptoms in Adolescence: Comparison of National Samples of Clinically Referred and Nonreferred Youths," *Journal of Consulting and Clinical Psychology* 65 (1997).

4. Paul A. Grayson and Philip W. Meilman, *Beating the College Blues: A Student's Guide to Coping with the Emotional Ups and Downs of College Life* (New York: Facts on File, 1992), 46–47.

5. Ibid, 47–48.

6. Ibid, 47.

7. Margaret S. Chisolm, "Colleges Need to Provide Early Treatment of Students' Mental Illnesses," *Chronicle of Higher Education* (15 May 1998): sec. B, p. 6–7.

8. Laurence Steinberg, *Adolescence,* 5th ed. (Boston: McGraw-Hill College, 1999).

9. Henry Wechsler et al, "Health and Behavioral Consequences of Binge Drinking in College," *Journal of the American Medical Association* (7 December 1994): 1672–77.

10. Jeffrey Cashin, Cheryl Presley, and Philip Meilman, "Alcohol Use in the Greek System: Follow the Leader?" *Journal of Studies on Alcohol* (January 1998): 3–70.

11. Jane E. Brody, "Researchers Unravel the Motives of Stalkers," *The New York Times,* Science Times section (25 August 1998), 1.

Chapter 10

If They Leave College, Will They Ever Get Back on Track?

The Challenges and Benefits of Taking Time Off

When my son flunked out of college, I thought it was the end of the world. I didn't know what to think. He'd always been such a good student. I was really worried for him and what this would mean for his future. I have to admit, too, that I was embarrassed and wondered if I could keep this a secret from his grandparents and my friends.

You may be surprised and alarmed when your child decides to quit school, is asked to leave, or wants to take a break from college. Most parents assume that their children will be successful and happy in college and never think about how they would respond if their child decides to quit or flunks out.

We've found that students who take time off, for whatever reason, usually come back with renewed and focused energy to do well in college. Many students can benefit from time off. It gives them time to mature, explore the "real world" through volunteer work or a job, test their academic ability in another setting, reevaluate their reasons for going to college, and learn from the opportunity to reflect on their skills and interests. Parents can play a key role in helping their child through this experience. Using your mentoring skills, you can discuss the options with your child and suggest activities that will ensure that the time off is productive.

This chapter will help you deal with this highly charged issue and understand some of the alternatives available if your child leaves college, including the possibility that he or she may decide not to return to school.

Being Asked to Leave

Few events are more disturbing than having your child fail. You will probably feel embarrassed, disappointed, worried, and helpless. While you cannot control your child's academic performance, you can respond as a mentor, helping your child learn from this experience and make decisions about his or her future.

Flunking Out

When your son Will called to tell you he'd flunked out of school, you were shocked:

WILL: Hi, Dad. How are things?

DAD: Okay, son. How are you?

WILL: Well, not so good actually. I got a letter from the dean today asking me to take a year off. The letter says "so that I can rethink my priorities and prove to them that I'm capable of doing college level work."

DAD: I don't believe this! What happened?

WILL: Well, you know last semester I got a 1.5 GPA, and they said if I didn't bring it up to a 2.0, they were going to ask me to leave. My grades came with the letter and I only got a 1.8 GPA this semester. I would have gotten a 2.0 if I hadn't blown my chemistry final. I'm sorry, Dad.

DAD: What does this mean?

WILL: It means I flunked out! What do you think it means?

DAD: I know that, but what are you going to do?

WILL: I guess I'm coming home. They said I have to take courses somewhere else to prove that I can get at least a B average before they'll consider letting me back in. I guess I'll have to go to the community college next year.

What's on your mind?

This is a nightmare.

How is Joanna going to take this? I hate to have to tell her when she gets home from work.

What will happen to Will. He sounds so discouraged.

Could it be that my kid isn't capable of getting a college degree?

What's on your child's mind?

I can't believe I actually flunked out.

What's wrong with me?

I'm so embarrassed and my dad sounded so ashamed of me.

DAD: I guess so. Gosh, I don't know what to say, Will. I find this so hard to believe. You were always such a good student.

WILL: I know, but college is really different. There are so many smart kids here; I guess I just got discouraged and stopped trying.

DAD: Why didn't you say something sooner? Maybe you could have gotten some help.

WILL: I just thought I could catch up, but I guess I was wrong.

DAD: I'm really sorry, Will. You must feel awful.

WILL: Yeah, pretty much.

DAD: So do you want me to come up on Saturday?

WILL: You can come earlier if you want. No need to stick around here any longer.

What's going on.

The first year of college is a real trial for many students. In fact, the number of students leaving college after the freshman year has hit an all-time high. While there are a number of reasons why a freshman may not return for his sophomore year, a significant one is failure to achieve a sufficient grade point average to remain in good academic standing. When students do not receive the minimum grades required, colleges typically will ask them to take a semester or a year off and take courses at another institution to prove that they are capable of doing college-level work. This can be a real crisis of confidence for your child and a difficult struggle for you as a parent.

What to do.	What to avoid.
• Listen to Will with empathy. • Ask him what you can do to help. • After both of you have come to terms with this situation, sit down and talk about what will happen next. • Engage Will in a discussion of the options available. He may want to enroll at a college near home to save money. • Make your expectations clear. If he's coming back home to live, you will want to discuss what you expect in the way of help around the house and adherence to family schedules and rules. • Try to focus on the next few weeks and months and helping Will get through this crisis. • Schedule an appointment with a family therapist to talk about how you will manage this new arrangement. • You may have to take the initiative in getting your son some tutoring and/or counseling help as well.	• Dumping all of your feelings of disappointment on Will. He feels humiliated and embarrassed enough. • Telling him how he's let you and the family down. • Calling the college and trying to get the dean to reverse the decision. • Losing faith in Will's ability to do college work.

What you need to know.

Only about two in five students complete an undergraduate degree in the standard four years. Overall, 58 percent of students finish college, but graduation rates vary a great deal from college to college. Some schools have close to a 100 percent graduation rate.[1] If your child attends a private college and leaves during his first year, he has a much greater chance of graduating after he returns than if he attends a public college or university. The National Center for Education Statistics reports that 76 percent of students who finished the first year completed their degree or were still enrolled in college after five years.[2]

Failing out of college can be a real crisis for families who sent a confident, bright child off to school and never expected to bring a defeated child home at the end of the year. There are many reasons why a student fails to achieve in college. Although bright and capable in high school, some students experience enormous challenges academically, personally, and socially in college. Some are simply not ready for the freedom and responsibility that are a part of college life and need more time to mature into successful students. This can be especially true for students who are not used to taking care of their daily physical needs and are overly dependent on parents to set guidelines and rules for their behavior.

Some students just need more time to grow up and learn to accept responsibility for the many demands of college life. A semester or year at home can provide that extra time and can be productive, if there are clear, realistic goals and expectations set.

Many colleges, realizing that some students come to school ill-prepared to tackle the rigors of college course work, have made concerted efforts to provide additional support to students having difficulty adapting to college work and offer information on where students in academic trouble can get help. Students enrolled at a large university, however, may fall through the cracks and not avail themselves of the assistance they need.

What's on your mind?

I'm glad that her time off was so helpful to her.
I'm relieved that she's going back to school.

What's on your child's mind?

I love the hotel business. Taking this leave was the best thing I've ever done.

A Leave with a Silver Lining

Your daughter Lynn was not doing well in her English major at the state university and she was asked to take an academic leave. She found a job at a local resort and loved her work in the hotel manager's office. She's now decided to go back to school and transfer to the university's hospitality program.

What's going on.

As we've said before, there are often great benefits when a child drops out of school for a time. In fact, we have never met a student who didn't feel later that this time off, for whatever reason, was a good thing. Students who come back from a leave are usually the most motivated and enthusiastic learners and many find that their time off has given them a whole new academic direction and career focus.

What to do.	What to avoid.
• Encourage Lynn in her new major. • Congratulate her on the successful job she's done. • Let her know how proud you are that she made such good use of her time away from school. • Remind her of how courageous it was for her to make something positive happen from this initially negative experience.	• Dampening Lynn's enthusiasm for her new career interest. • Telling her how hard the hotel business is. • Thinking this is not a very rigorous major and trying to convince her to stick with a liberal arts curriculum.

What you need to know.

There are so many success stories to be told about students who take time off and come back to school ready and able to excel in their college work. Let's face it, most eighteen year olds are not equipped to make the kinds of choices that are forced upon them in order to continue their education. Some find themselves dissatisfied with the major they've chosen, some don't yet have the maturity to manage the competing demands of school and social life, others need a bit of extra time to explore their interests.

A recent headline in *The New York Times: Education Life* section, asked, "What's the Rush? Why College Can Wait." The reporter asserts that "a growing number of students are opting to take time off from their studies in favor of real-life experiences. Educators applaud the decision. Parents, now that's a different story." In this article, Robert Gilpin, a teacher and president of Time Out Associates counsels students that "if you have the courage to opt out of the lemmings' rush to the sea, you're a special person." He believes that many young people are burned out and need a break from the relentless pursuit of education before they go to college. His favorite saying rings true for many: "College is the most expensive buffet in the world—$30,000 a year—and you'd better be sure you're hungry."[3]

While we don't want to downplay the disruption and anxiety that time off from college can cause parents and students alike, we do want to emphasize how valuable this experience can be and how important it is that parents support their children in considering alternatives and discovering ways to make time off a productive hiatus.

Choosing to Leave

You will probably be surprised and confused when your child decides to quit college or interrupt his or her college career. When your child is doing well academically, it's difficult to understand why he or she chooses to leave. You wonder if your child will ever go back and finish his or her degree. You are also annoyed that all the money you've invested in your child's education will go to waste.

> ## What's on your mind?
>
> Has she become so enchanted with life at the Zen center that she'll never be able to cope in the "real world"? She can't live in a meditation center forever.

> ## What's on your child's mind?
>
> I really feel at home at the center.
> I can always go back to college if I want to. Not everyone needs a college degree to be happy.

Dropping Out

You were shocked when your daughter Jacqueline announced that she has decided to drop out of school in her junior year to work at a Zen meditation center in upstate New York, where she had a summer job.

What's going on.

Jacqueline is finding it difficult to justify staying in college because she doesn't feel she belongs there. She had a wonderful summer at the meditation center and began to develop a part of herself—her spirituality—that she found rewarding and compelling. In the college world of achievers and strivers, she may have felt out of place. A year working in the bakery at the Zen center may be exactly what she needs to continue her identity and autonomy quest.

What to do.	What to avoid.
• Listen to her reasons for wanting to drop out of college.	• Telling her that you think she's crazy.
• Try to be as supportive as possible of Jacqueline's choices.	• Reminding her that people who live in these places are losers who can't make it in the "real world."
• Recognize that this may be a necessary and productive part of her development.	• Jumping to the conclusion that she has joined some dangerous cult.
• Find out more about the meditation center. Offer to visit her there and learn about the community.	• Making your expectations more important than her explorations.
• Remember that this is her choice and that your role is to raise questions but ultimately to be supportive.	

What you need to know.

Your daughter may be experiencing an identity crisis that is difficult for you to understand. The meditation center may offer her the time she needs to tackle the important task of deciding who she is in the world. Students who are not motivated to learn in college can benefit from time off. In fact, many students who stick it out in college would be better served by taking some time off and exploring their interests and passions. Parents can't give their kids motivation; in most cases, students who take time off return to college with increased energy and more focused goals.

Most colleges have a voluntary leave policy, in addition to medical and academic leaves. It may be a good idea for Jacqueline to take a leave of absence instead of just withdrawing. Taking a leave will make it easier for her to return if she decides to in the future.

Although this is not the plan you had in mind for Jacqueline, it's very important that you learn to accept and support her choice. Even though she's chosen to live in a cloistered community, she will learn life skills that will benefit her down the road, whether she chooses to stay or return to school.

College Seems Meaningless

What's on your mind?

Brandon has always been interested in what he calls "real people and real work."

I guess we can't force him to stay in school.

Will he be safe in Africa?

Your son Brandon has always been a self-starter with an uncommon curiosity about the world. He decided after his freshman year that college wasn't for him. Although he'd always done well in school, he didn't seem excited about the courses of study offered at the university and wanted to spend some time working with a not-for-profit development group that works on refugee resettlement in Central Africa.

What's on your child's mind?

There aren't any courses here that I really want to take.

I want to learn by doing, not by studying and taking tests.

I hope my parents will understand.

What's going on.

College can seem cloistered and unreal to some students. Brandon doesn't relate to the "careerism" found on most campuses and wants to do something meaningful in the world. He might have been a good candidate for taking a year or two off after high school and doing community service work. Now, much to his credit, he has realized that he isn't motivated to do college work and needs to pursue his education in another way.

What to do.

- Support Brandon, even though you may find his ideas unorthodox.
- Let him know that you are proud of his values and his desire to make a difference in the world.
- Ask him to share details of his plans with you.
- Review with him the pluses and minuses of his decision and ask him if he's thought about alternative plans.

What to avoid.

- Telling him that he's gone too far.
- Trying to convince him to stay in school.
- Letting your fear of uncertainty thwart his spirit and passion.

What you need to know.

The traditional college experience is not for everyone. While you may not be surprised if your child has come up with an unconventional alternative to staying in college, it still may be hard for you to understand and accept, knowing the risks and possible pitfalls of his or her decision. Your mentoring skills can be useful in helping your child assess his or her choices. A child who leaves college with well-defined goals will learn a lot more than one who drifts aimlessly about, becoming more and more dependent on his or her parents to set the agenda.

We recently read about a young man who dropped out of Oberlin College to enroll in what he called "the University of Planet Earth." He became an enthusiastic participant in a growing self-schooling movement, following his realization that "there were no courses in college covering the things I most wanted to learn."[4]

His self-styled curriculum is to "live in a different city every year. Attend a different place of worship every week. Seek out hundreds of mentors to help me find answers to my thousands of questions. Spend the rest of the time in the library and on the Internet. Create lists, make charts, and undertake the most ambitious projects I can think of. Create my own personal Bible, almanac, and telephone book. Live in the poorest neighborhoods in order to learn how to get along in the world and to save money. . . ."[5]

While this young man's story is an unusual one, it's also an indication of his curiosity, initiative, and desire for self-knowledge. His parents were not willing to give him the money they would have spent on his education, so he is working to support himself and accepting responsibility for his choices.

Although hard for parents to accept, there is no doubt that students who leave college to pursue an unconventional but well-conceived alternative can have some extraordinary learning experiences. It's normal to wonder what your child's future prospects will be without a college degree, but parents have at least as much reason to be proud of a child who exhibits such passion and motivation to take charge of his or her learning as they do a child who takes a more traditional route. And, remember, your child can always return to college later.

Transferring to Another College

Your son Arthur, who is a sophomore at the state university in
a nearby town, wants to transfer to a small, private college in
another state.

What's going on.

Your son is experiencing a rather common phenomena. He's
found that the college he chose is not a good fit for him. While
this means a disruption in his plans and the necessity of read-
justing to a new place, it's a good idea if you can support his
desire to transfer. Feeling at home is an important part of
doing well in college, and feeling in synch with a peer group is
a critical aspect of the college experience.

What to do.	What to avoid.
• Talk to Arthur about his reasons for wanting to transfer. • Listen to him and accept that he is the best judge of his comfort level. • Support him in finding alternatives to his situation. • Recognize that fitting in is critical to his well-being at school. • Reinforce the importance of planning this move carefully and making sure as many credits as possible will transfer.	• Dismissing Arthur's feelings as trivial. • Refusing to consider alternatives. • Reminding him that lots of kids do just fine at the state university and that he needs to learn to adjust. • Trying to make him feel guilty for choosing a more expensive college.

What you need to know.

Studies show that students who feel "at home" at college are significantly more
likely to remain in school and achieve. Parents should not trivialize their child's

desire to fit in and experience college with peers who share their values and goals. Colleges and universities have widely differing cultures, and even students who think they have made a suitable choice during the admissions process often find out later that they would be happier at another school.

Students need to be prepared for "transfer shock," even if they are quite familiar with the new campus. They may feel confused and need time to find a niche. It's important that transfer students take care in choosing their housing. It's best if they can be housed initially with other transfer students or students their own age. It's also critical that your child has good advising from the beginning so that his or her academic progress won't be interrupted.

Each year there are students who transfer, thinking that this move will solve all their problems. Parents need to be attentive to a child's reasons for transferring and be ready to talk about their child's motivation in a nonjudgmental, but realistic, way. For example, there's a big difference between a child wanting to transfer because he or she feels smaller classes will be of benefit and that he or she will have a better chance of being editor of the school's newspaper and a child who wants to transfer to avoid dealing with the breakup of a relationship.

Taking Time Off

Your daughter Mindy has decided to take a semester off from school and work in the Bahamas at a resort. She says she's burned out after so many years in school and that she really needs a break.

What's going on.

Mindy may need a break from the relentless demands of student life. Rather than just dropping out, she has a plan to do something productive and fun with her semester off. In our experience, students who take time off for a semester or a year invariably come back to college refreshed and more motivated to tackle their college work. Moreover, it can be a real advantage

What's on your mind?

Can she make enough money to support herself for a semester?

What will happen to her financial aid package at school?

What if she never goes back to school?

Should we let her do this?

What's on your child's mind?

I am so burned out with school. I need a break.

This may be my only chance to do something fun for a while.

I have it all figured out. I know I can get a good job.

for a student to live on his or her own, work, and get some job experience while in college.

As a parent, you may be used to things progressing in an orderly way and Mindy's decision to interrupt her education may worry you. Chances are good, however, that this break will give her a needed respite from college, and teach her some important things about living on her own in another culture and supporting herself. Remember that, in a few years, this will be remembered as an insignificant "blip" in her college years.

What to do.

- Try to listen to Mindy's desires.
- Support her in taking some time off.
- Ask her to give you a proposal for how she'll take care of herself.
- Make it clear that you expect her to return to school at an agreed upon time.

What to avoid.

- Letting her know that you think this is a frivolous idea.
- Ridiculing her for being a "slacker."

What you need to know.

Sometimes students who want to take a break from college are afraid to tell their parents for fear that they won't understand. Parents may be tempted to try to convince their child to stay in school. This often results in students taking a break anyway. They may stop going to classes, neglect their studies, get low grades, and eventually be forced to take a leave. It's important to listen carefully to your child and respect his or her needs.

You may have some pragmatic issues to deal with if your child decides to take some time off from college. While your daughter's financial aid package will probably not be affected by her decision to take a semester off, it is important that you look into her health insurance coverage. If she is covered under your policy or if she has her own plan through the college, her coverage will stop when she is no longer considered a college student. Your policy may have a provision for continuing coverage if you pay an additional monthly premium while she is on leave. You will need to check this out and make sure that she has coverage while she's away from school.

Dropping Out for Good

Your son Jackson is a computer whiz. He's decided to drop out of school and take a job for an enormous starting salary with a computer start-up company near his school.

What's going on.

Clearly Jackson is flattered and seduced by this great offer from the computer company. Most students today see college as a ticket to a well-paying job in the future and if Jackson has the skills to command a big starting salary without the college degree, he probably feels pretty good to have short-circuited the process.

What's on your mind?

I'm worried that Jackson's decision isn't a good one for the long term.

What if he regrets this later?

I know he's dazzled by the large salary, but how secure is this company?

What's on your child's mind?

Who needs college? I'll be making more money than my dad.

It's going to be so cool, having my own apartment and a new car.

What to do.	What to avoid.
• Congratulate Jackson on this great offer. • Talk with him about the pros and cons of leaving school without a degree. • Let him know that you support his right to make the choice, but share your concerns with him as well. • Ask him if he has thought of a fall-back plan if this job doesn't last or if this start-up company fails.	• Preaching to him about the importance of a college degree. It will undoubtedly fall on deaf ears. • Obsessing about all the things that could go wrong in his new job.

What you need to know.

You have probably read newspaper and magazine articles about impatient young people who leave college to strike it rich. Bill Gates, founder of Microsoft and the richest man in the world, dropped out of Harvard to start his company. The cover of a recent issue of *Forbes* asked, "College? Who needs it?" and the lead article, "The Tyranny of the Diploma," argued: "There's a lot to be said for going to college, but don't swallow the propaganda that the diploma is a great investment. It isn't."[6] The article highlights the success stories of a dozen or so individuals who either dropped out or never went to college. Each story celebrates the high salaries these individuals earn and argues that, had they finished college, they would be in much worse shape financially today.

While it's true that a few individuals each year leave college and go on to successful careers, it is certainly true as well that many college dropouts end up in low-paying, dead-end jobs. It can be compelling for a college student to be offered a high-paying job while he or she is still in school, and, for some people, this can be a good choice. But for most people, having a college diploma is still the most predictable route to enabling them to live satisfying and financially secure lives. It's easy, in a culture that celebrates and reinforces the notion that the good life means having lots of money, for a young person to go for the big salary and downplay the intrinsic rewards of education. However, if this young person finds that he or she has made the wrong choice, the person can always return to college later.

Parents are legitimately concerned when their child drops out of college and doesn't have a high-paying job prospect. But we know of many cases where a child dropped out and, after a couple of years of floundering around, landed a good job in an area that didn't require a college diploma. It can be difficult and disappointing, but parents need to recognize and accept the path their child has chosen. There is a difference between the student who drops out and spends the next year on your sofa doing nothing and the child who drops out and gets on with his or her life in productive ways. *Your* dream of your child being a college graduate may not mesh with his or her goals, interests, and ambitions.

Want to Know More?

Hall, Colin, and Ron Lieber. *Taking Time Off: Inspiring Stories of Students Who Enjoyed Successful Breaks from College and How You Can Plan Your Own.* New York: Farrer/Noonday, 1996.

The College Handbook for Transfer Students. New York: College Entrance Examination Board, 1997. Web address: http://www.collegeboard.org.

---

1. . . ."Graduation Rates for Athletes and Other Students Who Entered College in 1991–92," *The Chronicle of Higher Education* (20 November 1998): p. A42.
2. National Center for Educational Statistics, "Stopouts or Stayouts? Undergraduates Who Leave College in Their First Year," Washington, D.C.: U.S. Department of Education Office of Educational Research and Improvement, November 1998.
3. Linda Lee, "What's the Rush? Why College Can Wait," *The New York Times,* 2 August 1998, Education Life section, p. 24.
4. William Upski Wimsatt, "How I Got My Degree at the University of Planet Earth," *Utne Reader* (May–June 1998): 50.
5. *Ibid.*
6. Brigid Mcmenamin, "The Tyranny of the Diploma," *Forbes* (28 December 1998): 104.

Chapter 11

Understanding Your Child's Postgraduate Choices

Graduate School or Job?

Doonesbury
BY GARRY TRUDEAU

> *Caroline is graduating Phi Beta Kappa from an Ivy League school; she's editor-in-chief of the daily newspaper. She tells me she's decided to take an unpaid internship at the State Department in Washington and will support herself as a waitress. She's already been accepted to a prestigious master's program in public policy, but she wants to defer her admission for a year and waitress. It doesn't make sense to me.*

As your child's graduation from college nears, you may be filled with conflicting emotions. You're proud of your child's accomplishments and yet you wonder, what's next? Even if your child has a job offer in hand and seems focused on his or her future plans, this transition still looms ahead for you and your child. In fact, this may be the most challenging transition in your child's life. Most college students are uncertain about life after college; this chapter will help you to understand and prepare for this passage, whether your child is confident or confused as he or she approaches the end of the college years.

You probably have at least as many unanswered questions as your child. Is it best to attend graduate school immediately after college or is graduate school simply a way to avoid finding that first job? Do unpaid or low-paying internships make sense after spending so much money for a college education? What types of jobs are available for liberal arts graduates? How much financial support will you be expected to provide after college graduation? What about health insurance? What is your role as your child launches him or herself into a first job?

Indeed, parents can play a significant role in helping their children make informed choices about life after college. Our experience as career advisors revealed that parents have substantial influence as their children make decisions about postgraduate life. Using your mentoring skills and the information in this chapter, you can help your child assess his or her options and balance dreams with reality as he or she takes the first step on the path to becoming a self-supporting adult.

Graduate School—Now or Later?

It can be tempting to encourage your child to go straight to graduate school and "get it over with." In some fields that is a wise choice, while in others it's nearly impossible to gain admission to graduate school without work experience. We will discuss law school, medical school, business school, and other professional programs, as well as the traditional Ph.D. program. In addition, we will help you assess whether your child's decision to apply to graduate school is a response to senior panic or the logical next step in a chosen career path.

Fear of Job Hunting

What's on your mind?

Does it make sense for Ted to take both of these tests?

How much will this cost?

Shouldn't he be more focused before he goes to graduate school?

It's probably better for him to go directly to graduate school or he'll never go.

What's on your child's mind?

I am so confused.

I'm the only one who doesn't know exactly what I'm going to do next year.

At least the process of applying to graduate school is clear; I don't have a clue about how to start looking for a job.

If I go to graduate school, at least I won't have to take a low-level, boring job.

Your son Ted, who is majoring in political science, comes home during fall break of his senior year and reports that he has decided to keep his options open by taking the admissions tests for business school (GMAT) and graduate school (GRE). He plans to apply to business school and to graduate school for a master's in political science. He says that all his friends are going to graduate schools; he's sure that he'll find a program that's right for him.

What's going on?

It's not unusual for college seniors to feel that they are the only ones who don't know what they want to do after college graduation. If a student's major has not prepared him or her for a specific job, going to graduate school often looks more appealing than trying to find a job. And school is familiar. He or she has spent an entire life in school up to this point and knows how to take tests and fill out applications. The world of work looks scary and confusing. The student doesn't know how to get started. Not only does he or she not know how to look for a job, the student isn't even sure what kind of job he or she wants.

During the spring term of the junior year in college or early in the senior year, students usually come face-to-face with the scary question of "What's next?" It's not uncommon for panic to set in. For the first time in your child's life, he or she faces the unknown and uncharted future. Up until now, the next step has been relatively clear. But what now? That vast future looms ahead.

<table>
<tr><td>

What to do.

- Listen to Ted's fears about what he'll do after graduation.
- Remind him that he's not alone if he's confused about what comes next.
- Ask him if applying to graduate school is what he really wants to do right now.
- Suggest that he talk to a career counselor at school who can help him determine whether graduate school or a job is the best option.

</td><td>

What to avoid.

- Encouraging Ted to apply to graduate school, even if he's unclear about what he wants to do.
- Reminding him of how difficult it is to get a good job with only an undergraduate degree.
- Thinking that it's better to be in graduate school than floundering around in the uncertain job market.

</td></tr>
</table>

What you need to know.

It's normal for students, when facing this uncertainty, to want to delay it by going to graduate school. This is usually not a good idea, especially if your child's graduate school plans are vague and fundamentally a response to "senior panic." For one thing, graduate school acceptance is based on evidence of a serious commitment to a field of study, and graduate school admissions committees are fairly good at discerning who is exhibiting a true commitment to a particular course of study and who is merely applying to delay the inevitable entry into the job market. In fact, most graduate business schools require their applicants to have a year or two of work experience before they will consider admitting them.

With a master's degree in political science, your child may not be any more qualified for jobs than he or she would be with a bachelor's degree in political science. If a student wants a master's degree in order to work in government or public policy, it would make more sense to apply to one of a number of good graduate schools that award a professional (as opposed to a traditional academic) degree. There are schools that prepare individuals for careers in government or public policy work.

Because the professional world is based on a system of credentialing, an advanced degree that offers specific training is a more practical choice in preparing for a career in a particular field. The degrees offered in a traditional academic area are usually an M.A. (master of arts) or M.S. (master of science), while professional degrees are highly specific: for example, an M.P.A. (master of public administration); an M.L.S. (master of library science); an M.P.H. (master of public health); an M.R.P. (master of regional planning); an M.P.S. (master of professional studies in real estate, international development, or other professional areas); an M.A.T. (master of arts in teaching); an M.I.L.R. (master of industrial and labor relations); or an M.Eng. (master of engineering) to name a few.

If your child wants a career in social service work, the master's degree in sociology (M.S.) will not provide credentialing to work in this area. He or she needs a Master of Social Work degree (M.S.W.), which, after taking a licensing exam, will prepare the student to hang out a shingle as a therapist or to work in a variety of social service organizations. Or if he or she wants to work in publishing, a master's degree in English (M.A.) is not the credential one needs. Although most editorial assistants obtain their jobs right out of college, he or she may want to enroll in one of several highly respected postgraduate certification programs in publishing from which many publishing houses recruit their entry-level employees. In short, a master's degree in any of the traditional academic areas (English, history, psychology, political science, biology, economics, sociology, etc.) will not move your child closer to the credentials needed for work in a specific field. The desire to get a master's degree in any of these fields is usually evidence of a lack of understanding of how graduate degrees translate into careers.

Delaying the Decision

Your son Mick has decided that he's not going to take the LSAT and apply to law schools. He's going to take a year off and work in a ski resort in Colorado with a couple of his fraternity brothers.

What's going on?

Your son may be afraid that he won't do well on the LSAT and wants to avoid having to worry about it in his senior year of college. It's also likely that Mick is sick of school and needs a break before going on to law school.

What's on your mind?

I've spent all this money on a college education and Mick wants to be a "ski bum"? Is he copping out?

What's on your child's mind?

I can't face studying for the LSAT.
I can always go to law school later. What's the rush?

What to do.	What to avoid.
• Listen to Mick's fears and anxieties. • Let him know that you're proud of what he has already accomplished in college. • Be willing to accept his desire to have time off. • Offer a compromise. Suggest that he ski during the season and consider getting a job at a law firm during the off season. This may help him decide if law school is for him.	• Accusing him of being a "slacker." • Insisting that he explain why he's decided not to be a lawyer. • Threatening him with stories of people who aren't motivated to do something meaningful with their life after college.

What you need to know.

While this may be a surprising development for you, it's probably a good choice for Mick. It's not unusual for students to take time off between undergraduate studies and graduate school; by college graduation, most students have spent a continuous seventeen or eighteen years in school and can benefit from a break. It's appropriate to suggest, however, that Mick get a job that will help him decide if law school is for him. Working in a law firm or within the judicial or criminal justice system will not only give him an insider's view of the profession, but it will help him when he's ready to apply to law school.

Mick can enhance his chances of admission to law school if he has some "real world" experience, especially if his time off includes a job in a related field. While it may be difficult for you to understand his desire to put off law school, this break could be a valuable and maturing experience for him and mean that he will be truly motivated to do well when he eventually becomes a law student.

What's on your mind?

I'm afraid Bridget is going to
   make this big decision
   without much information.
Isn't there someone who can
   give her solid advice about
   graduate school?
I wonder if she really under-
   stands what's she getting
   into, working with such depressing cases every day.

What's on your child's mind?

I really love working with
   these kids.
I think this is what I want to
   do for a career, but I'm not
   entirely sure.
How am I going to figure this
   out in time to apply to
   graduate school?

What Graduate Program Would Be Best?

Your daughter Bridget, who is a junior in college, is trying to decide on graduate programs. When she was home over spring break, you had the following conversation:

BRIDGET: Mom, I really think I should be thinking about graduate school. If I want to go right after undergrad, I'll need to apply next fall.

MOM: What programs are you thinking about?

BRIDGET: Well, I'm pretty sure I want to work with abused kids. I really love my volunteer work at the family and children's center. There are so many kids who need help.

MOM: I'm really proud of you for wanting to do such a difficult job, but are you sure that you will want to do it full time for the rest of your life?

BRIDGET: I think so. It's just amazing what the psychologists do with those kids. I want to be able to help too.

MOM: Have you talked to any of the staff there about what graduate degree you need to work with abused children?

BRIDGET: Yeah, but I get even more confused when I talk to them. One of them has a master's in social work and one has a Ph.D. in clinical psychology. Both of them are really good with the kids, but I think the woman with the Ph.D. gets to do more and makes a lot more money.

MOM: Well, maybe you should consider a Ph.D. then.

BRIDGET: But, Mom, I've heard it's really hard to get into a Ph.D. program in clinical psych and my grades aren't all that good. I'm pretty sure I could get into an M.S.W. program though.

MOM: Is that what you really want?

BRIDGET: I don't know. I wish I knew if I could handle a Ph.D.

MOM: Could you talk to your faculty advisor about it? Or someone in the Psychology Department?

BRIDGET: I guess so, but I'm sure they're going to think I'm clueless.

MOM: Well, you do need some help figuring this out, and they might be able to give you some advice.

BRIDGET: Yeah, maybe I'll talk to someone when I get back to school.

What's going on.

Bridget thinks she has found a career path that will be meaningful and rewarding, but she's not sure how to obtain the credentials she needs. She feels the pressure to apply to graduate school when she doesn't have enough information to make an educated choice of programs. And she's not sure she has the academic qualifications to be accepted to the most competitive and rigorous programs. It's common for juniors and seniors to begin to explore graduate programs and feel pretty confused about what to do next with their education.

What to do.	What to avoid.
• Encourage Bridget to get as much information as she can in order to make an informed decision.	• Telling Bridget how depressing this kind of work can be and how many people burn out after a short time.
• Suggest that she talk to clinical psychologists and social workers who can share their own graduate school experiences with her.	• Suggesting that she settle for the master's in social work or insisting that she go for the more prestigious degree.
• Recommend that she talk to someone in the college's career center to get information on careers in both areas.	• Letting her know that you're frustrated with her indecision.
• Suggest that she talk to a faculty member in psychology about how she can get research experience.	
• Remind her that she may want to consider putting off the graduate school decision.	
• Suggest that she could consider working in a center for abused children for a while after college to see if this is really what she wants to do.	

What you need to know.

Ph.D. programs in clinical psychology are among the most competitive. It is usually much easier to get accepted to a Master of Social Work graduate program. This doesn't mean that your child shouldn't try for the Ph.D. The key here is that Bridget doesn't appear to be prepared to make this big decision; she needs time to investigate her options, even if it means working for a year or two after college and applying to graduate programs later. This time would allow her to work in some capacity in the field that interests her and to make her decision based on experience.

Bridget may decide that working with abused children is not for her but that she wants to work in another one of the helping professions. Having some experience will undoubtedly help her get into graduate school eventually; it will also give her the distinct advantage of having focused her goals.

Graduate Business School

What's on your mind?

He should have learned enough in college to prepare him for this test.

Am I going to have to pay for business school too?

What's on your child's mind?

I really want to get an M.B.A. Dad doesn't understand how important the GMAT is.

I want to get into one of the top ten schools. Graduates from those schools get the best jobs.

Your son Fred has decided that he's going to apply to business schools to get an M.B.A. and he wants you to pay for him to take an expensive course in preparation for taking the Graduate Management Aptitude Test (GMAT).

What's going on.

Eager and motivated students usually want to go directly to graduate school, and they understand the importance of the graduate school admissions tests for helping them get into a top school. It's usually a good idea to study a significant amount before taking these competitive examinations. Their specialized material requires additional study in order to achieve a good score. You can prepare for these tests in various ways, and some of them are expensive. It's a good idea to be wary, however, of the test courses that promise high scores and to investigate the reputation of any organization offering test preparation. Students can receive advice on this issue at their college career center.

What to do.	What to avoid.
• Suggest that Fred investigate the test preparation courses available and give you some more information, especially if he's asking you to pay for it. • Recommend that he talk to an advisor in the career center about applying to business school. • Congratulate him on taking the initiative to explore his options for postgraduate study.	• Telling Fred that you know he can do fine without the prep course. • Refusing to discuss this option before you know what's involved.

What you need to know.

While it might be a smart idea for Fred to take a preparation course for the GMAT while he's still in college, chances are that he will not be accepted to business school right after graduation. Most of the top business schools require that students have at least one or two years work experience before admitting them to the M.B.A. program. If he takes the GMAT now, he can use his test score for five years; he won't have to take it again—unless he wants to—when he applies to business school later.

Most professional schools, such as law and business, do not offer assistantships or fellowships to cover tuition and expenses. These are expensive degrees and often leave graduates with a significant loan burden. But most lawyers and business people earn enough money to pay off their graduate education in time. A graduate degree in these areas is likely to be a good investment financially; however, graduate degrees in other less lucrative career fields can create a real financial burden following graduate school. Fields such as social work, architecture, library science, and teaching do not have high-enough salaries to easily pay off a large amount in student loans. Students need to think carefully about how they will manage the costs of a professional master's degree.

Many organizations offer their employees tuition assistance, and some even send their highest performers to graduate school and pick up the cost. It may be possible for your child to pursue a graduate degree part time while employed, as many universities offer extensive night and weekend graduate degree programs.

Ph.D. in Science

What's on your mind?

Does Lily really need a Ph.D.?
What will she do with this degree?
I don't have the money to put her through more school.

What's on your child's mind?

I need a Ph.D. in order to teach physics at a university.
My professors think I can get accepted at a good school.

Your daughter Lily is an outstanding physics student and has been encouraged by her professors to attend graduate school and earn a Ph.D. in physics when she finishes her undergraduate degree next year.

What's going on.

Students who are seriously committed to a career in teaching and research in a college or university setting usually go directly to graduate school after college. If Lily knows that she wants to be a college professor, there is probably no reason for her to delay going to graduate school. She will benefit most from her professors' interest and encouragement if she goes directly on to earn her Ph.D.

What to do.	What to avoid.
• Congratulate Lily on her outstanding academic career.	• Telling her that graduate school is too expensive.
• Encourage her to get advice on which universities she should apply to from her current faculty members.	• Encouraging her to be satisfied with teaching physics in a high school where she won't need the Ph.D.
• Let her know that you are proud of her motivation and commitment to pursue such a difficult course of study.	• Reminding her of how hard it is to get a tenure-track faculty job today.

What you need to know.

While obtaining entry-level positions as tenure-track assistant professors is difficult in the current job market, it is not impossible, especially for the best students who graduate from prestigious universities with a network of respected scholars in the field. If your child is determined to make it in the academic world, he or she needs to have the best credentials possible. This usually means earning a Ph.D. from a high-quality institution and having the support of faculty who value his or her work and have confidence in the student's potential as a scholar and a teacher.

It used to be a given that a student accepted into a Ph.D. program would be fully funded with assistantships and fellowships. While this still remains true in some academic areas, particularly in the sciences, some Ph.D. programs no longer automatically provide financial assistance for every entering graduate student. These programs may require a student to assume the costs for a semester or a year so that the department can evaluate their academic performance before awarding financial support.

There are basically two types of aid: merit-based and need-based. Merit-based aid is awarded on the basis of academic accomplishment, talent, or promise. This type of financial aid comes in the form of grants, stipends, graduate assistantships, and/or fellowships. Assistantships are the most common type of graduate financial aid and usually translate into part-time teaching or research jobs. Students can investigate the availability of these types of aid before they formally apply to a particular graduate school. Fellowships are the most prestigious form of financial assistance at the graduate level. They are used by universities to attract students with the highest qualifications. Most assistantships and fellowships will include full tuition coverage plus a modest stipend to cover living expenses. Grants are sums of money awarded for specific activities on a project basis and are usually funded by government agencies, foundations, and corporations.

In assessing need-based aid, the university will calculate your child's financial need based on the difference between his or her total educational costs and financial resources. In order to apply for this aid the student will need to fill out the Free Application for Federal Student Aid (FAFSA) form. Need-based aid programs include work-study programs, private and federal loans, grants, fellowships, and tuition remission programs offered to students by the graduate school.

All students attending graduate or professional school are considered financially independent by the federal government; however, each year financial aid for graduate school becomes increasingly difficult to obtain. Applicants to graduate school need to be assertive in exploring all types of financial aid available and make sure that they have a good credit history before applying for some kinds of assistance.

If your child is applying to graduate school, encourage him or her to visit the college career center early in the process for advice on graduate financial aid and to research sources for support in the directories and publications available there. He or she should allow adequate time to explore the possibilities and to meet deadlines and application requirements.

Some students are intimidated by the Ph.D. degree and decide to apply for a master's degree instead. In the traditional academic graduate programs, assistantships are not usually available for students earning the master's-level degree because the department will award those to students pursuing the Ph.D. Most academic counselors will encourage your child to apply for the Ph.D. program directly instead of applying for the master's degree first. Students can always decide later if they want to complete their level of study at the master's degree, but the possibility of receiving financial aid increases dramatically when the applicant intends to pursue the Ph.D. degree.

Applying to Law School

Your daughter Jessica is a junior in college and has done well in her major course of study—American history. She's beginning to think about going to law school. While home for fall break, she shared some of her plans with you:

JESSICA: I'm so excited about going to law school. Where do you think I should apply?

MOM: Well, I'm not sure, honey. It's been years since I went to grad school. Where would you like to go?

JESSICA: I went to the career center and they had all of this information about applying to law school; it's amazing how many good schools there are. I don't even know where to begin.

MOM: It's pretty confusing at this stage, I bet. Maybe it's helpful to think about the decision in the same way you chose which colleges to apply to. Remember how you kept receiving catalogues in the mail and you wound up with three big boxes of college information? How did you make sense of that mess of college material?

JESSICA: Well, I had some help from the college advisor at school. He said I should apply to the most competitive colleges. We went on that college tour too, and that helped. I guess I just went where I felt the most comfortable when we visited.

MOM: So you had the college tour, and the advice of your high school counselor. Do you think the same kinds of things would help you explore law schools?

JESSICA: I don't know, Mom. I really don't have a lot of time to visit schools right now. I could ask my college advisor, but he's a philosopher and I think he got a Ph.D. in grad school. I'm definitely not interested in getting a Ph.D.!

MOM: So this is a different kind of decision, isn't it?

JESSICA: Yeah, I feel like I'm really on my own here. It's so confusing and I have to make some decisions pretty soon. I also have to study and take the LSAT, probably over holiday break. I wish there was someone who could tell me what schools are the best for what I want to do and where I'm going to be able to get in.

MOM: Your university has a law school, doesn't it?

JESSICA: Yeah, but I definitely don't want to stay there for law school.

MOM: That's understandable. I think it's smart to have another experience. I was just wondering if there was anyone else on campus you could talk to about law schools.

JESSICA: Yeah, maybe there is. Maybe I'll just walk over to the law school and see if anyone there can help me. Maybe I could also go to the career center—I think there's a grad school advisor there who might know something about law schools.

What's on your mind?

I can't believe Jessica is thinking about law school already. It seems like yesterday when we dropped her off at college.

I'm flattered that she's asking my opinion, but I don't know anything about law schools.

I hope she can get some guidance from the university.

What's on your child's mind?

I have so much to do to get ready to apply to law schools.

How do I know which one is right for me?

This seems so much more serious than going to college.

MOM: Sounds like another good idea. I think you're on the way to finding out what you need to know to make this decision. Can I help in anyway?

JESSICA: Well, you could write my statement of purpose for the application! Just kidding! I know this is going to be a lot of work, but I'm really getting excited about going to law school.

MOM: I'm excited about it too. You've worked hard in college, and I'm sure it's going to pay off when you apply to law school. I'm really proud of you, Jess.

JESSICA: Thanks, Mom.

What's going on.

Some students who are interested in a law degree go directly on to law school, while others decide to work for a year or two first. Although working can help students determine if they want a career in law, law schools typically don't require that their applicants have work experience.

In this dialogue, Jessica's mother used excellent mentoring skills in guiding and supporting her daughter in this decision-making process. Although parents don't always have the specific answers, they can encourage their child, suggest how to gather information, and sometimes even connect their child with someone they know who has been to graduate school in the same field.

What to do.	What to avoid.
• Listen to Jessica's dilemma. • Ask open-ended questions, such as: "How do you think you could get some advice on this big decision?" • Reinforce your child's ability to make good choices. • Remind her of situations in which she mastered a difficult decision and ask her to recall how she did it.	• Cutting off the dialogue by telling Jessica you don't know anything about getting into law school. • Suggesting that she wait a couple of years because she's obviously not ready to make a decision. • Asking why she doesn't ask her advisor at school. She'll probably just reply that her advisor doesn't know anything about law schools. • Telling her it will all work out and to stop obsessing about it now.

What you need to know.

With the increasingly high cost of a legal education and with the competitive job market that law school graduates face, it is important that your child thoughtfully determines if a law career is right for him or her. Each year many students decide to apply to law school because they can't figure out what else to do. This can be a costly and time-consuming mistake.

Encourage your child to explore the field through his or her career center library and on the Internet. The student should talk to practicing lawyers to find out what they do on a daily basis and to ask them about their satisfactions and dissatisfactions with their profession. A student may be able to get a summer job or internship in a law office in order to observe the personal characteristics needed to succeed as a lawyer, as well as to experience what lawyers do in a typical day's work.

There are over eight hundred thousand lawyers practicing in the United States and each year law schools graduate another forty thousand. The job market continues to be competitive for entry-level law positions, and the median salary for new law graduates is $41,000 a year.[1] If your child aspires to a corporate law position, he or she needs to be aware that most corporate lawyers work long hours, six or seven days a week. Although the starting salary may be in excess of $60,000 a year, they may have to make significant sacrifices in their personal lives. If they aspire to a public interest law position, the starting salary will probably be in the $30,000 to $35,000 range and they may have difficulty managing on that salary, especially if they have accumulated a large amount of debt. Typically, law students do not receive assistantships or institutional financial aid, even if they need it; they usually have to take out loans to finance their law school education.

Medical School

What's on your mind?

What if Ron doesn't get into medical school? He has his heart set on being a doctor.

What's on your child's mind?

I have to get into medical school.

I know my grades are good enough to get me in, but what if my MCAT scores are not high enough?

Your son Ron has wanted to be a doctor since he was a little boy. He's done well in college and, now, in his junior year, he's preparing to take the MCAT examination and apply to medical schools. He seems both excited and anxious about this process.

What's going on.

Some of the most driven and competitive individuals on campus are the premed students. They usually come to college committed to being doctors, or they decide early in their college years to apply to medical school. Knowing how difficult it is to be accepted to medical school, many students work hard and are extremely intense about doing everything they can to ensure they will be among the few who go on to medical school each year. Because of this strong commitment, many premed students do not want to consider alternatives and are devastated if they don't get in on the first try.

What to do.	What to avoid.
• Empathize with Ron's anxiety. Let him know you appreciate how hard he is working and that you're proud of him.	• Putting any more pressure on Ron to succeed.
• Suggest that he think about a fall-back position if he isn't accepted on the first try.	• Dismissing his fears.
• Prepare yourself for the possibility that he might not get in right away, and be ready to deal with his feelings of disappointment.	• Telling him you're sure he'll get in and to stop worrying about it.

What you need to know.

Nationwide about 40 percent of first-time applicants to medical school gain admission. While application numbers may vary from year to year, the number of places in medical schools stays the same and, hence, the number of students accepted is fairly static. A key variable may be the type of college your child is attending and the quality of its premedical advising program. Prestigious colleges and universities that are well-known for the high quality of their students and faculty and for their rigorous course of study usually have acceptance rates significantly higher than the national average.

Some colleges have a formal premedical major and others do not. Medical schools do not require or even recommend any particular course of study, although they stipulate that certain courses, such as general and advanced biology, introductory and organic chemistry, introductory physics, English composition, and in some cases, mathematics, must be completed to be considered for admission. It is a common misconception that students must major in science to be considered seriously. In fact, recent medical school admissions requirements data show that 38 percent of biological sciences majors, 44 percent of physical science majors, and 43 percent of nonscience majors who applied were accepted to medical school. Medical school admissions committees overwhelmingly recommend that students select a major area of study primarily because it interests them, not because they feel a certain major will enhance their chances of acceptance.

Most colleges have a health careers program that provides information, guidance, and advice for students who want to go to medical school. Encourage your child to contact his or her school's health careers program as early as possible. They will be able to offer invaluable assistance as he or she experiences the complex and stressful process of preparing to apply.

Even if your child has a stellar academic and cocurricular record in college, there is still a chance that he or she won't be successful in gaining admission to medical school on the first try. As a parent, you can be extremely influential in helping your child consider alternatives to medical school. Your child will need all of your emotional support and thoughtful guidance during and after this process. There are many ways that he or she can use the time after college and before applying to medical school again to enhance his or her chances of getting accepted on the second try. A student can gain experience by working as a laboratory technician in a hospital, teaching biology or chemistry in a private school, or joining the Peace Corps as a health worker, to name a few possibilities. His or her health careers advisor may be able to suggest other options as well.

The First Job—and the Floundering Period—After College

Few students graduate from college with a job offer in hand. In fact, only about 20 percent have jobs upon graduation, but 95 percent are employed within a year of graduation. Students in preprofessional programs, such as engineering, nursing, or physical therapy, are much more likely to find jobs before graduation than students whose college major has not trained them for a particular job. There are also students in some traditional liberal arts majors, such as economics and mathematics, who are actively recruited for positions with banks and consulting firms before graduation.

All parents, especially those who have sacrificed financially to put their child through college, wonder how their college graduate will land that first job and be self-supporting. These scenarios will help you understand the job search process, why it may take your college graduate several years to land their first career-related job, and what you can do to help during the transition period.

Clueless and Confused

Your son Trevor is about to graduate from college and every time you ask him about his plans, he says he doesn't want to think about it. It's clear that he doesn't have a plan and you're worried about him taking up permanent residence on your couch after graduation.

What's on your mind?

What is wrong with Trevor? He can't just come back home and wait until a job drops out of the sky for him. He's got to find a job to start paying off his student loans.

What's going on.

It's very common for seniors to go directly into denial when facing life after college. For the first time in Trevor's life it's not clear what follows, and he may be embarrassed to admit that he's clueless. He may need some gentle prodding to confront the first real job search of his life. If he hasn't had internships or summer jobs to help him define his career interests, he will need some counseling and support to obtain that first job. Fortunately, colleges have career offices to assist in this effort, but your child will need to take the initiative in getting help.

What's on your child's mind?

I don't want to think about what comes next.

I wish my parents would stop asking me what I'm going to do. I don't know!

What to do.

- Ask Trevor if he has been to the career center for counseling.
- Encourage him to take advantage of any services offered on campus.
- Let him know that you appreciate how scary and difficult this transition is, but remain firm in your expectation that he will be able to find a job and support himself.
- Talk with him about his options and offer to help him make contacts if you have friends or associates who can provide information and guidance.
- Try to be patient as you observe his indecision and denial.

What to avoid.

- Criticizing Trevor for being so clueless and disorganized about his future.
- Taking over and begging a friend to give him a job without consulting him.
- Telling him he can't come home and veg out until he "finds" himself.
- Threatening him that you'll cut him off at graduation if he doesn't get his act together.

What you need to know.

The transition from college to the first job is usually a stressful time for student and parent alike. Graduation from college does not, unfortunately, guarantee that your child will be offered a secure job. Although the job market is significantly better than it was in the early nineties, students still need to be assertive in pursuing that first job after college. This can be particularly confusing for students who have majored in an area that doesn't translate easily into an entry-level job or for students who are unfocused about what they want to do. This doesn't mean that your child will languish on your couch forever. It means that he or she needs to take advantage of the career services and advice available while he or she is still on campus.

There are students who feel dissatisfied with the assistance they receive from their career office on campus. The quality of advice and assistance certainly varies from counselor to counselor, and students may have to be persistent in finding a counselor who can meet their needs. However, it's also true that students are often overwhelmed when they realize that finding their first job requires extensive work and that career offices do not hand out jobs to seniors! In our experience, students who have developed job search skills during college find this process significantly less daunting than students who present themselves to the career office in a panic during their senior year. Your child is entitled to assistance and support from career office counselors, but your child should not expect that counselor to find him or her a job.

Try to support any attempt your child makes to deal with his or her prospects for employment. Your graduate may have to come home for a period of time to concentrate on the job search. In the meantime, it is entirely reasonable for you to insist that he or she get a job of some sort. Temporary agencies can offer short-term employment that will get your child off the couch, engaged in work, and earning some money. And temporary jobs often lead to a permanent job offer in a month or two. Your child may need some time to sort through his or her options and earn enough money to be able to relocate to an area where jobs are available.

If graduates know where they'd like to live and search for a job they should check out employment agencies and internship possibilities in that area. It may mean that parents will have to partially support them while they get their feet on the ground in another city, but that may be well worth your effort in the long run. Getting a child launched into the world of work may require tremendous patience and understanding, as well as some temporary financial support.

If your child is covered on your family health insurance plan, you will need to make arrangements to continue that coverage or get him or her personal health insurance coverage. Students covered under a family or student plan lose that coverage automatically the day they graduate from college. If they are covered under the family's health insurance, the family can extend that coverage through the federal COBRA plan. If they are not covered under the family plan, families will need to investigate other options. You may want to buy short-term, month-to-month, catastrophic coverage, which is usually less expensive than a full coverage plan, until your child gets his or her first job with health insurance benefits.

Following Your Heart

Your son Roger's great passion has always been basketball. He played on the high school team, but realized he wasn't good enough to have a career in professional basketball. He decided to major in economics and has been a good student in college. He went to the career center to check out the job possibilities, and the career advisor gave him a battery of skills and interests tests. Not surprisingly, he's still interested in sports, but he has also developed skills in math and analytical reasoning. He's wondering how he can put both his interests and skills to work after college.

What's going on.

Roger is coming to terms with balancing his dreams with reality as he prepares for life after college. It's easy for students who have had limited "real world" experience, or who have widely disparate interests and skills, to think there is only one predictable path for them to follow when looking for a job.

What's on your mind?

Roger is still as avid a basketball fan as ever.

It's too bad that he wasn't good enough to be a professional basketball player.

I wonder what he'll do with his economics degree.

What's on your child's mind?

I still wish I could have been a pro basketball player.

I can't see myself being a financial analyst, no matter how much money they offer me.

What am I going to do?

What to do.	What to avoid.
• Encourage Roger to return to the career center and have a counselor explore with him creative ways to combine his skills and interests. • Recommend that he gather names of alumni who work in sports management and set up informational interviews with them. • Suggest that he look into postgraduate internships that may be available with some of the major sports franchises.	• Telling him that it's time to grow up and forget about a career in basketball. • Suggesting that he should just accept the fact that he's probably going to have to work in a bank or financial services organization.

What you need to know.

Many students find creative ways to combine their passions and skills when beginning their job search. While it's true that Roger had to give up his dream of being a professional athlete, it's not necessarily true that he will have to settle for a job with no connection to sports. Roger could potentially find a position in the financial division of the NBA.

One of the fastest-growing sectors of the economy in the United States today is sports and entertainment. Students who have a strong interest in sports, film, television, theater, or music can often use their business and finance skills to find work in one of these industries. It simply takes some creative thinking about alternatives and the willingness to work hard to research and uncover possibilities.

Career center staff at most colleges can help your child explore ways to combine his or her dreams with the reality of finding an entry-level job. Skills and interest inventories can identify areas of strength, and contacts with alumni can provide useful advice and networking opportunities. If your child has a relatively unusual career objective, it's important that you encourage him or her to take advantage of the assistance he or she can receive while still in school.

Studies show that most people find jobs through personal contacts. Your child will need to become skillful at networking and informational interviewing to be able to find a job that combines his or her analytical skills with a love of sports. Contacting alumni of the college and setting up appointments to ask them questions about their careers in sports management is a good place to start. An alumnus may even agree to allow your son or daughter to spend a day or two at work, observing his or her daily activities and accompanying him or her to meetings.

While your son or daughter may have to abandon the dream of being the next Michael Jordan or Olga Korbut, he or she doesn't necessarily have to give up a job in sports. There are jobs available for people with analytical and communication skills in sports administration, and behind-the-scenes work can be rewarding for individuals who have a passion for sports and entertainment.

Career Confident

Your daughter Romy is an art history major but has always had a great interest in journalism. She worked at the local newspaper last summer and has announced that she plans to take a low-paying internship as an arts and leisure reporter for the *Daily Journal* in Tupelo, Mississippi, after she graduates.

What's going on.

Romy doesn't have a journalism degree, but she's convinced that she wants to be a newspaper reporter. She wants to take this internship and is eager to try living in another city in a different part of the country.

What's on your mind?

I can't believe Romy wants to go so far away for such a marginal job.

Is this a sound idea?

What's on your child's mind?

I loved working at the newspaper last summer.

I know this is what I want to do after college.

What to do.	What to avoid.
• Suggest that Romy see a career counselor on campus to learn more about journalism as a career. • Encourage her to try for this internship, even though it sounds strange to you. • Suggest that she talk to alumni who are journalists to find out more about this career path.	• Discouraging her because you don't understand the field. • Telling her that she should have majored in something more practical. • Thinking that she's crazy to want to go to a place she's never been before.

What you need to know.

Students who want to pursue a career in journalism usually have to start out working as an intern at a small town newspaper. Few aspiring journalists, even those with graduate degrees in the field, start out their careers working for big city newspapers. This is how beginning journalists acquire experience and build a portfolio of clippings to advance their career. Romy will probably spend a year or two in Tupelo and then be ready to apply for a better job in a somewhat larger city.

Journalists are divided over the issue of whether a graduate degree is necessary to become a successful reporter at a prestigious newspaper. Most agree, however, that beginning journalists have to "pay their dues" in the profession by working in small markets and covering less exciting stories to gain the experience and track record they need to move to the next level in the newspaper business. Most individuals spend several years with small- and medium-sized newspapers before they are ready to apply for jobs in the bigger markets with large-circulation newspapers. This is usually the pattern in the fields of photojournalism and broadcasting as well.

Working Abroad

Your daughter Leslie is graduating with a major in European history and wants to live and work abroad for a couple of years. She spent a semester in Spain and thinks she can find a job there. She's willing to take practically any job in order to live in Spain again.

What's going on.

Many students who had a wonderful semester, summer, or year abroad want to go back there and live after college. They are convinced that they can get a job, but are unsure of how to go about doing an international job search.

> ### What's on your mind?
> How in the world can Leslie find a job in Spain?
> This idea seems so unrealistic.

> ### What's on your child's mind?
> I loved Barcelona.
> I should go now before I have to settle down and find a real job.

What to do.	What to avoid.
• Encourage Leslie to talk to someone in the career center about her international job search. • Listen to her dreams, but insist that she get some good advice. • Offer to help if you have friends or associates who work abroad.	• Telling her she's crazy to even think about working in Spain. • Saying no to this idea before getting more information from Leslie.

What you need to know.

An international job search is difficult at best. Most countries have legal requirements or ethical commitments to hire their own citizens; this can make it tough for a foreigner to obtain a work visa. There are programs, however, that do help American college graduates find jobs abroad. For example, the Council on International Educational Exchange (CIEE) helps American students and graduating seniors obtain work permits to allow them to work for three to six months in Britain, Ireland, France, Germany, Canada, Costa Rica, New Zealand, or Jamaica. For a modest fee, students will receive orientation, job leads, and housing assistance after they arrive; however, many students end up working in menial and relatively low-paying jobs. There are also countries (Japan, China, Taiwan, and some Eastern European countries) who offer American students jobs teaching English. Many, however, require some proficiency in the native language.

In general, it is extremely difficult for students to work abroad for an extended period of time without extraordinary personal connections or qualifications. It is possible for some students to obtain placements abroad while working for an American company, but these assignments are usually reserved for employees who have some seniority or a special area of expertise. If your child is determined to work and live abroad after college, it might be more realistic for him or her to join the Peace Corps or another type of international aid organization that places people in foreign countries for a year or two after college.

Your Son, the Banker

You were surprised and happy when your son Marshall called last night with the good news that he had received two excellent job offers as a result of interviewing with companies on campus.

What's on your mind?

I can't believe it. Marshall has two job offers.

This is great. I'm so proud of him.

What's on your child's mind?

I am so excited to finish school and move to the city.

I can't believe I have two good offers. I'm really glad I majored in math.

The training program sounds hard, but I know I can do it.

MARSHALL: Hey, Dad, I've got some great news!

DAD: What's up, son?

MARSHALL: I just got two job offers.

DAD: Wow, that's great! What are the jobs?

MARSHALL: Well, one's with Crouse-Barden and the other's with J & S Banking.

DAD: So what would you be doing?

MARSHALL: They're both entry-level analyst positions, and they both have training programs so I can learn all about the investment banking business.

DAD: Where are they located?

MARSHALL: They're both in New York City. Isn't that cool, Dad? I'm going to live in the city. I can't wait. I'm so excited.

DAD: This is such great news, Marshall. I'm really proud of you.

MARSHALL: The only problem is trying to decide which offer to take. I have to decide in a week. Right now I'm leaning toward the Crouse job because I've heard their training program is the best. And their salary is a little higher too. I'm going to need money to live in the city.

DAD: Well, that's for sure. It can really be expensive to get an apartment there.

MARSHALL: I've already decided to live with a couple of my friends. They have job offers in banking too. The three of us should be able to scrape up enough money for rent.

DAD: Sounds like you're already on your way.

MARSHALL: Yeah, I'm really psyched to move to the city and start working.

DAD: Your hard work has really paid off. Good for you.

What's going on.

Marshall is one of a relatively small number of students who will have a solid job when he graduates from college. Many banking and investment firms travel to campuses each year to interview and choose outstanding students for their entry-level training programs. Although this is not the typical experience for a college senior, Marshall has been diligent in researching opportunities and preparing for interviews and now is in the enviable position of having two attractive job offers.

This is the kind of phone call that most parents would love to receive. It's a great relief to know that your child is on the way to becoming self-supporting in a career that offers financial rewards and growth potential.

What to do.	What to avoid.
• Congratulate him on his job offers. • Let him know how proud you are and that you have great confidence in his ability to succeed in this next phase of his life. • Give yourself some credit too for all of the support and guidance—and perhaps, money—you've provided along the way.	• Second-guessing his decision or trying to influence which job offer he accepts. • Telling him that living in the city is going to be really hard and expensive.

What you need to know.

Marshall is an example of a highly focused and confident student. His job offers were most likely the result of his participation in an on-campus recruiting program that coordinates interviews for jobs in areas such as banking, engineering, consulting, and insurance. His mathematics major and economics minor have prepared him to be a good candidate for a training program in investment banking.

There is significant support on most college campuses for students interested in participating in the on-campus recruiting program. Most career centers have staff that help students make contact with hiring organizations and prepare their students for interviews. It is likely that Marshall registered early with the career center's recruiting program, attended preparation sessions, networked with alumni, and probably had some summer job experience that made him an attractive candidate.

Many students who are not in these highly sought-after fields of study don't realize how much they can gain from the services offered by their college career center. Parents can have significant influence by encouraging their children to take advantage of the services offered while they are still on campus. Most career centers have an array of helpful services, including a resource library and employer information, alumni databases, practice interview sessions, résumé referral services, on-campus recruiting programs, job listings, graduate and professional school counseling, individualized career advising sessions, interest testing and computerized career guidance assistance, internship programs, career fairs, and workshops on writing résumés and cover letters, networking, informational interviewing, interviewing skills, and negotiating job and salary offers.

Making Sense of Getting That First Job—Parent to Parent

You received a call last night from a friend whose child is graduating from college in the spring. He sounded pretty exasperated about his daughter's prospects:

DAN: Hi, George. How are things?
GEORGE: Well, pretty good, Dan, but my daughter is making me crazy these days.
DAN: You mean Jenna? What's going on?

GEORGE: She's decided that she's going to move to Washington, D.C., after graduation and take an internship in the Environmental Protection Agency that only pays her a hundred dollars a week! I don't think she has a clue about what it costs to live in a city.

DAN: Yeah, I remember those days of worrying about your kid's plans for after college. A few years ago, Meg told us she was going to move to Chicago after college and work at the art institute for five bucks an hour. I thought she was nuts!

GEORGE: What happened?

DAN: Well, she moved to Chicago all right and found out how hard it was to pay the rent on five bucks an hour. I could have told her that, of course, but she had to find out for herself.

GEORGE: What did she do?

DAN: She found another job waitressing four nights a week. And she lived with six other girls in a run-down old house. It wasn't in the best neighborhood, but she didn't seem to mind. She was having a ball living in the city, and she figured out how to make ends meet most months.

GEORGE: So what's she doing now?

DAN: Well, it's taken a few years, but she just landed a great job in a community arts organization, and she's thinking of going to graduate school at night to get an M.B.A. in arts administration. She has her own apartment now and she's doing fine. She seems really happy.

GEORGE: So everything turned out all right for her, huh?

DAN: Yeah, sometimes you just have to let them go, ya know? Jenna's a smart kid. She'll figure it out. It's you that's gonna suffer for a while!

GEORGE: Yeah, you're right about that!

What's on your mind?
How is Jenna going to survive in the city?
I'm really worried about her.
Should we insist that she come home and work until she gets on her feet?

What's on your child's mind?
I am so excited about this internship and living in Washington.
I know I can find a place to live and take care of myself.
My parents are such worry warts.

What's going on.

Jenna is excited about moving to Washington and getting on with her life after college; her parents aren't so sure this is a good idea. They can't imagine her being able to support herself, and they worry about her safety and security.

What to do.	What to avoid.
• Talk to Jenna about the internship she wants to take. • Let her know that you're proud of her taking charge of her life after college, but that you're concerned about how she'll manage living in the city. • Sit down with her and map out a plan for where she'll live and how she'll support herself on her internship salary. • Suggest that she may have to get an additional job to make ends meet. • Let her know to what extent you are able to help her financially.	• Telling her she can't do this. • Begging her to come home and work until she has enough money to move to the city. • Assuming that she won't be happy unless she has a nice apartment and a car.

What you need to know.

Many college students head off to a marginal job or low-paying internship in a city after graduation with great hopes and dreams of living on their own and being independent from their parents. Although you might consider this a risky proposition, your child probably sees it as a great adventure. It's hard to set aside your fears and believe that your child can make it, but this is the beginning of your child's path to independence. Many solid careers result from taking this first step, but the first year or two can be difficult for you. Launching a child into the real world means that you have to believe in your child's ability to cope with less-than-ideal living circumstances in order to make his or her way in her world.

This floundering period can take months or years, but very few college graduates, five years out, are living in marginal neighborhoods and subsisting on macaroni and cheese as they contemplate another day at a low-paying, dead-end job. This dose of reality can be a very positive experience that motivates your child to focus his or her goals and work to achieve them.

Life in the Big City After a Trip to Europe

Your son Jamal is going to move to San Francisco at the end of the summer, but first he plans to travel around Europe for a couple of months. He doesn't have a job yet in San Francisco, but hopes to rent an apartment with three friends who already have good jobs in the Bay Area.

What's going on.

Many students who can afford it take the "European tour" during the summer after college, especially if they don't have a job offer at graduation. Jamal is more than ready to strike out on his own and move to the city with his friends after his trip. His youthful enthusiasm overrides any concerns he may have about whether he can find a job and support himself in San Francisco. Every year, soon after graduation, thousands of students move to the big cities on both coasts, full of energy and ready to take on the world.

What's on your mind?

Should Jamal take this trip?
Will all of the jobs be taken when he gets back?
I'm worried about him moving so far away.
How will he pay the rent and eat?

What's on your child's mind?

I really want to take this trip to Europe.
It will be so cool to live in San Francisco with my friends.
I'm sure I'll be able to get a job when I get back.

What to do.	What to avoid.
• Encourage him to take the trip and enjoy his last summer of freedom from job responsibilities.	• Telling him he can't go on the trip until he has a job.
• Have a frank talk with Jamal about how he plans to support himself in San Francisco.	• Refusing to help him relocate because you think this is a crazy idea.
• Take his plans seriously, but ask him to consider all of the possibilities before he makes the move, including a fall-back plan if he's unable to find a job immediately.	• Letting him know you think he's incapable of taking care of himself.
• Find out what the costs will be and let him know if you are able or willing to help him with relocation money.	
• Suggest that he visit the career center on campus to find out about the job market in San Francisco and get some counseling to focus his job search.	
• Recommend that he gather names of alumni in the Bay Area that he can contact.	
• Let him know that you are proud of his courage, even though you are concerned about the risks.	

What you need to know.

Students who do not have job offers at graduation will not suffer from putting off their job searches until late summer or early fall. In fact, most organizations do little hiring during the summer. Late summer and early fall are far more productive times to begin a job search, and it will be much easier for Jamal to find a job when he is actually in San Francisco.

Although moving to a city without a job is frightening for parents who understand the risks, it is not uncommon for students to take this leap of faith when they graduate from college. And most learn a lot about themselves and coping on their own. Some students in this situation need a significant amount of support and financial assistance from parents. For example, in order to rent an apartment, your child will probably need to come up with a chunk of money for his or her share of the security deposit and the first and last month's rent—and possibly even a broker's fee. This can amount to several thousand dollars, in addition to the money he or she will need to move and to take care of him or herself until getting a paycheck.

There are various ways that students can produce the money they need to establish themselves. Some parents are able to give or lend their child the money; others insist that their child come home after college, get a job, and save the money necessary to relocate later in the summer or early fall. Some students, who don't have family resources, run up credit card debts or attempt to borrow money on their own. It can be tough on students who get themselves heavily indebted, especially if, six months later, they have to begin paying off student loans. It's important that parents take the initiative in talking about the costs involved, mapping out a plan, and then allowing their child to experience the consequences of his or her decisions.

Most students can get a job immediately when they move to a new area through a local temporary employment agency. Many organizations actually use temp agencies to find new employees. Employing someone on a temporary basis gives the organization a chance to observe his or her work and make a decision on offering permanent employment later. Temp agencies (and employment agencies) usually specialize in a particular career area, such as public relations, marketing, sales, or advertising. A student can choose a temp agency that most closely fits his or her career focus. If there is a good fit between the organization and the temp worker, that worker may receive a permanent job offer when the temporary work contract has been fulfilled. Even if this doesn't occur, your child will have gainful employment while he or she looks for a permanent position in another organization. Temporary jobs often allow flexibility in hours so that the employee can pursue a job search and coordinate job interviews elsewhere.

When your child arrives in a new city, he or she should immediately contact employment agencies who specialize in his or her area of interest. These agencies often serve as recruiting departments for organizations who don't have the time and staff resources to conduct searches for new employees. Employment agencies are paid by the employer to provide this service; prospective employees should never agree to pay an employment agency fee. The agency does not collect a fee, however, until they have placed an individual in a job. It's to the agency's advantage to move quickly, and prospective employees may need to be assertive in taking the time they need to ensure that a job is a good match for them. It's important that the student be well prepared for interviews with employment agencies, just as he or she would be with a prospective employer. A good résumé, appropriate attire, and excellent interviewing skills are necessary to make a good impression with an employment agency and, hence, ensure that the applicant is referred to appropriate companies with job openings.

What's on your mind?

Why can't Chelsea make up her mind about what to do after college?

I'm afraid she's going to be unhappy in a dead-end job.

I guess her major in philosophy didn't exactly prepare her for a job.

What's on your child's mind?

Why can't I make up my mind about a career?

I feel so clueless. Everyone else knows what they're going to do.

The Uncertain Future—Parent to Parent

Yesterday you had the following conversation with a friend about your daughter's plans for life after graduation:

JANE: Hi, Marge. How are you?

MARGE: Fine, Jane. I just got off the phone with Chelsea at school. She's trying to figure out what she's going to do after graduation.

JANE: Oh, boy, I remember those conversations with Marcia when she was a senior in college. Scary, huh?

MARGE: Yeah, I just can't believe how confused she is. One day, she's all set to head to Boston with her friends and take the job she's been offered as a buyer trainee at Filene's. The next day, she's convinced that she should apply for a job with a consulting firm so that she can make more money.

JANE: It's great she has a job offer, at least. I thought Marcia was going to end up on the street when she graduated five years ago. She's certainly been through some changes, but look where she is now. She just got another promotion and loves her work. She's an assistant vice president for training with a computer software company. Who would have thought a Spanish major would work in computers?

MARGE: Wow, that's really great. You must be so proud of her.

JANE: Yeah, I am. It's easy to forget how panicked and confused she was a few years ago. You know, it takes awhile for kids to settle into a career these days. It's not like when we were graduating back in the Dark Ages.

MARGE: I just wish everything weren't so up in the air.

JANE: I know, but look at Marcia. Give Chelsea some time; she'll find her niche.

MARGE: I guess you're right, but in the meantime, I'm going crazy!

What's going on.

Chelsea is going through the typical confusion surrounding what to do after college. It's hard for parents to cope with the lack of decisiveness when students face the prospect of life after college. It's important to keep in mind that Chelsea's task is simply to choose a first job and not to decide on a life-long career. Her career will evolve over time and cannot be predicted with certainty at the beginning.

What to do.	What to avoid.
• Listen to your child's worries, empathize with her confusion, and let her know that you have confidence in her.	• Thinking this is an all-or-nothing choice for Chelsea.
• Remind her that this decision is not a lifetime commitment.	• Growing exasperated with her lack of direction.
• Help her consider the alternatives by asking open questions, such as: "What parts of the retailing job are most attractive to you?" or "What aspects of the job worry you?"	• Letting your anxieties add to Chelsea's burden.
• Suggest that she look into some counseling at the career center.	

What you need to know.

A few years out of college, most graduates are not doing anything related to their college major or their first job. In fact, the average person today will change careers six to eight times in his or her working life. And those changes are likely to be most dramatic during the first ten years out of college. Most college graduates go through a floundering period during which they experiment with various vocational paths. This is a natural developmental process, even though it can be an unsettling and frustrating experience for you.

Change is an absolutely predictable phenomenon in today's world of work. The days of accepting a job upon graduation, and sticking with it until retirement are over for most people. As your child ventures out into the challenging and ever-changing world beyond college, you can be an invaluable mentor and guide, offering support, encouragement, and unconditional love in the trials and triumphs to come.

Your role will certainly change and evolve as your child continues along the path to fully independent adulthood. One of the great joys of parenting is observing your child on this journey and continuing to act as a trusted mentor and guide. We hope this book has helped you begin this journey and that you'll find yourself celebrating the many rewards and possibilities along the way.

Want to Know More?

Martz, Geoff. *How to Survive Without Your Parents' Money: Making It from College to the "Real World."* Princeton, NJ: The Princeton Review, 1996.

---

1. National Association for Law Placement's *Class of 1997 Employment Report and Salary Survey.*

About the Authors

Helen E. Johnson founded and directed Cornell University's first Parents' Program. She has worked for more than twenty-five years in higher education as a writer, career center director, assistant dean of students, and program manager. She has written and spoken widely on careers and the liberal arts, parent-adolescent communication, and parenting college-aged children. She earned a BA degree, summa cum laude and Phi Beta Kappa, from Wells College and did her graduate work in Corporate Communication and Training at Ithaca College. She is the parent of two recent college graduates.

Christine Schelhas-Miller teaches adolescent development in the department of human development at Cornell University and is a consultant to independent, secondary schools on issues related to adolescent development. For over twenty years she has worked in higher education, providing academic, personal, and career counseling to students at Cornell University, Ithaca College, Harvard University, and Indiana University. She lived and worked as an advisor in residence halls at several universities. She earned a BA degree, cum laude, from Bucknell University, a master's degree from Indiana University, and a doctorate in Human Development from Harvard University. She is the parent of two children.

Index